D1068163

Desert Kingdom

Desert Kingdom

How Oil and Water Forged Modern Saudi Arabia

Toby Craig Jones

Harvard University Press · Cambridge, Massachusetts, and London, England · 2010

Library of Congress Cataloging-in-Publication Data

Jones, Toby Craig, 1972–
Desert kingdom : how oil and water forged modern Saudi Arabia /
Toby Craig Jones.
Includes bibliographical references and index.
ISBN 978-0-674-04985-7 (cloth : alk. paper)
1. Saudi Arabia—Politics and government—20th century.
2. Natural resources—Government policy—Saudi Arabia—History—20th
century.   3. Water resources development—Government policy—Saudi
Arabia—History—20th century.   4. Water—Government policy—Saudi
Arabia—History—20th century.   5. Petroleum industry and trade—
Government policy—Saudi Arabia—History—20th century.   I. Title.

DS244.52.J66   2010
953.805—dc22   2010013253

For Sandy, Mackenzie, and Danielle

Contents

The Nature of the State

1

In November 1976, flush with billions of dollars from the recent boom in oil prices, Saudi Arabia commissioned a study of the improbable, a project so fanciful that one engineer would characterize it as horrifying. He went on to remark that the project lay "several orders of magnitude beyond anything within [the] experience" of the experts assembled to consider it.[1] The study aimed to measure the feasibility of towing a 100-million-ton iceberg from Antarctica to the Red Sea, where it was hoped the melting ice would slake the desert kingdom's desperate need for freshwater. Over the next several years Muhammad al-Faisal, a nephew of the Saudi king, collaborated with a French polar explorer and a French engineering firm to advance the endeavor. So bullish was al-Faisal on the project that he invested millions of his own dollars in the creation of Iceberg Transport International, a company whose sole purpose was to haul icebergs to the water-poor. He bragged to the *New York Times* that he thought tugging icebergs "a better enterprise than oil," believing he could deliver drinkable water from the South Pole, and do so on the cheap.[2]

In spite of massive logistical challenges, the forty-one-year-old prince insisted that he could bring to Saudi Arabia a mile-wide iceberg, towing it on a 5,000-mile voyage in six months to a year, for a cost of around $100 million. Much like the iceberg itself, the scale of the task was enormous. The most daunting challenge was delivering the berg without its melting from the combination of the sun's powerful glare and the ocean's battering waves. The prince's technical team aimed to thwart the threat by wrapping the colossus in an eighteen-inch-thick layer of plastic, in the hope that it would deflect the sunlight and shield the ice from the dissolving power of the salty ocean. Supporting engineers advocated using six or seven of the world's most powerful tugboats, the same as those used to pilot oil supertankers into harbor, to pull the iceberg on its epic journey. Al-Faisal fancied affixing paddlewheels directly to the iceberg itself, a suggestion that led one observer to declare snidely that he was "surprised the prince didn't suggest little oarsmen like [on] Roman triremes."[3]

The closest the prince ever got to delivering his prize to Saudi Arabia was Ames, Iowa. In October 1977, at considerable personal expense, he arranged for the transportation of a 10,000-year-old "miniberg of blue ice" from the Portage glacier field near Anchorage, Alaska, to the campus of Iowa State University, where more than two hundred delegates had gathered for a conference on iceberg utilization.[4] American national media reported that the Alaskan iceberg elicited considerable curiosity from the Ames community. Bemused observers, including children bused in from local schools, chipped away chunks of ice for souvenirs. A married couple stored several handfuls in a portable cooler. They told one reporter they would serve the ice in cocktails at their annual holiday party. For those who took the proceedings more seriously, the Ames conference generated more skepticism than support and may have inadvertently killed whatever momentum the project possessed. Wilford Weeks, from the U.S. Army Cold Regions Research and Engineering Laboratory, remarked at the conference, "Once you get north of the equator, you'll have nothing but a rope at the end of your tow."[5] Aside from al-Faisal, no other significant major Saudi decision makers attended the conference.

Al-Faisal proved to be a bad gambler. Before founding Iceberg Transport International he had served as director of the kingdom's program on desalinating water, a position he resigned in order to pursue his polar ambitions. It was a poor decision. Those in power never seriously pursued towing icebergs for water relief.[6] Instead, they turned to al-Faisal's past project, desalination, to meet future needs. While al-Faisal pressed his case in Iowa, the Saudi government allocated $15 billion to build dozens of massive desalination plants designed to supply billions of gallons of water over the coming decades.[7] The first such plant had already been built in Jidda, one of the kingdom's most important commercial entrepôts on the Red Sea, and one that suffered from chronic shortages of freshwater. The Jidda plant was designed by the U.S. Department of the Interior's Office of Saline Water. A subsidiary of the Coca-Cola Company completed the plant's construction in 1970. The Jidda plant proved the first of many. Today more than thirty desalination plants operate in Saudi Arabia, providing the majority of the country's water.[8]

Whatever led the Saudis to choose desalination over towing icebergs, neither the price tag nor the scale of the respective projects seemed to matter. Turning seawater into drinking water has always come at considerable expense. The outlay for construction in the 1970s was in the hundreds of millions of dollars for a single plant—a sprawling complex of pipes, pumps, storage tanks—and for generating the electricity to run it. Beyond construction costs, the expense of operation also proved exorbitant, and not just financially. The kingdom had settled on a technical approach to desalination (osmosis) that was particularly energy hungry, and it quickly discovered that desalination required not only money but also a vast supply of energy to fuel the process.

But by the late 1970s the country possessed massive quantities of both. What Saudi Arabia lacked in water it made up for in oil, the twentieth century's most important source of energy. Home to more than a quarter of the world's oil reserves, Saudi Arabia was flush with enough oil to easily meet both global and domestic energy needs. Saudi Arabia used its extensive energy stores to turn nature on its head, using its oil to fire the energy-hungry desalination facilities. The process virtually turned oil into water. The Saudis had been pumping oil in commercial quantities since the 1940s, and getting rich doing so. Saudi Arabia had a foreign partner, a conglomerate of American oil companies that came to be known as the Arabian

American Oil Company (Aramco), on which it relied to perform the actual work of drilling, pumping, refining, and exporting its petroleum. Although the kingdom needed Aramco for its capital and expertise, at least for a time, the oil underground remained the property of the Saudi government.[9] After Aramco pocketed its share of oil revenues, the rest went directly to the Saudi treasury, where the wealth steadily accumulated. The real windfall came during the oil boom of the mid-1970s. From late 1973 to the end of the decade, when Saudi Arabia and other oil-producing countries wrested control over oil pricing policy from the major Western oil companies, prices soared to previously unimaginable heights. Petrodollars flooded into the central coffers of oil-producing countries in what amounted to one of the most dramatic transfers of wealth in human history. The oil boom liberated Saudi Arabia from the restraints of pecuniary caution, and the government eagerly sought ways to spend its mounting fortune.

The need for water relief was acute. Arabia's people have long made do in a land with no natural rivers or lakes. Their apprehensions about water have been grave and perennial. For Saudi leaders, meeting their water needs and ameliorating their anxiety have been ongoing concerns. Considering the singular role of water in sustaining human life, projects to find—and ultimately to create—freshwater have been of considerable import. The sole sources of freshwater for most of the country's nine million residents were prehistoric underground water aquifers with a limited and nonrenewable capacity. Once drained, the country's existing water resources would be gone forever. Rainfall was almost nonexistent, hardly enough to dampen the arid landscape let alone replenish lost water. Growing cities, rapid urbanization, and the construction of infrastructure and some industry intensified demand on already stressed resources. In its $142-billion budget for the five-year plan spanning 1975 to 1980, the Saudi government called for the same amount to be spent on water as on education.

The turn to desalination partly reflected a real desire to address a pressing need. But it was also much more than that. The pursuit of freshwater, including commissioning research to span the globe to find it as well as spending extravagantly on desalination, was more than a quest to satisfy the needs of the thirsty. It was, foremost, a political enterprise, one that served to secure political authority.[10] In the heyday of the oil boom, finding, making, and providing water came to serve as a form of political patronage. And water was not the only focus. Having more water opened the door to additional projects. After the boom, the Saudis spent $85 billion subsidizing wheat agriculture. The kingdom's intemperate climate made wheat farming particularly daunting, but the government proved so committed to the project that the country eventually became the sixth-largest wheat exporter in the world. Water and agriculture were two principal means through which Saudi Arabia's rulers redistributed some of the country's fast-growing wealth. In spite of their cost, such expensive environmental projects offered a way of cashing in domestically on the abundance of oil at home as well as the petrodollars generated by its sale abroad.

The redistribution of oil wealth served various ends, from rewarding those most loyal to the Saudis to further enriching members of the extended royal family. The state also used some of its largesse in an effort to stave off criticism, dissent, and potential revolution. The Saudis redistributed oil wealth as a way of offering something in return for their unrelenting grip on power—a devil's bargain with the people of Saudi Arabia. Popular pressure was an ongoing concern for the country's ruling elite, which had created a closed political system, a tyranny in which the kingdom's subjects had limited access to power and virtually no influence on decision making, and paid a heavy price for attempting to assert their interests. Since the 1940s, oil wealth had lubricated the system, providing just enough capital to enable the Saudis to sustain their dynasty and their authoritarian impulses, although not without challenge.[11] The spectacular new levels of wealth generated by the oil boom helped further entrench Saudi authoritarianism. While the central government commanded total authority, it also demanded very little from its subjects. The government bartered various social benefits, including food and water, in exchange for public quiescence.

For a time the bargain worked. During the 1970s, when oil prosperity peaked, many of Saudi Arabia's subjects were caught up in the awesome scale of the wealth being generated by oil and the possibilities it seemed to portend. There were no apparent limits. For the greatest oil power on the planet, desalination, towing icebergs, and harvesting wheat in the desert merely required capital and commitment. Like the Iowans in Ames who gawked in awe at the prospect of transporting icebergs globally, taken in by the sheer magnitude of the project and its blatant disregard for the laws of nature, Saudis, too, were enraptured by the spectacle, but for different reasons. For many in Saudi Arabia the prospect of towing icebergs and the reality of turning oil into water was sublime, a conspicuous exhibition of oil's and their country's newfound power. Many Saudi subjects took to the new wealth enthusiastically, spending on previously unaffordable consumer goods, cars, and real estate. The Saudi bargain also heightened expectations, establishing a permanent sense among the populace that the state would forever indulge their material desires.[12] These expectations were unrealistic, however. The peaks of the 1970s did not last. The price of oil collapsed by the mid-1980s and undermined the government's ability to sustain high levels of patronage. But even before global markets had leveled off, some Saudis were unhappy with the new wealth or how it was being used. The government met opposition in some quarters from those opposed to the boom-time materialism and consumption. Many others grew disillusioned with the way the wealth was distributed. It turned out that not everyone enjoyed equal access to the spoils. The combination of hostility toward the new wealth and frustration at being left out of the windfall led to a violent reckoning.

The impact of the oil boom on Saudi Arabia was not exceptional. Oil producers everywhere experienced similar economic and political fallout, in the end paying a heavy price for their oil wealth. Oil turned out to be as much a curse as a blessing. Economically, the bonanza resulted mostly in disappointing outcomes. Rather than fueling long-term prosperity, the boom intensified an unhealthy dependency on oil itself and left producing countries like Saudi Arabia vulnerable to unstable energy markets abroad and corruption at home. For a variety of reasons, oil wealth stymied efforts to stimulate diverse economies. Oil-producing governments became wholly tied to their prize, unable to use the wealth it brought in to grow the economy in new directions. Likewise, citizens became dependent on bloated states for salaries, subsidies, and the provision of cradle-to-grave services. The political consequences of oil wealth were also familiar. The oil crisis of 1973 and 1974 enabled the Saudis to use oil wealth to purchase support and consolidate their grip on power, securing the autocratic character of their regime.[13] But wealth alone does not explain the full impact of oil on politics in Saudi Arabia. While oil money helped strengthen autocracy in the kingdom, oil's impact on the political order and on political authority has a longer and more complicated history.

Political authority in Saudi Arabia derived from a number of sources, historically. Saudi Arabia was founded on conquest and violence. In the first three decades of the twentieth century, the Saudi family and its supporters waged a series of bloody campaigns to conquer the Arabian Peninsula. From their perch in the central Arabian Desert, they built an empire through war. But because the Saudis brutalized Arabia's denizens and used force to compel their submission, the result was the establishment of a weak polity vulnerable to various pressures, including from a mutinous army, a contentious clergy, and legions of imperial subjects who bristled against Saudi rule. Other than its extended family and tribal alliances, the ruling family had no social, ideological, or political base of support outside central Arabia until late in the century.[14] The Saudis compounded the effects of their imperial violence by imposing a strict Islamic worldview, one that demanded uncompromising conformity.

Violence and religion were not enough to guarantee the long-term political authority or stability the Saudis craved, however. They also sought other means to institutionalize and secure their power and build a modern state. Among these was gaining control over the peninsula's natural resources, including sustained efforts to manage and remake the environment. Establishing authority over resources and the environment has been central to the Al Saud's calculus of power and its approach to governance since the early twentieth century.[15] In this respect, Saudi Arabia's modern history has hardly been exceptional.

Saudi Arabia is perhaps better known for the influence of its clerics than the politics of its environment—for good reason. Since early in the twentieth century, when Saudi Arabia's founding monarch, Abd al-Aziz ibn Saud, stormed Riyadh with a small band of warriors, wrestled power away from his family's rivals, and launched his quest for suzerainty, the legitimacy of his rule has been based on a grand bargain. In exchange for their blessing of his right to worldly power, Abd al-Aziz ibn Saud granted central Arabia's conservative clergy, the legatees of the eighteenth-century founder of Wahhabism, the power to oversee and police the social and cultural life of those the new polity came to rule. Islam and its Wahhabi interpreters played a key role in sanctioning the legitimacy of the new regime and have done so ever since. But religion was not the only instrument of power. Often, it was not even the most important.[16]

Even before the consolidation of the Saudi state, the environment's place in the political reasoning of the Saudis was evident. During the first two decades of the century, when the future founders of the kingdom led a series of campaigns to conquer the Arabian Peninsula, establishing the territorial foundation for the modern state, the Saudis used water, land, and agriculture as incentives to recruit, maintain, and control their armies. Most of the warriors known as the Ikhwan (Brotherhood), who filled the ranks of the Saudi fighting forces, were former nomadic tribesmen from central Arabia, near the Al Saud's center of power. Their recruitment as a fighting force was partly the result of an intense missionary campaign.[17] Religious zealotry accounts for only part of why they signed on to the Saudi imperial project, however. As part of their program to gain Ikhwan support, political authorities offered them physical relief from the perils of desert life. They did so by guaranteeing the Ikhwan access to water and fertile agricultural land, often as the spoils of battle. In exchange for such access, Saudi leaders mandated that the Ikhwan settle in permanent farming communities *(hujjar)* across the peninsula, forgoing their peripatetic past for a sedentary present and future. The political imperative for settling the Ikhwan was clear. A settled army, even one spread across vast Arabia, was easier to call to action than one constantly in motion. It was also easier to oversee, and to combat in the event of mutiny.[18] In the end, the Ikhwan warriors made miserable farmers, and they abandoned the *hujjar* after the consolidation of Saudi control across the peninsula. In spite of the Ikhwan's rejection of settled life, the experiment made it clear that the Saudis possessed an instinct for using the environment to achieve political ends.

The pattern persisted well after the era of conquest. Arabia's people, the subjects of Saudi imperial rule, needed and expected regular access to freshwater. The young Saudi government, which desperately desired to build a social foundation of support, used water as a means to build its political credentials and base of power in cities such as Mecca, Jidda, and Medina. The Saudis co-opted the services of the powerful urban guild of water carriers historically charged with a range of responsibilities. The water carriers were responsible for providing liquid relief to those performing the annual hajj pilgrimage. They also collected an array of taxes—including the head tax on pilgrims, the primary source of revenue for the Saudis before oil, as well as taxes on religious trusts and buildings—which they turned over to the Saudis "with great alacrity and at little expense."[19] By co-opting the water carriers, the Saudis secured not only the services of the most powerful and established force for the extraction of revenue but also the means to discipline and control those they served. In securing the water carriers, they also gained the services of the largest police force in the Hejaz and thus the ability to impose their political will on the people. The combined powers of the guild—the ability to nourish, to tax, and to punish—made water carriers the ideal surrogates for the emerging Saudi state.

Control over water was particularly critical, but it was just one part of what would become a much larger environmental imperative in Saudi Arabian state and nation building in the twentieth century. Equally important was power over the lands that sustained or enabled agriculture and, thus, agriculture itself. Saudi leaders came to see, like all modern state builders, that having power over the environment was instrumental to centralizing control, providing a source of tax revenue, accessing labor, and ensuring national security.[20] It was also tantamount to having power over people, their bodies, their purses, their movements, and the ways they used space and land, all basic elements of modern governmental authority. Controlling nature, as well as working to administer and order it, has long been a basic instrument of domestic statecraft worldwide. Saudi Arabia's history was consistent with patterns of global development and the emergence of political authority across the third world and the developing world in the twentieth century. Power over land, property, and resources went hand in hand with the power to determine, govern, and police the territoriality of the nation-state, and thus the sovereignty of the state itself.[21]

Saudi efforts to master and remake the environment spanned the twentieth century. Over the course of the century, the imperative was primarily Saudi-driven, embraced and formulated by the kingdom's ruling elites, who had clear political and economic goals. They understood well that the security of their regime, and their political authority, depended in part on achieving control over the environment and the region's resources. Ambitious and visionary, the Saudis were nevertheless unable to go it alone, at least not early on. The government lacked the human and technical resources to turn its leaders' vision into practice. Eventually the country would come to possess the skill and technical capacity to undertake its own work in managing and engineering the environment. Thanks to oil, it turned out that the Saudis would have help getting there.

Oil wealth eased the financial costs of mastering the environment, turning an empire into a state, and securing political power.[22] The Saudis secured financial support when they signed lucrative agreements allowing American oil companies to prospect for crude oil in 1933. Advance royalties from the American oil company Standard Oil of California, as well as timely loans, lifted some of the burden on the Saudi treasury. The discovery of oil in commercial quantities in 1938 guaranteed the Saudis a sound source of financial security for the foreseeable future. But oil played a key role in strengthening political authority in other more fundamental and often unseen ways as well. Oil was a powerful magnet, attracting the interest and energies of thousands of people from around the country, the region, and the world. Oil work took numerous forms, from wildcatting to building oil pipelines to staffing various facilities.

Among the most politically influential of those who worked in Saudi Arabia were the scientists, engineers, and experts who came to prospect for oil and to build the country's oil-industry infrastructure. They did that and much more. Saudi Arabia's eager leaders also tapped into their expertise to map the country's nonpetroleum natural resources and develop plans to use them. The efforts of foreign and domestic experts, an international network of technicians and technocrats connected through their technical missions *and* oil, were instrumental in helping the Saudi government achieve its environmental and political ambitions. It was in great measure through their work that the Saudis secured their realm.[23]

It is difficult to overestimate the impact and the scope and scale of their efforts. Over the course of the twentieth century, scientists, engineers, and social scientists helped shape the basic institutions of Saudi Arabia's political system, from its treasury to its military to its agricultural and environmental planning. They also often oversaw and managed the building of the kingdom's material infrastructure, from irrigation networks and dams to roadways and cities. Many of those who worked in the kingdom also traveled in the region and plied their expertise elsewhere as well. Throughout the century Saudi Arabia was integrated into global networks of capital, institutions, consulting firms, research institutes, and expertise as a result of the work undertaken by the scientists and experts who passed through and worked in the kingdom. Saudi Arabia's history was not only similar to that of other developing states but it was also often connected to them through complex transnational networks.

Knowledge production was as important as the work of constructing infrastructure and development projects. Scientists and technicians assumed leading roles as advisers and consultants to the government and, for a time, even headed key institutions. Well paid, they helped produce reams of data about water resources, soil salinity, agriculture, and so on. They also offered an equally voluminous range of suggestions for how to manage and exploit the kingdom's environment. Their efforts shaped the way the country's leaders would think not only about their natural resources but also about the people who depended on them. The Saudi government learned as much about its farmers as it did soil types and water aquifers. Such information was critical to a government that sought increasingly layered and more direct ways to assert its power and link its subjects to the central authority. In addition to producing knowledge about the environment and society, Saudi Arabia's experts influenced and shaped the creation of the country's agricultural and environmental markets. They imagined and helped diagram various ways that communities could be better connected with one another and the central authorities, creating a national market in which the government would have considerable influence and control—another means of strengthening its power.

Many of those who carried out the work of exploring, cataloging, and engineering Saudi Arabia's natural resources—for example, Federico Vidal, a Harvard-trained anthropologist who worked for Aramco—appear in few works of history. Others have featured more prominently, such as Karl Twitchell, an American geologist who was an early believer in the idea that Saudi Arabia possessed significant oil deposits. Vidal and Twitchell played important roles in shaping Saudi Arabia's environmental policy as well as its political power; their stories are related in several of the chapters that follow. Scientists and technical experts like Vidal and Twitchell did not consider themselves to be players in Saudi Arabia's political drama. Unlike the executives who made decisions about the operations of Aramco and who sought to influence political outcomes in Saudi Arabia, particularly by rooting out Arab nationalists who wished to assume ownership of the oil company's operations, men like Twitchell and Vidal claimed to be doing the dispassionate work of science, applying the principles of quantification, neutral observation, and reason in the service of improving the function and performance of humans and nonhumans.[24] But their work and its outcomes were as political as the work of Aramco's decision makers. They made significant contributions to the character of the political order. While they gathered and passed along valuable data about water, agriculture, and other natural resources, they helped shape the very terms by which Saudi Arabia's future administrators would think about the environment, how to manage it, and those engaged with it. Saudi Arabia not only incorporated the knowledge but also embraced the science as a means to manage its interests, to order nature *and* society. The claim and widespread belief that science was by its very nature apolitical proved convenient for the Saudi government, which used scientific expertise as a justification for increasingly intrusive efforts to manage and remake nature and society. Oil turned out to be not just a prized natural resource that generated great wealth; it also generated a set of relations among politics, big business, global capital, labor, and scientific expertise, all of which interacted to forge the modern state of Saudi Arabia.

Saudi Arabia was not exceptional regarding the relationship between science, technology and political power. In the mid- to late twentieth century, postcolonial and developing states leaned heavily on science and technology in building the machinery of modern governance.[25] State officials and advisers to the royal family jumped aboard the development bandwagon.[26] They came to see technology, technical expertise, and technical management as instrumental in solving environmental, agricultural, economic, and social and political challenges. Efforts to conquer and control nature bore significant fruit, institutionalizing political authority and making the country's subjects dependent on central authorities for services and goods. The building of dams, the construction of hydroelectric and desalination facilities, irrigation and drainage projects, and the extension of agricultural loans, as well as the design and implementation of sedentarization schemes, led to the creation of both physical and administrative networks that connected Saudi Arabian subjects across the Arabian Peninsula to the central government.[27] Saudi Arabia's citizens, many of whom continued to work the land for their livelihood late into the century, came to depend on the government for access to water, land, loans, and technology. This is just what the kingdom's central authorities desired.

While the environment was viewed as an object, something to be made and remade in order to secure control, the work carried out to exploit and engineer the environment shaped political authority itself.[28] The modern Saudi state was as much the outcome of the various efforts to order nature and society as the engine driving them.[29] This was true even though many Saudi Arabian development projects turned out to be technical disasters. As was the case throughout the world in the twentieth century, even in failure technology served political ends. Efforts to put into place the work undertaken by scientists and engineers had the effect of defining the nature of political authority. Saudi Arabia became not just an oil state but also a modern technostate, one in which science and expertise, scientific services, and technical capacity came to define the relationship between rulers and ruled. The result was a strong technopolitical central authority that used science and technology as instruments of power, but was equally dependent on them for its political authority and credibility. Saudi authoritarianism, then, was more of an outcome of its efforts to order nature and society than either a characteristic of the political order from its founding or the result of a peculiar relationship between Islam, the clergy, and the Al Saud.[30] And science and expertise also influenced how political authorities came to "see" society, as officials and technocrats embraced quantification, the principles of scientific management, and the pursuit of making nature and society legible.[31]

Saudi Arabia's leaders believed that mastery over the environment would translate into credibility, both at home and abroad, legitimizing the government to its subjects and its neighbors. The domestic audience, though, was paramount. As the work of exploring and engineering nature and society intensified at midcentury, Saudi leaders increasingly spoke of the state's service and commitment to its subjects, although they also demanded in return a commitment to honor the authority of the country's rulers. Authorities attempted to forge an image of a central government looking after the best interests of its citizens, providing services and protecting their interests. Environmental services, including irrigation projects, loan programs, dam building, and training, formed an important part of the kingdom's image-building program. Saudi Arabia's leaders marketed their environmental power as a promise to always do more. As early as the 1950s, political authorities attributed meaning and value to nature, to technology, and to the work of engineers and scientists. Moreover, Saudi leaders also promoted science, technology, and development as key markers of the Saudi nation, along with being part of the contract that bound ruled to ruler. In part, efforts to attribute meaning to technology filled in where Islam fell short. Although Saudi leaders hoped and then subsequently claimed it was the case, Islam was not a unifying force in Saudi Arabia. While Saudi leaders and officials claimed otherwise, the kingdom was not culturally or religiously homogeneous.[32] Many of its subjects bristled against the strictness of the official religion of the state, and while religion legitimized Saudi power in some communities, it was alienating in others.

Well aware of this, the leading members of the ruling family, as well as a generation of technocrats who led and staffed what became the country's bureaucracy, relied on scientists, technologists, and their knowledge and craft to further buttress the family's legitimacy. In spite of these efforts, the government failed to foster a widespread sense of national belonging or nationalism. Instead, even before the oil boom, it succeeded mostly in raising expectations among its subjects that they would and should receive increasing amounts of technical and material support, better-run state programs, and, above all, more access to the country's oil wealth in the form of services and privileges—more and better water, land, and other vital resources. By focusing so much energy on capturing resources and developing the environment, indeed in giving meaning to the idea of a national environment, the government made the environment an object of public attention and concern. Some of the kingdom's subjects, such as those in the Eastern Province, an especially important region that was home to all of the kingdom's oil as well as the country's richest water reserves, proved acutely aware of efforts by central authorities to use not only oil but also other resources, such as water and land, as political instruments. As their expectations about the work that oil could and should do rose, one of the ways they measured the sincerity of the government's commitment was through its handling of their concerns about agriculture, land management, sewage, water quality, public health, and pollution.

It turned out that many of the Saudis' promises were empty. Not everyone benefited from the state's largesse or its efforts to remake nature and society. This was true in many parts of the kingdom where oil wealth was distributed unevenly and where the effects of the government's efforts to order nature and society were detrimental. It was perhaps most notably true in the oil- and water-rich Eastern Province. There, disappointment with the state's handling of its oil wealth and its environmental development efforts took on various forms. In the middle decades of the century, as residents in the east took stock of the early impact of oil and environmental change, disappointment was channeled in constructive and hopeful directions. Locals took to the pages of the regional newspapers in efforts to detail their plight and to express early frustration that they were being left behind other regions and communities. There emerged a kind of environmental subjectivity, an effort by some residents to define their place in the nation and the idea of the nation itself by their relationship with oil, water, and land. Not only did the government ignore their entreaties for environmental relief and access to the growing spoils, but it actively worked to shut down opportunities for critics to express their frustration. By the late 1960s the central Saudi state was openly antagonistic to such calls from the region. The impact on local politics was profound. In less than two decades, residents in the Eastern Province went from seeking better terms with the government and a place in the nation to embracing radical Islamism and revolution. The height of their anger overlapped with the height of the kingdom's prosperity in the late 1970s amid the oil boom and Saudi Arabia's greatest financial windfall.

The connections between oil and efforts to manage and transform the environment were felt across the kingdom. It was a national story with dramatic consequences everywhere. Even so, the effects were not everywhere the same, with some regions experiencing greater dislocations than others. The chapters that follow explore both the national and the local dimensions of Saudi Arabia's oil history. At the local level, several chapters examine the impact of oil and environmental politics on the Eastern Province. Similar examinations of Saudi Arabia's other regions would certainly be merited and would yield considerable insight, but the Eastern Province occupies a particularly important place in Saudi Arabia's modern history. All of the kingdom's massive oil reserves are located in the region, and as a result, it has been the heart of the country's oil operations. The impact of Aramco's work in Saudi Arabia was most profoundly felt there, although the company's scientists worked further afield as well. In addition to oil, the Eastern Province possesses some of the richest water and agricultural resources in Arabia. Even if Saudi Arabia had no oil, the Eastern Province would have been a treasured prize in a country dominated by desert. Enabled by oil, some of the kingdom's biggest environmental engineering projects were undertaken first in the east. The region was often a testing ground for new development initiatives, a place to measure success, failure, and the political effectiveness of scientific experiment. Perhaps more than others in the kingdom, those living in the Eastern Province experienced the stark unevenness of Saudi oil and environmental policy, and this led to dramatic political outcomes. This was partly because the region has traditionally been home to a religiously diverse community in a country that has typically been hostile to such diversity. Unlike anywhere else in the kingdom, the Persian Gulf coast has been, and remains, home to both Shiites and Sunnis, with the former historically being in the majority. Relations between the Saudis and the Shiites have long been tumultuous. The religious worldview embraced by the royal family has viewed Shiites and Shiism with deep acrimony, with the leading religious figures periodically calling for their forced conversion to Wahhabism or their extermination. Official Saudi historiography has completely erased the existence of the despised Shiites.[33] Religious difference, and hence religious politics, became an important factor in how the environment became politicized. It might be tempting to argue that because of the region's special religious character, indeed its peculiarities, the impact of oil and environmental politics there was exaggerated or exceptional. The chapters that follow argue, however, that this was not the case.

Much of the focus on the Eastern Province is also the result of opportunity. Saudi Arabia's twentieth-century history, and especially the details of local social and political life there, remains something of an enigma. Although the kingdom has had a vibrant and tumultuous history, and although it played an important role in shaping the course of events in the Middle East in the second half of the century, scholarship on Saudi Arabia, as well as on most of the other Arabian Peninsula and Persian Gulf countries, for that matter, lies outside the mainstream of Middle East studies.[34] That Saudi Arabia continues to be a puzzle and remains on the margins of study is not entirely the product of scholarly disinterest, although historians and observers of the twentieth-century Arab Middle East have focused most of their analytical attention elsewhere. To some extent this lacuna can be explained by the closed door that scholars have historically come up against when attempting to carry out research inside Saudi Arabia. Until recently, researchers have been forbidden to enter the country and undertake any critical inquiry.[35] And even for those who have gained entry into Saudi Arabia, access has proven no guarantee that the sources necessary for thoughtful analysis are available or even exist. In addition to being an enigma, Saudi Arabia is a black box, a country that closely guards its secrets, particularly those that bear on the sources of political authority for the ruling family. *Desert Kingdom* attempts to partially pry open this black box, to explore the connections between political power, expertise, oil, and the environment. It begins with the story of Karl Twitchell, an American technical expert who helped set in motion the realization of what would become Saudi Arabia's political-environmental imperative.

2

In late December 1948 Karl Twitchell, an American geologist and mining engineer with close ties to the Saudi government, dispatched an urgent letter to his friend and the second most powerful person in Saudi Arabia, Minister of Finance Abdullah Sulaiman. Twitchell was alarmed by the drawing of the kingdom's southern boundary as it appeared in atlases and on globes in use throughout the United States and the United Kingdom. He alerted the finance minister that various mapmakers, including the cartographers from the American Geographical Society who drew the map of Saudi Arabia for the U.S. State Department in 1947, had either mistakenly drawn the country's southern border too far to the north or had wrongly marked it as "indefinite." These were grievous errors, mistakes that potentially left Saudi Arabia's boundaries vulnerable to dispute or seizure. Twitchell urged Sulaiman to lodge a protest with the "State Department in Washington and the Foreign Office in London, as well as [with] various map publishers . . . *immediately*."[1]

To most casual observers, and probably to most of the mapmakers in question, Twitchell's alarm would likely have seemed overwrought. Most of the area in question, a desert known ominously as the Empty Quarter, was a barren wasteland known best for its mountainous sand dunes and unforgiving heat, a place so treacherous that it was almost entirely uninhabitable. But Twitchell and his Saudi patrons had compelling cause for alarm. All believed that there was a very high likelihood that there was more oil awaiting discovery in the area. The geologist pointed out that "the importance of the Empty Quarter area south from Jabrin is now much greater than previously, as a[n oil] structure between Jabrin and Hofuf is now being drilled, and I was told that still further southerly there are other attractive structures."[2] Twitchell was more right than he knew. The structure being drilled in 1948 turned out to be the Ghawar supergiant oil field, the single largest oil field on the planet.

The prospect that more oil was trapped deep beneath the Empty Quarter's sediments made the uncertainty about Saudi Arabia's southern border an urgent matter. Though Twitchell was unnerved by the idea that the boundaries depicted on various maps could undermine the kingdom's claims to future oil discoveries, he also saw something of an opportunity in the uncertainty. He encouraged the Saudi finance minister to make an aggressive new territorial claim, suggesting that the Saudis use the indeterminacy of their southern border as an opportunity to demand that their borders be drawn as far south as possible, disregarding competing claims to sovereignty in the region from neighboring states. Already possessing an appetite for expansion, Saudi leaders needed little encouragement to push the kingdom's frontier. In the next few years Riyadh asserted bold new claims to territories in the south. In 1951 Riyadh staked a claim to the Buraimi oasis in present-day Oman, citing historical ties to the territory.[3] The Saudis had some interest in Buraimi itself, but they had even greater interest in the large oil fields that had been discovered in nearby Abu Dhabi. Drawn by the prospect of another El Dorado along the shores of the Persian Gulf, the Saudis sent in their army and seized the area from the local tribes. The kingdom's oil grab was eventually rebuffed by the British in 1955, who responded by marching in their own forces and driving the Saudis out.

There is no evidence that Karl Twitchell played any direct role in the siege of Buraimi. It is unlikely that an American scientist was privy to the political deliberations of the royal family or the governing elite when it came to matters of conquest. But it is nevertheless remarkable that the geologist felt suitably close to Saudi Arabia's power brokers to offer unsolicited advice that bore directly not only on the kingdom's boundaries but also on its very sovereignty. It is also noteworthy that Twitchell's advice was not predicated merely on the possibility that the deserts of South Arabia were home to more oil but was informed by his expert opinion and capacity as a geologist. Science, he assured the Saudis, justified both his own intervention and whatever attempt the Saudis made to secure their southern reach.

Twitchell and subsequent generations of both foreign and Saudi engineers, scientists, and experts were instrumental in securing Saudi Arabia's empire. Their efforts in support of the ruling family not only helped consolidate, institutionalize, and centralize Saudi political authority but also helped turn expertise, science, and technology into a key source of royal power. The work of experts, a transnational network of scientists and engineers active over much of the twentieth century, helped enroll millions of Saudi subjects in the state's emerging administrative order. They helped secure the country's borders, created vast new stores of knowledge and information about nature and society, consulted on and engineered the construction of infrastructure and other material manifestations of central authority, and assisted in the organization of a centrally controlled economy. In a place better known for the power of its clerics and the influence of faith, it was the work of experts and the influence of science that secured the political fortunes the ruling elite. And it was the work of experts and scientists that helped turn the Saudi empire into a state.

Saudi rulers increasingly demanded and paid for information about territory, resources, and people, information that scientists such as Twitchell happily provided. Information served the quest for control. But experts like Twitchell were not just compilers of data—data used by central authorities to know and oversee their dominion. They also influenced the very terms by which the authorities came to understand and see the territory, resources, and people they sought to command, shaping the terms of power and the nature of the relations through which power was wielded. Natural resources, territory, and people emerged as not only things to control but also as problems to be solved, objects to be developed, subjects to be managed. Experts argued that the Saudis' objectives could be achieved, and both their and the governments' interests served, only through a strong central state. The result was that managerial ability was collapsed with political authority. The two became one and the same. More important, the political nature of the relationship was obscured, masked within the language of rational, apolitical, dispassionate science.

Neither Twitchell nor those who followed him, nor most historians who have taken account of the work of science and expertise in the making of modern Saudi political authority, considered themselves political agents, let alone advocates for the creation of what amounted to a strong authoritarian state in Arabia. Like most who have thrown their weight behind science and technology, experts, and the knowledge they create, Saudi Arabia's experts claimed to be doing the work of progress, guiding the kingdom toward modernity, lifting up an isolated people. Twitchell and his chroniclers have gone a step further, too, routinely repeating the tale that the geologist was doing the work of philanthropy in Arabia, work that was "gifted" to the kingdom so that it might see a better and more prosperous day. Claims of scientific beneficence, the mid-century equivalent of the civilizing mission, set aside the material motives of those who traveled to and travailed in Arabia. Given the Saudis' oil and oil wealth, there was profit to be made in consulting for Arabia. In the service of the empire, men such as Twitchell certainly sought a share of the spoils. It was here, at the intersection of knowledge production and the application of science and technology, that the second element of Saudi political authority was achieved, through the creation of a national economy and an integrated market.

The story of experts and expertise in Saudi Arabia is a global story, one in which actors from within the kingdom, and without, drove events. The effect of their efforts helped secure Saudi power and shaped the nature of governance. The idea of a centralized Saudi state was, in many ways, the result of their work. But while the centralized state was served through the labor of experts, it is important to keep in mind that the experts themselves were fully integrated into the political order. By serving Saudi Arabia's rulers, Twitchell not only helped shore up Saudi authority over space, people, and markets but also was a key component of the new relations that took hold. Twitchell was a cog in the Saudi imperial and authoritarian regime.

Scientists and engineers were engaged in many endeavors in Arabia in the middle of the twentieth century. But most important in the 1930s and 1940s was the production of knowledge about the environment, and attempts to conquer and to remake the environment, that formed the early foundation for Saudi authority. Indeed, the equation of political power with control over the nonpetroleum natural resources produced in the Arabian Peninsula has been a central part of the calculus of Saudi power from early in the twentieth century. Most notably, authority over water and the lands that sustained or enabled agriculture, and thus agriculture itself, was essential to political power. Saudi rulers pursued control over both throughout the twentieth century as a means to strengthen and secure their reign, and they emphasized the importance of water and agriculture to their political fortunes. Given the paucity of life-sustaining natural resources on the overwhelmingly arid Arabian Peninsula, the Saudi desire to dominate them is not surprising. Both settled and nomadic communities depended on and often struggled violently to gain access to water resources for their survival. No less important was the role of agriculture, which occupied the energies of the vast majority of nomads and settled farmers alike, who farmed and herded intensively just to sustain the most meager of livings. Beyond asserting their authority over established farms and farmers, Saudi rulers integrated agriculture, especially its expansion across the peninsula, into their strategy for deepening their power.

THE CONQUEST OF WATER

At its founding in 1932, Saudi Arabia occupied around 80 percent of the Arabian Peninsula (just under 900,000 square miles), stretching from Iraq, Kuwait, and Jordan in the north to Yemen and Oman in the south, with the Persian Gulf on its east coast and the Red Sea on its west. Throughout history more than half of the peninsula has been desert.[4] So arid is Saudi Arabia that it has no permanent natural lakes or rivers. In recent centuries rainfall has been minimal, except in the southwest region of Asir, where remnants of Indian Ocean monsoons annually drop a small amount of rain, only twelve to twenty inches. The rest of the region has historically received considerably less precipitation, making water the peninsula's scarcest resource. Considering the harsh climate, it might appear absurd that agriculture would become one of the Saudi government's most important preoccupations in the twentieth century. But what water there was, usually located in oases spread across the peninsula, supported agriculture that, although hardly bountiful, did prove sufficient to feed large communities and was even adequate enough to allow the export of some crops. Except for the western region of Hejaz, home to the holy cities of Medina and Mecca and the commercial port of Jidda, most non-nomadic communities in the Arabian Peninsula lived in agriculturally dominated oases or at least close to underground springs that allowed for limited farming and the herding of sheep, horses, and camels. Even before the twentieth century, when they intensively and successfully asserted their dominance over the region's precious hydrological resources, Saudi leaders understood that their political fortunes were linked to the control of water, the agricultural production it made possible, and, most important, the people who depended on both.

Although markedly different in scale and ambition, Saudi efforts to capture, consolidate, and develop the Arabian Peninsula's agricultural resources in the twentieth century were not unprecedented. Nor were the political ends for which agricultural resources were put to use. Given the environmental challenges of life in the Najd region in central Arabia, the desert homeland of the Al Saud and their base of power from the late eighteenth through the twenty-first century, the expansion of agricultural production was often a matter of life and death. Arid by any measure, the Najdi climate severely restricted the quantity and quality of agricultural production for the region's inhabitants. Until the mid-twentieth century, settled Najdis eked out a living by tapping as much nourishing power as they could from the region's limited natural resources. Indeed, before the founding of the kingdom, the discovery of oil, and the integration of Saudi Arabia into the global economy, agriculture was the central pillar of economic life.

In the nineteenth century the cities of Najd "were merely big villages, where economic life was based on agriculture and modest trade with Bedouin and the trading centers in the surrounding regions."[5] Agricultural lands were situated in the oases within or close to the towns.[6] Small groves of date palm trees cut lush swaths of green through an otherwise dusty landscape. Dates were the staple crop, although small cultivators also grew wheat and barley, as well as millet, vegetables, and some fruits, including limes and figs. In addition to date production, which continued to dominate the local economy until the mid-twentieth century, the breeding of camels, horses, and sheep also constituted important parts of the Najdi economy. Water was drawn from hand-dug wells. With the assistance of animals, typically donkeys, farmers constructed barely adequate irrigation networks that delivered only enough water to maintain modest production. Outside the oasis towns and villages, the nomadic Bedouin also practiced various forms of agriculture, mostly animal husbandry, producing livestock, hides, wool, and milk. They traded with settled farmers and merchants in the region's towns.[7]

Although Najdi agriculturalists mastered the limited resources available to them, they faced considerable difficulties in producing enough food to satisfy local demand. One historian has noted that "although every piece of cultivable land was used as intensively as traditional techniques allowed, Najdi towns were seldom self sufficient."[8] Farmers and merchants engaged in cross-peninsula trade, trekking periodically to either the Red Sea or the Persian Gulf coast to hawk their own wares and buy sufficient stores for their families and customers back home. Wealthy Najdis even cultivated exotic tastes.

Local consumption patterns, particularly the heavy consumption of rice by elites, demonstrated that imports not only formed a valuable part of the local diet but also helped define the social hierarchy. Most food imports came from South Asia, although a good many vegetables and even superior varieties of dates were harvested in eastern Arabia. Traders and merchants were not solely preoccupied with the purchase of foodstuff. They imported other things as well: coffee, tea, textiles, tobacco, weapons, and ammunition. Najdis delivered various goods to the market, exporting horses, camels, sheep, and hides.[9]

In addition to being stark, the Najdi climate was cruel. That cruelty helped set in motion rivalries that shaped subsequent Saudi political strategy. Periodically heavy rains devastated local towns, destroying infrastructure and savaging the already vulnerable gardens. The floods that resulted from seasonal downpours also wiped out city defenses, rendering local towns open to attack by Bedouin raiding parties. Raiders stole livestock, especially horses, seized other loot, and killed citizens. Perhaps most devastating, and seemingly harmful to their own long-term interests and need for food, the Bedouin raiders also often razed the palm groves, destroying vital date-producing trees. Because date palms take years to mature and produce in good quantity, the effects of such raids were often catastrophic. The mortal threat posed by Bedouin raiders helped shape Saudi agricultural policy in the twentieth century, when the rulers sought to settle the nomads in agricultural settlements to subdue them. But well before they set out to use agriculture as a tool for consolidating their political power and defeating potential rivals in the twentieth century, the Al Saud sought to expand its sphere of influence by capturing rich agricultural resources beyond Najd. The two oases of the Eastern Province, al-Hasa and Qatif, were particularly alluring prizes.[10]

In contrast to the aridity of Najd, the oases of eastern Arabia were resource rich, seemingly drenched in life-giving water and abundantly stocked with lush palm groves and vegetable gardens. Hundreds of thousands of palm trees filled the eastern oases, and water, which bubbled up from artesian wells, gushed through the groves. While dates were the dominant crop, local cultivators also harvested an array of fruits and vegetables, including pomegranates, apricots, peaches, figs, cucumbers, tomatoes, lemons, oranges, various melons, green beans, and even cotton.[11] Over the course of two centuries, Saudi leaders routinely set their expansionist gaze eastward and set out to seize the region's rich resources.[12]

The conquests of the Arabian Peninsula in the twentieth century raised the challenge of how the Saudis would administer the natural resources and agricultural areas they now ruled over. While state leaders did periodically seize produce from farming communities such as those in the east, it was probably a rare occurrence. There are no available and reliable sources regarding forcible seizures and their frequency, but conducting violent raids on farms and farmers would have been counterproductive as a long-term strategy for a state that until the 1940s was strapped for revenue. In desperate times, such as during depression or war, the forced surrender of crops made economic and political sense to the royal family, whose fortunes were undermined by such global crises. For the most part, however, the Saudis seem to have preferred to allow farmers to farm and trade their produce in a secure—if rigidly controlled—environment, promoting economic security and as much commercial vibrancy as possible, given the climate.

One reason for the Saudis' preference for maintaining a healthy agricultural environment in the twentieth century is clear; they relied on it for tax revenue. From 1902 to the 1940s, the Saudi state was cash poor. Although the kingdom entered into an agreement with the consortium of American oil companies that would eventually become the Arabian American Oil Company, or Aramco, in 1933 and relied heavily on them for loans drawn on future oil revenues, it was not until after World War II that the first significant revenues from oil sales began to pour in. Until the end of the war and the subsequent rise in oil revenues, the main source of income for the central government was the tax revenue generated by foreign visitors making the hajj, the annual pilgrimage to Mecca.[13]

In addition to serving the financial need for the limited funds provided by agricultural taxes, the struggle to control nature and farming was part of a political struggle to subdue potential rivals. Among the key threats to Saudi power were the settled farming and merchant communities on the periphery of the peninsula. The Saudis sought early on to integrate the agricultural hinterlands into a unified national economy under their control. They did not fully succeed until midcentury, when efforts to co-opt the merchants and farmers bore fruit, but the understanding that economic integration would strengthen Saudi power was well understood in the first few decades of the century.[14] Part of the strategy resulted from Saudis' claiming broad ownership rights over the most fertile lands. They did not eject farmers from their fields, but they did fundamentally transform the land-tenure system, claiming direct ownership. Local farmers were poorly equipped to resist Saudi military and police power and typically had little choice but to comply, surrendering ownership. By claiming ownership and appointing regional overseers to observe and police local affairs in the first few decades of the century, Saudi rulers did not aim to disrupt or undermine production. Rather, they sought to make clear their authority, to capitalize on existing success, and to expand production, an approach they continued during the decades that followed.

The forced incorporation of the natural-resource-rich oases into the new polity was only one part of a broader set of objectives having to do with agriculture. Rulers also decided early on to use water and agriculture as tools to subdue potential political rivals among the nonsettled population. Most important, the Saudis and their backers used agriculture to rein in the tribal and Bedouin forces that threatened their newfound, and still loose, grip on power. The Saudi Arabian historian Abdulaziz al-Fahad notes that "in writings about the country, the Saudi state is typically identified with the Bedouin, the tribe or nomads, and 'tribal values' are supposed to suffuse the state, at least at its inception. Such identification is difficult to sustain notwithstanding its prevalence, for this state had been (and continues to some extent to be) an exclusively *hadari* [settled] endeavor with profound anti-tribal and anti-Bedouin tendencies, and circumscribed roles for the Bedouins and their tribes."[15] Indeed, the founding of the kingdom, and successfully securing it, depended on quelling tribal tensions and defusing the threat posed by communities that had historically enjoyed freedom of movement and whose income derived in part from raiding *(ghazu)*, an activity wholly destabilizing to the Saudi polity.

Less than a decade after establishing control over Riyadh in 1902, the Saudis launched a two-pronged strategy to bring the Bedouin under control. The first plan was to promote their loyalty to the ruling family by exposing them to an intensive proselytizing and recruiting campaign that used faith to gain fealty.[16] The second part of their strategy was to restrain and manage the Bedouin through settlement, by transforming them into a *hadari*, or settled, farming and warrior class subordinate to the centralized power in Najd.[17] As warriors, they were indoctrinated as the Ikhwan and became a terrifying military force that proved instrumental in helping the Al Saud conquer the Arabian Peninsula.[18] Adept at war, the Ikhwan proved less adept at farming, taking slowly if at all to agriculture.

In spite of the inability or unwillingness of the Ikhwan to take the agricultural imperative seriously, the strategic significance that the Saudis attributed to the settlement policy marked a major turning point in the political history of the Arabian Peninsula. Encouraging sedentarization and using settlements as mechanisms to end politically threatening raiding practices not only reflected broad strategic thinking on the part of Saudi leaders but was also most likely unprecedented—especially the emphasis on permanency that they hoped would be made possible through cultivation. The Saudis, in partnership with religious scholars, had asserted peninsula-wide authority in the past, but they had not so boldly attempted to create both a political and a socioeconomic framework to justify their rule. The sedentarization scheme possessed a clear political goal: the protection and projection of Saudi power. The struggle to convert nomads into farmers also reflected the first large-scale social-engineering project imagined and sponsored by the Saudis. It was no less remarkable for its cultural ambition, which was not only to overturn deeply ingrained anti-*hadari* prejudices among the Bedouin, feelings that had been commented on for centuries by Arab chroniclers, but also to take an additional, previously unthinkable step and convert the *badu* into *hadarūn,* the very thing the Bedouin had historically loathed.[19] Although the agricultural component failed for the most part, the fact that the rulers connected religion and agriculture reflected the scope of their much grander political vision and ambition.

The sedentarization-cum-agricultural program also reflected a specifically spatially oriented strategic thinking. While supporting and eventually compelling the settlement of Bedouin near water sources was clearly necessary for their survival, the location of water came to assume a significance all its own. Although there is little documentary evidence to show it conclusively, it seems that the Al Saud learned to see the location of water as strategically important, especially when it sought to dispatch the Ikhwan on expansionist missions. It made little sense to have settlements clustered tightly around the seat of central authority, although that would have made administrating and governing the communities considerably easier. Knowing about and establishing control over well-spaced water resources made it possible to maintain *hujjar*-military outposts at strategically vital locations, some closer to the Hejaz and others nearer al-Hasa. It is also illustrative that in the 1930s and especially the 1940s, well after the first sedentarization programs had been completed, Saudi officials turned to Western geologists to map more completely the water resources across the peninsula. Although it is ahistorical to read later strategic thinking into an earlier period, it is reasonable to conclude, and even patronizing not to, that Saudi leaders had already realized that nature, water, and agriculture could be harnessed for political ends with regard to *both* settled and nomadic communities.

Later in the century Saudi leaders continued to keep a close watch on farming for the same reasons. And the targeting of agriculturally based communities made clear sense, as most of those residing in the peninsula were engaged in some form of agriculture. Periodic surveys and studies revealed a consistent pattern over the course of the twentieth century. The United Nations Food and Agriculture Organization (FAO) reported in 1956 that 78 percent of the kingdom's citizens made their living from agriculture.[20] According to the FAO only 22 percent of the national population was urban. Even as late as 1970, as much as one half of the population worked either as agricultural day laborers or on their own farms.[21] The Saudi Ministry of Agriculture reported in 1974 that out of a population of about 7 million inhabitants, around 45 percent of the entire labor force was in agriculture.[22] While much Saudi energy was spent on bringing farming communities into their sphere of influence, most pastoralists were not permanently settled. No figures are available for the percentage of the population constituted by nomadic and seminomadic communities at the beginning of the century, but the FAO report claimed that at least 66 percent of the population continued to be nomadic as late as 1956. Although settled farming communities were not always easily pacified, the Saudis and their supporters eventually quelled most of them.

GEOLOGY AND POWER

In the 1930s and early 1940s the Saudi concern with tapping the economic and political power of water and agriculture expanded to include other natural resources they believed would prove to be the lifeblood of the regime. The discovery of oil in Iraq, Iran, and Bahrain by American and European geologists, and the material rewards it brought, eventually galvanized Saudi interest in exploring for oil in their own country. Before the discovery of oil and the "petrolization" of the Saudi state, however, the kingdom's leaders turned to the science of geology, and to American geologists in particular, in the hope that something of value could be unearthed from beneath the arid landscape.

The turn to geology reflected practical interests, especially the desire to harness resources and benefit economically from them. But it also reflected a deepening understanding of which natural resources were fundamental to power. That understanding came to be shared, and indeed shaped, by the kingdom's external relations. The quest by Saudi officials to expand their knowledge of the kingdom's geological and natural environment marked a continuation of the strategic thinking that first evolved while they attempted to settle the Bedouin. Partly as a result of the failure of the Ikhwani experiment and partly in an effort to perfect it, Saudi leaders came to see that having a more systematic knowledge of their natural environment was a precursor to controlling the political environment.

Although the full implications of the decision to invite foreign geologists in to perform the work on behalf of the state were unpredictable at the time, they would prove to be profound and would establish a foundation for economic and political relations that have endured until today. Saudi-American relations, in particular, were shaped in the 1930s by the work of the first American geologists in Arabia, most of whom simultaneously served American and Saudi Arabian political and commercial interests. The nature of U.S.-Saudi relations shifted over the course of the twentieth century, subject to a variety of global and local political crises and challenges, but the basic formula, in which maintaining Saudi rule was critical to U.S. national security, was established early on.

At the heart of the geopolitical relationship was oil, of course. Saudi Arabia's possession of the world's largest oil reserves guaranteed that the United States would go so far as to wage war in its defense. Oil was just too vital to the American economy for the United States to leave the fate of Saudi oil to chance, subject to cold war rivals or Saudi Arabia's allegedly predatory neighbors. Oil also played an important role in shaping American behavior inside Saudi Arabia. Since World War II, when the kingdom's oil riches became clear, the U.S. government has placed a high priority on the security and stability of the Saudi regime, no matter its brutality or excesses. A stable authoritarian Saudi government beholden to American oil companies and to U.S. security assurances was eminently preferable to a more liberal polity that would potentially attend to its citizens' needs and interests first. For American businesses, including big oil as well as the private consultants, scientists, and engineers who went to work for the Saudi government, ensuring the stability of the Saudi regime also meant ensuring their own access to some of the windfall generated by the sale of oil. The pursuit of profit and patronage went hand in hand with efforts to strengthen the capacity and reach of the central Saudi government.

Although it is tacitly understood in most analyses of U.S.-Saudi relations, the significance of science and geology to the two countries' relations—to the shaping of Saudi Arabia's national economy, the territoriality of the nation-state, and what Saudi authorities knew about the space over which they ruled, and thus their authority itself—is underappreciated. Moreover, the full import of the work of scientists and engineers for the countries' shared relations and, especially, for Saudi Arabia's political philosophy throughout the twentieth century has been overlooked completely.

Observers have tended to mythologize the role of Americans in Saudi Arabia, lionizing the contributions of geologists and businessmen (there were no businesswomen). A common trope in the literature is the intrepid American scientist or engineer who braved unforgiving conditions and exotic surroundings to bring modernity to benighted locals.[23] Aside from the racism bound up in such characterizations, the focus on the alleged heroism of the scientists overlooks both the profound impact that their work had on the evolving political logic that eventually took root in the kingdom and their role in enabling the more complete realization of Saudi political dominance. The single-minded obsession with the American version of the colonial civilizing mission, recast as a modernizing mission, has also tended to ignore the ugly side of the encounter.[24] This approach has not only overlooked but also misrepresented the material nature of the relationship between American experts and the Saudi government, as the former pursued an ever-increasing share of the spoils from oil sales and Saudi Arabia's privileged position in the global economy. A relationship that many have cast as mutually beneficial—as an exchange of expertise for oil—boiled down to the pursuit of financial gain. The pursuit of wealth was not and is not in itself problematic. What merits greater scrutiny, though, are the political consequences of that pursuit.

The material incentives that galvanized the interest of American engineers were often hidden. As was the case elsewhere in the post–World War II era, engineers, scientists, and technicians were swept up in the fervor of increasingly powerful and compelling theories about modernization and development. Science, technology, and expert planning, they believed and argued, offered Saudi Arabia a route to prosperity, stability, progress, and happiness—values they accepted as universal, transparent, and without complication. But for all the talk of development and progress, carried out in the name of science and service to Saudis everywhere, the bottom line was that American scientists served Saudi political power in the building of an authoritarian political system, one that used science and knowledge and technology and the environment as means to shore up centralized Saudi dominance. While it might be tempting to conclude that this relationship reflected the initiative of the American experts who worked in the kingdom, it is important to note that the Saudis understood, like modern state builders everywhere, that their authority and power stemmed not only from their physical control of the environment but also from their ability to integrate, remake, and place the environment within a broader set of relations—state bureaucracy, institutions, and so on. American geologists contributed to, but did not direct, the further entrenchment of the Saudi strategic thinking that had taken shape earlier in the century.

In addition to their talk of progress, Americans in the kingdom introduced corollaries that had valuable implications for future Saudi environmental and scientific strategy. Geologists and engineers enjoyed the favor of Saudi leaders because they had special expertise and knowledge, which enabled them to offer new and useful information about the kingdom to its rulers. Their scientific and technical knowledge did allow the visiting Americans to employ their skills and know-how, revealing details about the natural environment and constructing technologies to exploit it. At the time, there were few in the kingdom who could lay claim to similar abilities. But more important than the initial difference in technical expertise between Americans and Saudi Arabians was the establishment of the connection between that expertise and authority, a connection that state leaders would subsequently seek to establish for themselves. The first wave of Western scientists and engineers who worked in the kingdom helped introduce a belief that achieving progress through science and technology was an apolitical act. Even though they reported directly to Saudi rulers and officials—serving the interests of the state—they believed uncritically and unyieldingly in the vision of progress that could be wrought through science and technology. State leaders would come to mimic the progress narrative, claiming openly that they were serving the interests of the nation through scientific and technological means.

Abd al-Aziz ibn Saud first invited an American geologist to survey his territory's natural resources several years before he became king. In late 1930 he requested a conference with Charles R. Crane, a former U.S. representative to China, a philanthropist deeply involved in the political changes that swept the Middle East after World War I, to ask for his aid in undertaking an inventory of the peninsula's water resources. In 1926 and 1927 Crane had visited Yemen and helped finance surveys of that country's mineral resources. Crane had hired the American Karl Twitchell as his chief geologist and engineer, dispatching him on several expeditions to Yemen to carry out the surveys as well as to complete other projects, including investigating the possibility of building a road network, building agricultural demonstration posts, installing water-pumping windmills, and erecting "the only steel truss highway bridge in Arabia."[25] According to Twitchell, who later recorded his experiences in a volume on Saudi Arabia and its natural resources first published in 1947, "reports of these unusual gifts reached Saudi Arabia," and "Mr. Crane accepted an invitation of King Ibn-Saud to visit him in Jidda" to explore ways of rendering assistance to him. "It soon appeared" to Twitchell that the Saudi regent's "principal desire was to find ample water supplies, especially flowing artesian wells in the Hijaz and Najd." Eager to accommodate the Saudi ruler, Crane "donated" the services of Twitchell, who in April 1931 began a comprehensive survey, spanning 1,500 miles, of the Hejaz's water resources.[26]

Twitchell, accompanied by his wife, Norah, who "was ill part of the time," filed a "pessimistic report" that found "no geological evidence to justify the hope for flowing artesian wells." The American reported his findings directly to the powerful Saudi finance minister, Abdullah Sulaiman. Sulaiman lamented the disappointing news and apparently confided in the geologist that the kingdom was near-desperate for sources of income. Twitchell recalled that the powerful minister stated that "the King and the Saudi government quite realized that practically all their revenue was then dependent on the annual pilgrimage to Mecca; that this fluctuated from year to year, and might become much less in the future than it had been in the past." It was clear to Sulaiman, according to Twitchell's recollection, that his reports "did not encourage anticipation of any large agricultural increases in the Hijaz."[27]

Twitchell did have some promising news to report, however. Based on his field research, he suggested that there were encouraging geological indications that the Hejaz held mineral riches, including what he believed were King Solomon's gold mines. His preliminary findings, which led Twitchell to propose a gold-prospecting expedition to both the Saudi ruler in Jidda and Crane, who was in New York, led to a mining mission in Taif, a city east of Jidda. He and his team of miners initiated work in October 1931 and spent six months "drilling, pitting and sluicing," to disappointing results. He later recorded that "nothing developed which would be profitable to even local groups of Saudi Arabia."[28] Undaunted by the absence of gold, Twitchell relocated to Jidda, where he and Norah worked "to rehabilitate the city's water supply . . . the Waziria." Although Twitchell relegated the Jidda water-reclamation project to secondary importance in his later writings, the fact that he was charged with its undertaking so soon after the completion of the mining expedition reflected its significance to Saudi political leaders, who saw the restoration and augmentation of water delivery to the commercially vital port city as essential to their power over it.

The Saudis had demonstrated their concern with water in Jidda within two years of their conquest of the port city. Between 1926 and 1928 they commissioned the construction of two plants for condensing seawater, that produced an impressive but insufficient 135 tons of freshwater every twenty-four hours.[29] Upon his return to Jidda, Twitchell and his wife began repairing damaged terra-cotta pipes and water tunnels that the Turks had built sixty years previously at a location about seven miles east of the city. In the years since the original construction of the network, the water level had receded considerably. Local minders had also been forced to abandon the well site as a result of frequent Bedouin raids.[30] To raise the water output, the Twitchells supervised the construction of a "16 foot diameter American windmill . . . along with an auxiliary pump-jack and Diesel engine" that he claimed "raised an average of 40 gallons per minute into the water tunnel and flowed to Jidda 7 miles to the west, making an appreciable addition to the city water supply."[31]

The failure to locate much-hoped-for natural riches in the Hejaz hardly dampened Saudi hopes that the peninsula was home to mineral and natural wealth. Nor did the absence of water resources in the west challenge the Saudi belief that it was the key to political power elsewhere in the region. Twitchell, who finished building the Jidda water delivery system in late 1931, was then contracted by Abd al-Aziz to "advise him on the water resources and oil possibilities in his province of Hasa along the Persian Gulf. Although this would be a thousand mile trip over rough country, where no American had ever been, the invitation was readily accepted."[32] The geologist-engineer left his wife in charge of ongoing drill testing for water resources east of Jidda, and set out for al-Hasa in early December.

It was in the east where Twitchell and his geologist colleagues would make their most significant discovery. Twitchell spent several weeks surveying al-Hasa's geological features and even traveled to Bahrain, a small island, located twenty-five kilometers off the eastern shore of the peninsula, that shared similar characteristics with al-Hasa and where oil prospecting had already begun. After returning to Jidda, Twitchell advised the Saudi monarch to wait for the results of the Bahraini test drills before proceeding with any development plans in the east. The king agreed. Twitchell later recalled that Abd al-Aziz sent word "that on account of the depression, with the lack of pilgrims and consequent fall in revenue, he could not afford to follow out the development previously planned and agreed upon. Furthermore he wished me to try to find capital to carry out the development previously discussed [more mining, surveys for water resources and test drills for oil]."[33]

Twitchell returned to the United States in early 1932. Driven by his firm belief that oil was awaiting discovery in Arabia, the geologist once carrying out the work of a philanthropist now saw an opportunity for wealth. In July he began exploring in earnest U.S. commercial interest in prospecting for minerals and oil in the Arabian Peninsula. After a wave of initial rejections by mining and oil companies, his efforts eventually led to the signing of Saudi Arabia's oil concession agreement with the Standard Oil Company of California (Socal) in May 1933, out of which emerged an operating company that ultimately came to be known as the Arabian American Oil Company (Aramco).[34] The story of the concession agreement has been widely featured in accounts of the period and will not be repeated here. A few details are of interest, however. The Saudi Arabian government agreed to grant Socal exclusive drilling rights in al-Hasa (over an area of 318,000 square miles) in exchange for royalties on oil if any was discovered in commercial quantities and an initial loan of £33,000 in gold sovereigns. Late in 1933 the first team of geologists sent to search for oil began operating in al-Hasa. After several years of disappointing results, they eventually struck a commercially profitable amount of oil at Jabal Dhahran in 1938. Within decades, Aramco would discover the largest oil field in the world at Ghawar, making Saudi Arabia home to the largest oil deposits on the planet.

The location of oil in al-Hasa, and its subsequent development, clearly proved the most important geological discovery in the kingdom's brief history. The wealth it eventually generated provided more security for the Saudis than agriculture could have accomplished even in the best-case scenario. Saudi rulers appreciated this fact early on, but it did not diminish their efforts to learn more about sources of water, which was still much needed, and to pursue agricultural expansion. Oil revenues did not take off until the late 1940s and early 1950s, and before then and even for several decades afterward, Saudi leaders did not view oil revenues as sufficient either to protect their authority or to enable them to firmly assert it across the vast peninsula. Most of the young kingdom's subjects continued to be engaged in agriculture and dependent on water for their livelihood. Even though the state now looked at its citizens less as a source of revenue—it halved the *zakat* taxes in the 1950s—it still continued to believe that they needed to be productively engaged and that providing the necessary resources was key to security. Particularly important was the emphasis placed on building an integrated administrative and economic network controlled or at least monitored by the central government, such as it was. This would become especially true in the 1950s, when various communities became more politically restive and grew frustrated with the central state. In the hope that it could wring more water from the desert, King Abd al-Aziz and his top lieutenants continued to probe the country for it. Aside from filling the Saudi purse with much-needed revenue, the discovery of oil also helped heighten Saudi faith in science, and especially geology, and strengthened the belief that it would be geologists who would help the kingdom locate and harness whatever resources remained undiscovered.

In 1940, King Abd al-Aziz and Abdullah Sulaiman once again turned to Karl Twitchell, who was visiting Riyadh, in the hope that he might be able to assist in finding the desired resources in Najd and to introduce water drills, pumps, and other farming and irrigation technology. Twitchell eventually returned to the United States and began another exhaustive search for partners who would be willing to undertake the necessary exploratory work. Twitchell traveled more than 15,000 miles in the southwestern United States, including visits to Texas, New Mexico, Arizona, and California, in his attempt to drum up capital from American mining firms—to no avail. The unwillingness of American mining companies to invest the money and time in Saudi Arabia did not prove fatal to the project, however. Instead, the U.S. government sponsored the mission, which would set out to "examine and report upon the agricultural and irrigation possibilities of Saudi Arabia, and submit to [the king] recommendations regarding methods of development."[35]

Before returning to the United States and being commissioned by the U.S. government to analyze Saudi Arabia's resources, Sulaiman contracted Twitchell to carry out an extensive survey of the kingdom's southwestern province of Asir. Asir was rugged country and virtually inaccessible. Because of the difficult terrain, Saudi leaders dispatched Twitchell, along with a Saudi mining engineer, Ahmad Fakhry, to undertake an exhaustive study of the Asir's countryside. The two engineers, along with teams of local guides and assistants (rarely acknowledged by Twitchell), were charged with several objectives, including mapping, measuring, and marking the area's steep mountain grades for a future road network, prospecting for future mineral mining, and surveying the area's potential water resources and agricultural prospects. Twitchell, Fakhry, and their team spent more than three months negotiating Asir's difficult passes, with the American corresponding regularly and directly with the king, providing progress reports on his findings. They planted flags where future roads would pass and noted depressions where future dams might be constructed to capture seasonal rain that ran off the mountainsides. Twitchell and Fakhry's work in Asir foreshadowed the kind of work Twitchell would do for the next few years, surveying for resources and reporting back to the central government. It was important work and served the central authorities well.[36]

Twitchell and Fakhry's exploratory work in Asir was particularly valuable to Saudi Arabia's rulers. The province was a contentious place, one vulnerable to dispute. Riyadh's grip on the region was tenuous at best. Saudi dominion over the region had been established less than two decades before the engineers traversed the countryside there. A Saudi army had conquered the territory, wresting control of the province away from local powers in the mid-1920s, but Asir proved hard to subdue. In 1934 the Saudis were forced to defend their hold from a rival claim leveled by forces in nearby Yemen. Because Asir had fertile soil and the potential for future mineral mining, the Saudis sent in Twitchell and Fakhry to carry out the preliminary work of fortifying the central government's presence. Not only did Twitchell and Fakhry investigate and inventory resources, but they also initiated the process of road building. The early roadwork carried out by the Twitchell-Fakhry team made passage as well as the extraction of resources and revenue much easier. Plus, the new roads would make it far easier for the central government to police and secure the vulnerable region.

Two years after completing the survey of Asir, Twitchell returned as part of a team for the U.S. Department of Agriculture, to carry out even more extensive surveys of the kingdom's natural resources. The American component of the U.S. Agricultural Mission, as it was called, included J. G. Hamilton, an agronomist from the U.S. Department of Agriculture, and A. L. Wathen, an irrigation specialist from the U.S. Department of the Interior, in addition to Twitchell; they arrived in the kingdom in May 1942.[37] As was the case with the Twitchell-Fakhry team that covered Asir, the Americans were accompanied and assisted in their work by local inhabitants who possessed their own knowledge of and expertise in the region. Perhaps unsurprisingly, the published report produced by the mission offered little insight into the local experts' influence on the survey team's findings or experience. With the backing of the U.S. government, the survey team's mission was considerably expanded beyond Najd to cover the breadth of Saudi Arabia. From May 15 to December 5, 1942, the team traveled almost 11,000 miles by car, camel, and on foot, investigating the peninsula's geological and agricultural possibilities.[38] With help from Aramco, which provided logistical support, the team had the use of two Ford cars, and as Twitchell wrote, they had to "carry gasoline, lubricants, water, spare tires, spare car parts, as well as food and cooking equipment, tents for our soldier escorts, chauffeurs, mechanics, cook, and helper in addition to the several months' food for ourselves."[39]

The team's field research covered thousands of miles, but it still provided only a preliminary estimate of the water and agricultural potential of the kingdom. More comprehensive surveys carried out in subsequent years would yield greater insight and detail. Yet, although hardly exhaustive, the survey report itself, its particular details and the suggestions it made, provided the first systematic account of the region and established a foundation for future scientific work and, more important, for more effective centralized control over the region's natural resources and territory, key concerns for the Saudi sovereigns. Twitchell and his colleagues saw themselves as a force for progress, but their work also served well-understood political goals, especially the strengthening of the royal family and the polity.[40] Beyond cataloging water resources, soil information, and the geological features of the peninsula, the U.S. Agricultural Mission's work and its report, filed in 1943 in both English and Arabic, also served political ends.

The U.S. Agricultural Mission's report is an impressive inventory of water, land, and agricultural resources. In spite of the limitations placed on the survey team by the demands of time, poor transportation, and the elements, the report is remarkably authoritative. In varying amounts of detail, the mission surveyed many of the communities and locations on the peninsula already actively engaged in settled farming, including al-Hasa, Najd, the Hejaz, and Asir in the southwestern corner of the kingdom. They cataloged a number of features, including annual average rainfall in each region, the kinds of soil and the extent of soil fertility, water resources, and the types of crops being grown, and they offered some limited commentary on technique, especially that used at an experimental farm set up in al-Kharj southeast of Riyadh. Although their primary objective was to outline where and how intensive efforts might expand the areas being cultivated, the mission also helped create the foundation for a new kind of political language and knowledge, one in which science overlapped with and reinforced geostrategic interests. In doing so, the U.S. Agricultural Mission contributed to the ongoing development of the Saudi strategic thinking that had emerged earlier in the century.

Of particular interest, Twitchell argued that the kingdom's four different regions—the territories that had historically maintained cultural, social, and political autonomy and that were conquered by the Saudis only a decade before (al-Hasa, Hejaz, Najd, Asir)—also served as a convenient classification system for describing the kingdom's geologic features and water resources. This was not unexpected. Al-Hasa in the east was historically the most fertile area in the Arabian Peninsula and the site of its richest underground water resources. Likewise, there are real topographical and geological features that distinguish the western provinces (Hejaz and Asir) from the center (Najd) and the east, although they blend together at some point, making the actual distinctions somewhat arbitrary. The westernmost shore of the peninsula (the Tihama plain) was a fertile coastal strip that varied from ten to forty miles wide and then yielded abruptly to a mountain wall whose height reached 8,000 feet. In the Asir, the range climbed to 9,000 feet. The mountain plateau stretched eastward into the Najd, but the fertile shores disappear into sandy wastes. The western shore and the areas adjacent to it also received the most rainfall in the kingdom, enabling limited amounts of rain-fed farming—unique in Saudi Arabia. Although they had likely never measured the mountain heights nor gauged the average rainfall in any particular area, the report's findings were hardly surprising to Saudi leaders, who would have been well aware that there were considerable environmental and geographic differences between the center and the periphery.

While it had a superficial geological and geographical plausibility, Twitchell's classification system did have political implications. The use of geology to justify the existing geopolitical classification reinforced to the Saudis the idea that these areas were objectives to be captured and exploited. This was further underscored by the decision of the report's authors not to discuss people, emphasizing geology and water over actual communities. The Americans created a powerful new knowledge system for the central government that prioritized descriptions and classifications of nature over descriptions of social and cultural life. This would continue to be a feature of state-sponsored agricultural work throughout the twentieth century. Just as important as the knowledge system itself were the details it revealed about the location of the water resources being surveyed. Previously, various communities, including the Saudis, had to compete for resources, a competition whose outcome was largely determined by knowledge of where things were as well as the ability to police them. The U.S. Agricultural Mission eliminated the need for Riyadh to bother with the process of "discovery." While not a comprehensive survey of all water sources, the mission did pinpoint with considerable precision some of the major sources and provided valuable details about water depth, sustainability, and usability, all vital information for a central government that considered control over such sources part of its power. In addition, the report emphasized the very strategic logic that the Saudis had already begun developing themselves: that because the center was natural-resource poor—the Najd was the least fertile region and had the fewest sources of water—capturing resources from the periphery would be a key to power.

But the U.S. mission sought to do much more than simply help the central government capture resources from its provinces. In its final report the team provided a scientific framework, a language, and a set of recommendations that would help the central government more fully incorporate disparate areas within its sphere. It accomplished this by pointing out the allegedly disappointing production levels of local agricultural areas and by offering specific suggestions for how those levels could be raised, not to serve local cultivators but to serve the government, which sought to increase revenue and establish its own presence. The Americans encouraged the Saudis to engage in various "reclamation" projects that would increase output in virtually every corner of the kingdom.[41] And their focus was on water: its use, improving access, and implementing extensive irrigation and pumping systems. The report pointed out that "it is [probable] that an inadequate water supply in all of its aspects, including quality, has caused the greatest damage" to agricultural production.[42] But in spite of Arabia's scarce water resources, the report's authors were adamant that better water management would yield considerable returns. Better irrigation, they wrote, would "conserve the precious gift of Allah—water—and will result in the springs and wells flowing for many years instead of flowing less and less each year until some day in the future they will stop flowing."[43]

In one important and hopeful example, the mission's report concluded that the agricultural area in Qatif in the Eastern Province could be expanded by 33 percent, from 9,000 acres to 12,000, bringing thousands of additional date-producing palms into production. An additional 10,000 acres could be "reclaimed" in al-Hasa. They advocated similar increases in other parts of the kingdom. Scientific management, Twitchell and his colleagues argued, was the key to achieving this. They called for the introduction of drainage and irrigation networks all across the kingdom, in addition to ongoing efforts to find additional water resources through continual test-drilling. The successful operation of an extensive national network of irrigation systems would require constant observation and data collection. Maintaining regular hydrological and climatic data would serve scientific ends, and it would also offer an opportunity for central authorities to assert themselves and maintain control over space and resources. The report's authors even suggested collapsing data collection with the work of occupation: "The work of collecting and recording these data could be assigned to the commandants of the various army posts throughout the country."[44] Of course, they envisioned the technology to be in the service and under the control of the central government. They made clear that, to benefit the kingdom, all of this work demanded the presence and active engagement of representatives of the central state.

The underlying logic that informed the mission's thinking was that the Saudis needed to strengthen the territorial reach and control of the central government in order to maximize the productivity and proficiency of the land. The scientists also brought with them an understanding, almost certainly the product of Twitchell's friendly relationship with the Saudi monarch, that they were making suggestions about the need to set in motion the creation and boosting of Saudi Arabia's national economy and the government's capacity to plan and operate at a "national level." Citing the example of the U.S. president Franklin Roosevelt, the authors wrote, "In Saudi Arabia as in the United States there have been valid reasons why planning on a National scale has not been practical in the past. Under the present strong and well organized Government however it might be of great and lasting benefit to Saudi Arabia and its people if planning on a National scale for the development of all resources were undertaken."[45] They emphasized that achieving this could not be done by expanding local production alone but also called for the integration of local markets into a national one. A national economy did not necessarily mean one that was tightly controlled by a central authority (a veritable impossibility, in any event). The mission did not imagine that Riyadh could or would carry out all development work on its own. But the central authorities would have a guiding, managerial role to play, one in which they shaped patterns of practice, determined areas of need, and firmly steered the populace toward outcomes useful to the state. Given that the overwhelming majority of the country's subjects were engaged in some form of agriculture, the pursuit of expanded productivity would best be served by improving the farmers themselves, their methods, and linking them in both material and less tangible ways to the state.

One way to do this, the mission proposed, was to create a system of national credit, with interest rates controlled by a central regulatory authority. Citing the United States as an example of a system in which farmers were able to safely borrow from the government, they argued that "full development of the agricultural resources is only possible through government assistance." Such assistance would pay various dividends to the government, by "adding to the taxable property and thereby securing an increase in the tax revenues," for example, as well as by eliminating "a certain consumptive group from becoming relief clients [parasites]" on the central purse.[46] In addition to raising tax revenues and curbing efforts by some to skim from the government, the report also lauded the potential "intangible benefits" to be gained through a government-run credit system. The report averred that "one of the most important is that for each successful irrigation project developed a certain group of people now existing on a bare subsistence level are changed into a contented and relatively more prosperous group upon whom the government can depend for whole hearted support." The authors sensed that turning conquered subjects into loyal citizens was even more urgent for the central authorities than the potential taxable benefits to be gained through a planned agricultural economy. They wrote that the intangible "benefit is of far greater real value to the government than the two previously mentioned gains of adding to the taxable wealth and eliminating potential relief clients."[47]

The Americans presumed a national space, and they wrote and thought about the kingdom as a unified whole, a territorial fait accompli, that simply lacked the infrastructure and systems to make it more efficient. It was not. In the 1940s the kingdom was still new and Saudi authority, if feared by most of those who resided within its boundaries, was hardly accepted. It is unlikely that many cultivators across the peninsula would have agreed with the U.S. Agricultural

Mission's objective of expanding fertile areas in the interest of a national economy, although they may have appreciated the additional revenue to be brought in by newly cultivatable fields. But this was not what the Agricultural Mission had in mind. Twitchell's team did not advocate greater privatization for local farmers nor the creation of "free markets." Rather, they called for more oversight and presence on the part of the central government, and they provided a detailed balance sheet about local resources that would guide the government on where to concentrate its efforts. On the surface, the argument for greater centralized control over markets contradicted the capitalist, free-trade model of development that was emerging in early twentieth-century American foreign policy and that would become a staple of the postwar period.[48] It is plausible that Twitchell and his colleagues did not consider the kingdom ready for the creation of open markets and believed the state was needed to lay the groundwork for a more mature national economy, though they did not remark openly on this. In reality, the argument put forward by Twitchell served American interests, both government and business, particularly well, and the American preference for centralized Saudi control over its domestic market remained a staple of U.S. policy. The argument in favor of strong government oversight was connected to the American desire for political stability in Saudi Arabia. Even in the early 1940s, before the terms of U.S.-Saudi relations had crystallized, the United States understood that because of its rich oil deposits the kingdom would be a critical partner and a key front in the battle to control the postwar petroleum-based order.[49] After World War II, Aramco, which enjoyed more political influence in Saudi affairs than the American government, continued to support state control over the economy, which it saw as a bulwark against instability and threats to its operations in the kingdom.

But for individuals like Karl Twitchell, there was another powerful motive for helping to create a national economy in Saudi Arabia, for encouraging the development of its natural resources and strong Saudi oversight. While he was often described as a philanthropist or as a scientist devoted to the principles of progress and to helping develop one of the United States' most important allies, Twitchell also sought to profit from his ties to the kingdom and its growing oil revenues. When he is seen as someone on the payroll of the state, as an entrepreneur in the pursuit of a small share of the oil bonanza, Twitchell's arguments for and influence on the creation of centralized control over the national economy are stripped of any veneer of scientific service or objectivity. Instead, he emerges as someone whose material interests almost certainly shaped the kind of expertise and advice he provided. In the decade following the U.S. Agricultural Mission to the kingdom, Twitchell continued to serve the Saudi government as the vice president of American Eastern Consortium (AEC), a business that provided expertise on mining and mineral extraction, as well as a personal consultant to the finance minister. Finished with the work of surveying and exploration, Twitchell turned to the work of extracting resources and playing a more direct role in shaping the country's development planning. He was particularly concerned with various mining activities in the Hejaz and Najd, committing considerable personal energy to the mining of various minerals while working for AEC. He also maintained an active presence in consulting for the government on agricultural, hydrological, and other geological matters. In May 1949, at the request of Abdullah Sulaiman, Twitchell met with the new minister of agriculture, Saleh Gazaz, to assess the kingdom's agricultural strategy and to offer his own insight on future efforts. He followed up their meeting with a personal letter to Sulaiman in which he outlined a long list of things the government should give priority to, from road building and dam building to the use of fertilizer and the creation of demonstration farms. A month later, again at the request of the finance minister, Twitchell even drew up a detailed "Three Year Plan" for development, a comprehensive blueprint advising the Saudis on when and where to focus their energies on matters including agriculture, mining, transportation, education, communication, health care, and even Saudi Arabia's prisons. Twitchell wrote authoritatively on which regions needed the most attention and even called for a specific amount of spending, $55.5 million U.S. dollars, suggesting he had an intimate familiarity with the holdings in the Saudi treasury.[50]

The letter to Sulaiman was hardly unusual. Throughout the 1940s and well into the 1950s Twitchell actively corresponded with Abdullah Sulaiman about mining and agriculture, not only offering insights on the country's "needs" but also playing the role of a purchasing agent, establishing relationships between the Saudi government and American suppliers, ensuring that the Saudi and American markets were firmly interconnected. Beginning in the late 1940s Twitchell spent less time in the kingdom, offering advice mostly from afar. Mining work continued into the 1950s, although it is unclear how successful any of these efforts turned out to be. The Saudis never discovered large veins of gold, nor did they turn up any sources of mineral revenue that rivaled oil. The failure of the mining operations to yield anything of value never diminished Twitchell's efforts to explore further. In 1954 Twitchell even briefly entertained a proposal to explore Saudi Arabia for uranium, a project that ultimately failed to materialize.

Karl Twitchell's work was not universally appreciated. At least one of Charles Crane's relations harbored some uncertainty about the nature of the work and whether it was appropriate. In 1938, as head of the Saudi Arabia Mining Syndicate based in the kingdom, Twitchell sent a letter to Charles Crane updating him on the status of the waterworks in Jidda, the project that Crane had originally dispatched Twitchell to oversee in 1931. Although Crane's philanthropy had come to an end as a result of the Great Depression, Twitchell had felt obliged to update him periodically on the work that he had inspired. Twitchell's letter to Crane detailed the successes of the project as well as some of its ongoing shortfalls, but mostly Twitchell sought to communicate the heartfelt gratitude of the country's rulers, including the king. Apparently somewhat recovered from the global economic downturn, Crane responded with his own letter of thanks and an offer of an additional financial contribution to help further the waterworks project. But Twitchell received a second, less amiable letter from John Crane, the elder philanthropist's son, a letter that expressed clear disregard for what Twitchell was doing in the kingdom.

John Crane discouraged Twitchell from taking his father up on the offer of additional financing. He wrote, "I rather hope that you will consider this offer in the nature of what he calls a 'symbolic gesture.'" John Crane's discouragement was partly the result of his own anxiety about his father's financial standing and the Depression's impact on the family's wealth. But his response also addressed, if even inadvertently, some of the political uncertainties surrounding Twitchell's work in Saudi Arabia. Crane noted sharply that "it is my feeling that such undertakings under present circumstances should be carried on by governments and not individuals, and you will probably agree with me that he has already done more than enough to provide a practical demonstration of their utility in Arabia. I trust therefore that you will understand my reasons for suggesting, on my own responsibility, that you simply acknowledge the offer and let it go at that."[51]

Twitchell made no such reply. In a response to his former patron, Twitchell made no mention of any need for additional gifts, although by not mentioning further aid he left the door open for Crane's charity. He also mentioned that he had "received an interesting letter from" John, although he noted none of the younger Crane's concerns.[52] More interesting was the geologist's defensive response to John Crane's slight. Stung by the suggestion that he was doing work more appropriate for governments, Twitchell hit back in a letter to John:

Regarding water supply, there is a local Commission which has followed out our first recommendation. A few months ago I ordered an additional pump for them and for which they are paying. Furthermore, I ordered on their behalf last Summer a "Star 71" drill which can put down a well to 2,000 feet if necessary. The Saudi Arabian government bought and paid for this. The Standard Oil Company of California, who are operating their oil concession in El Hassa [*sic*], have sent two men to operate this drill. These men arrived yesterday. So you can see that the people are, as you hoped—the Federal Government as well as the Municipal Government—developing their water supply.[53]

That there was a contradiction in his response to Crane's criticism—that he and an oil company were not just doing the bidding of the government but were making it possible for the government to operate in a development capacity at all, and that doing so was helping to define what the government actually was for thousands of its subjects—seems never to have occurred to Twitchell. He never considered his relationship with the Saudi government—that he was doing its political bidding—as problematic. It made sense to the geologist that a developing country, one with potentially rich natural resources and a need for expert guidance on how to use them, had turned to an American expert for help. Twitchell understood that he was fortunate to have ended up in a privileged position, close to the Saudi king and his power financial adviser. Good fortune or not, and aware of it or not, Twitchell was an important political actor in the early making of Saudi political authority, turning expertise, planning, and development, as well as the environment more generally, into political categories that helped secure the government's centralized power. The Saudi government learned the lesson well and demonstrated over the following decades that science, technology, development, and the remaking of nature continued to be at the heart of its political authority.

3

Saudi efforts to conquer and engineer nature in Arabia accelerated quickly in the decades after Karl Twitchell carried out most of his work. Development of the environment, particularly agriculture, emerged as one of the most important areas in which the government attempted to bolster its political authority. In conjunction with the oil company Aramco, Twitchell's work reinforced the Saudi belief that the conquest of nature and the control of the country's limited natural resources were vital to the consolidation of the ruling family's power. Armed with much of the new knowledge produced by Twitchell and other experts, and with their direct assistance, in the early 1960s the kingdom launched a series of intensive programs—experiments in environmental engineering—as efforts to subdue the environment. Over the middle decades of the twentieth century, these efforts came to form an important component of key new political institutions and bureaucracies in the emerging state machinery. Foreign experts and expertise would prove to be central to the consolidation of the Saudi Arabian state and, in particular, the development of a new environmental technostate. Foreign experts worked alongside an emerging group of Saudi technocrats, and together they built and brokered a modern polity.

Starting at midcentury, Saudi and foreign experts constructed an elaborate political machine that used nature as a means to shore up the power of the Al Saud and to subdue the kingdom's subjects. Specifically, from the 1960s through the early 1970s the government and its foreign advisers devoted considerable attention to developing land and agricultural resources, and to turning farmers into not only productive subjects, but subjects whose productivity depended on the state. The centralized and bureaucratized state was, in turn, the product of the very experts it employed. In important respects, Saudi political authority took shape through the development and institutionalization of technical expertise. In addition to shaping authority and political power, science and technology, development work, and the principles of modernization assumed increasingly important roles in the way that Saudi leaders articulated what it meant to be Saudi. This too possessed a political component. The principles of science and expertise, at least as practitioners articulated them, lent themselves to the project of legitimizing Saudi political authority because of the claim that science and expertise were, in fact, apolitical. Experts, engineers, and scientists claimed that they sought no political objective but only carried out the dispassionate work of their trade. The state adopted a similar position, using the depoliticized language of science to justify its increasingly intrusive role in the lives of its subjects. Engineering and environmental projects were cast as services provided by the state, the foundation of a sociopolitical compact that sought to bind ruler and ruled through the pursuit of material prosperity. In this way, Saudi leaders aspired to construct an ideological foundation for their political legitimacy by depoliticizing the work of state building, to provide a normative framework in which the kingdom's subjects would accept and even embrace Saudi authority, by emphasizing the claim that science and technology are politically neutral. Remaking the environment and expanding agriculture were particularly important in this regard because they engaged the energies of the kingdom's subjects directly. Not all of the development projects succeeded technically, but they did serve valuable political ends, most importantly by expanding the presence and reach of the central authorities.

At midcentury, the accelerated pursuit of development work and the expansion of the country's environmental imperative took shape amid considerable political transformation. Saudi Arabia's founding monarch and principal power broker, Abd al-Aziz ibn Saud, died in November 1953. His death set in motion a new phase in the kingdom's political history and the transformation of the Saudi polity into a modern state. His eldest son, Saud ibn Abd al-Aziz ibn Saud, succeeded his father almost immediately. Although Abd al-Aziz had forged what would turn out to be a family dynasty in Arabia, his son did not inherit a particularly strong government. Saud's rule would be beset by internal family rivalry and uncertainty about the kind of government that would ultimately take shape and rule the country. In 1953 Saudi Arabia had only begun to build the institutions and bureaucracies necessary to administer the sprawling territories and peoples that made up the kingdom. Much work remained to be done. Among the most important of Abd al-Aziz's legacies was a shared sense of urgency around the idea that the government and the Saudi royal family's political primacy were connected to the control of the country's natural resources. Another legacy was the belief that science was not only an important tool for subduing and remaking the environment but also a powerful political instrument. Oil of course remained the kingdom's most important resource. But nonpetroleum resources, such as water and agriculture, also held vital significance. In fact, oil was both a blessing and a potential problem. The wealth it generated eased financial anxieties, but it also engendered nervousness about dependency on foreign oil companies as well as on the commodity itself. Saud and those closest to him, as well as his rivals, came to see oil as a means to expand the country's nonpetroleum productive capacity. And they all came to see the science, technology, and expertise that went into the modern oil industry as vital assets in their quest to strengthen their own political authority. Within a month of assuming power, Saud provided some insight into his political priorities. He told an interviewer that, after oil, "the country depends on the 'development of our agricultural resources by adapting modern methods, providing water for irrigation through the construction of dams and canals, and connecting the agricultural areas of the country with other parts of the kingdom by modern communication facilities.'"[1] Saud would be ousted from power before he accomplished any of these goals. By the end of the 1960s, however, Karl Twitchell's earlier lessons about the priority of expertise, the need for centralized technical management and economic planning, and the importance of nature and the environment to the royal family's fortunes had taken clear hold.

In spite of the Saudis' intensified interest in knowing about and locating natural resources, the information yielded by the efforts of Karl Twitchell went mostly untapped for more than a decade. For a variety of reasons, the Saudi government was unable to take advantage of the new knowledge handed to it, and the initiation of widespread agricultural modernization projects had to wait until the early 1960s, when it intensified development work as well as its relations with foreign experts. Initially, the most important limitation faced by interested authorities continued to be a lack of capital. During World War II very little revenue made its way into the kingdom. Although it had discovered commercial quantities of oil in 1938, Standard Oil of California drew down its personnel in Arabia and minimized its drilling and pumping efforts while the war raged. Oil revenues did not begin their initial take-off until the late 1940s and early 1950s, after the oil company, then known as Aramco, returned to full operation.[2] The lack of capital also led to an emphasis on other aspects of state building, particularly efforts by the Saudis to enroll merchants from the periphery of the peninsula in the new political system. "Najdiization," the program designed to establish the royal family's political and cultural hegemony in the Hejaz and al-Hasa as well as to extract whatever wealth it could from those regions' residents, continued throughout the war years, even though money for extensive programs was often in short supply.[3] Spending for agricultural projects took a backseat during the 1940s and early 1950s to efforts to co-opt traders, merchants, and tribal leaders, who increasingly cooperated with the Al Saud in exchange for the preservation of some of their own regional political autonomy. This trend was most pronounced in the Hejaz, historically the richest commercial center in the peninsula.

With the growth of petrocapital in the late 1940s, the Saudis began bestowing patronage on the allies it was cultivating in order to shore up the family's political security, a strategy that would intensify after the oil boom in the 1970s. The emphasis on patronage and on building personal networks with wealthy and powerful families meant that the government itself remained institutionally weak, however, and that the long-held goal of increased centralization had yet to be fully achieved. The government continued to be dominated by the king, the extended royal family, and a close group of advisers, although this began to change in 1950, when Abd al-Aziz established several new ministries and a cabinet. Saudi Arabia even lacked a uniform monetary system as late as the 1950s. The Saudi Arabian Monetary Agency was founded in 1952 with assistance from the U.S. Treasury. It was also in this period that the kingdom's first road networks, ports, and communications facilities were built. The Ministry of Agriculture was established in 1954.[4]

There were several exceptions to the decision not to pursue national agricultural development schemes in the 1940s and 1950s, although their focus was local and they often proved too politically charged to be effective. From 1950 to 1954 the U.S. government sustained a Point Four development program in the kingdom aimed at helping the Saudi government undertake infrastructure projects, including road construction, water surveys, and agriculture.[5] But the Point Four program ran into political difficulty with Saudi leaders and was shut down in 1954. The kingdom also commissioned at least seven hydrological surveys in the area around Riyadh. Aramco carried out the first in 1948 and another in 1960 when it mapped the geologic features of the Wasia aquifer, a massive reservoir of water deep underground that many believed was adequate to provide Saudi Arabia with all the water it needed for years to come.[6] Others followed every few years, including a survey by the U.S. Geological Survey in 1963.[7] The focus on Riyadh underscored the fact that although Saudi leaders understood the importance of geology and water to their authority, many of their initial efforts were limited to strengthening the central province and their immediate base of power. That was also true with regard to efforts to develop agriculture. The largest and most discussed agricultural project in operation in the 1940s and 1950s was at al-Kharj, a community about 150 kilometers southeast of Riyadh. An experimental farm at al-Kharj, often cited as the kingdom's first large development program, operated until 1959, but while both the government and Aramco helped operate the farm, it did little more than provide a private source of produce for the royal family.[8]

The challenge of securing their rule was complicated by rivalry and conflict within the royal family, especially after the death of Abd al-Aziz in 1953. The first Saudi monarch was succeeded by his eldest son, Saud, shortly after his death. Saud would prove to be a controversial figure, best known for his political idiosyncrasies and unpredictability. Saud ruled from 1953 to 1964, when he was forced to abdicate power by his rivals within the royal family. Throughout his reign, Saud faced periodic challenges from his younger brother and the heir to the throne after him, Crown Prince Faisal, as well as from other members of the royal family and the slowly growing Saudi bureaucracy, most notably a group of junior family members who desired the creation of a more liberal polity and a handful of technocrats who occupied influential posts in various ministries. Saud's critics charged him with being a wastrel and lacking a coherent politico-ideological philosophy. In particular, they said he used the kingdom's newfound wealth to build lavish palaces for himself and his hangers-on instead of funding productive programs that would strengthen the state and the national economy, and secure the family's authority. Saud's support for road building and infrastructure programs was important but hardly sufficient, they believed. The domestic economy, already limited, also suffered a setback during this period. Under Saud's guidance, the kingdom witnessed a growth in imports rather than a growth in its productive base. Tim Niblock has noted that "large sectors of the economy—especially agriculture, pastoralism and handicrafts" were "affected detrimentally."[9]

The rivalry between Saud and Faisal led to several difficult political periods, with the two jostling for greater personal authority and control over the mechanisms of governance. Faisal eventually replaced Saud as king in 1964, but it was when he became prime minister, from 1958 to 1960, that he first grabbed political power. Faisal held that post for only a short time before Saud regrouped and forced him out, although the crown prince would occupy the position again in 1962, wielding even more power than previously. The rising pressure being directed against Saud intensified as a result of other developments within the royal family and within society more generally. Within the family, princes besides Faisal had begun challenging Saud and the nature of the political system. Most important, Prince Talal and a group that came to be known as the Free Princes advocated the creation of a constitutional monarchy and the liberalization of the regime.

Ominous threats to Saudi power also emerged in the 1950s outside the royal family. Social distress was visible in different parts of the kingdom, especially in al-Hasa, where a combination of poor treatment of workers by the oil company and other social crises within local communities led to public demonstrations of frustration and anti-Saudi sentiment. A series of labor stoppages at Aramco in the 1950s threatened both Saudi power and the production of oil.[10] Frustration in the east was manifested in the creation of local and vocal political organizations whose very existence threatened the established political order.[11] Frustration took other forms as well, with the local media in the east providing an outlet for locals to voice additional grievances.

The draining of the royal purse and the emergence of serious threats within Saudi Arabian society prompted a political showdown within the House of Saud. Between 1958 and 1962 the camps led by Saud, Faisal, and Talal competed for primacy within the royal family. Saud's power was increasingly weakened during this period. The liberal-minded Talal would eventually be forced into exile; his progressive views on the need to reconstitute the political system proved too radical for most of the royal family, who had no interest in parting with power. Faisal and his supporters forced Saud out in 1964, when the eldest son of Abd al-Aziz ingloriously abdicated and left Saudi Arabia to live out the rest of his life in Switzerland and Greece. Faisal's triumph represented the family's support for his more serious demeanor, his commitment to more rigorous stewardship, and his personal piety—Faisal was a man of sincere faith.

Although Faisal's victory was clearly a political one, it is less clear that he represented an ideological vanguard, particularly when it came to dealing with restive elements of Saudi society and his vision for the future development of the country. Niblock has written that Faisal and his supporters "sought to defuse discontent by extensive programs of industrial and agricultural development accompanied by social welfare programmes."[12] The ascendance of Faisal to the throne has been lionized in Saudi historiography as the beginning of the kingdom's "renaissance" and the birth of modernity, although it did not constitute as radical a departure as was commonly assumed.[13] Importantly, Faisal's tenure in power did not mark an ideological sea change. Initially at least, Faisal had mixed feelings about development and whether the kingdom should pursue administrative reform or more rapid technological development. In reality, during his decade in power (1964–1975) he would oversee both.

Faisal first outlined his development agenda in full in November 1962, less than a month after his appointment as prime minister, when he announced a ten-point program aimed at steering the kingdom onto a new political and economic track. While much of the plan focused on the Islamic character of the Saudi polity and the scriptural foundations for political authority, the most important and innovative provisions included Faisal's unprecedented public commitment to "raising the nation's social level"; establishing regulations for economic, commercial, and social development; promoting an economic upsurge; and abolishing slavery. The plan promised a "sustained endeavor to develop the country's resources and economy, in particular roads, water resources, heavy and light industry, and self-sufficient agriculture."[14]

Faisal's political rhetoric and strategy were orchestrated partly for public consumption. They represented a response to the growing social discontent that had first emerged in the 1950s and that continued to find expression in the early 1960s. That Faisal determined that a public declaration of his intent was necessary was remarkable.[15] Never before had the kingdom's rulers felt publicly accountable to the people and communities over whom they ruled, at least not to those who held no position of power or influence. The ten-point program proved only the first such public statement, reflecting the arrival of a new political reality in Saudi Arabia in which the government would have to respond to public pressure and at least appear to be interested in ameliorating grievances, and would have to justify its authority. Just as important, the ten-point program revealed both to the public and to the rest of the royal family the development-focused political strategy that would frame domestic policy for at least two decades.

The development turn was not a new innovation. It included elements of King Abd al-Aziz's strategic thinking, particularly the emphasis on using material incentives to secure support from potential threats. And, to be sure, development remained a political program, one that aimed at shoring up central power and authority. While it constituted a fundamental shift in thinking and practice, its goals remained consistent with those pursued since the beginning of the twentieth century.[16] Although it was business as usual in some respects, the shift was nevertheless historically profound. Under Faisal, the kingdom pursued and achieved more effective centralization of power, one of the key long-term objectives that his father had not realized. The building of infrastructure and the implementation of national development projects helped achieve that centralization. Institution building and development went hand in hand, and government institutions, particularly those related to various aspects of development, underwent intensive expansion under Faisal's watch. A technocratic class educated in scientific and secular domestic and foreign universities emerged in the 1960s and then proliferated in the 1970s. The government determined that a need existed and then set in motion the training and equipping of a class of experts to achieve it. The kingdom continued to rely on foreign companies, both American and European, to do much of the work involved in development, but it had begun the process of building up its own capacity. There was a familiar spatial logic to much of the work that followed from the development turn. Many of the first large infrastructural and modernization projects took place in the border regions of the kingdom, where Saudi power was still the weakest.

Perhaps the most remarkable new feature of Saudi Arabia's development approach to governance was its ideological substance. Saudi leaders did not imagine development as merely a more sophisticated framework for the projection of power, although it was that. Development was also intended to create a new framework for the citizens of Saudi Arabia, to shape their thinking about their relationship to political authority and the nation. Development and modernization became central elements of a new type of narrative. The 1962 ten-point plan made it clear that Islam remained the glue that bound ruler and ruled, and that religion would remain the centerpiece of the relationship between state and society. It was from within Islam that the Saudis continued to justify their rule and the basic structure of the state. Because religion had been at the core of the sociopolitical contract, the Saudis had not engaged in an ideological program of nation building. But the ten-point plan, as well as the programs that followed, crafted and shaped a message in which Islam and development, science, and modernity were to come together in forging a new era of Saudi prosperity, which depended on cooperation between state and citizens as well as the inculcation of the idea of service. This was emphasized heavily in public statements and also in the work of institution building, development planning, and the actual carrying out of projects. It was also reflected in the government's tendency to send in scientists and engineers to solve social crises and to achieve political objectives, when in an earlier era it had sent in clerics and religious missionaries.[17]

GREENING THE KINGDOM

During the 1960s Saudi leaders, Saudi technocrats, and foreign experts determined to expand the productive base of the Saudi national economy and to shore up centralized control over it. Whereas in the 1950s agriculture had withered, the 1960s witnessed efforts aimed at rescuing it and the kingdom's struggling farmers. New institutions emerged and existing ones were strengthened, including ministries whose purview included broadly conceived notions of development and modernization. In 1965 Faisal created the Central Planning Organization (CPO), which was to have a hand in overseeing the formulation of national development projects, coordinating among other ministries in shaping a national vision, and helping determine budgetary allocations for individual projects. In the 1960s and 1970s the CPO worked with the government in apportioning considerable fiscal resources for city planning, education reform, and the construction of urban health facilities. The CPO was also involved in preparing programs for stimulating and expanding the kingdom's economic base, including industry and agriculture. Industry proved a difficult challenge as the kingdom lacked the necessary materials, natural resources, and private capital to sustain large industrial projects. In later years, it did prove capable of and reasonably successful at developing a petrochemical industry, which operated as a derivative of the oil industry. Although it was involved in agricultural development, the CPO played a secondary role to specific institutions created to serve the kingdom's farming and herding communities. In 1964 the kingdom created the Saudi Arabian Agricultural Bank to help farmers on small and midsize farms acquire the necessary capital to intensify production. That year it also added water to the portfolio of the Ministry of Agriculture. The ministry later recorded that "from that time onwards the Ministry of Agriculture and Water became responsible for the execution of both agricultural and water programmes, the provision of services and the protection of the agricultural and water resources of the Kingdom of Saudi Arabia."[18]

A look at the Agricultural Bank's operations over its first ten years, the last year coinciding with the massive increase in revenue that flowed from the oil boom, underscores the scope of the central government's efforts to expand cultivation, as well as offers data about its specific intent. The Agricultural Bank was one of the many institutions in which Saudi and foreign experts collaborated in the reengineering of nature and, in doing so, helped create new political-economic relations between subjects and the state. In its first annual report, the bank noted its general objectives and its reason for being, stating that "it is important to work to develop the agricultural sector [along with industry], making the national economy [al-iqtisād al-watanī] better capable of facing economic difficulties [al-suʿūbāt] and crises [al-azamāt]."[19] There were also political and practical reasons for the bank's existence. With a total cultivated area of 200,000 to 300,000 hectares in the 1960s, according to U.S. sources, as many as 60 percent of landowners were renting out their land to others and only 40 percent of them were doing their own cultivating.[20] The vast majority of farmers who owned land maintained plots that ranged in size between 1 and 2.2 hectares.[21] Since the 1950s agricultural production had become mostly subsistence oriented, and small farmers did not produce sufficient quantities to sustain a national market. The growth of imports created a series of challenges for the expansion and development of local agriculture, and as imports flooded into the country, it became difficult for smaller cultivators to break into the market.

The problem was compounded by the steady disappearance of small landowning farmers and the rise of tenant farming, a disenchanting existence and a subject of particular concern to the central government, especially considering the rise in social discontent that had led to civil disobedience just a few years before. Often, at the base of those protests were disillusioned former farmers who had taken up jobs in the oil fields or other oil facilities. According to a Russian analyst, large and midsize landowners, those who held more than five hectares, owned more than 60 percent of the total cultivated area by the early 1960s.[22] They rented most if not all of their holdings to tenant farmers, who paid in cash, or to sharecroppers who had previously owned small parcels but could no longer sustain their smaller farms. In spite of their size and potential for productivity, even large farms were not oriented to widespread production and continued to serve mostly subsistence needs. Agricultural laborers could expect to earn between 1,500 and 3,500 Saudi riyals (SR) annually, an amount too low to "ensure a tolerable standard of living of their families."[23] Better-off "middle peasants," who did own their own land and constituted around 11 percent of all peasant families, did better, with two to five hectares each and earnings of SR3,000 to SR5,000 a year. The most successful peasant farmers (around 5 percent of the total) owned five to ten hectares and earned SR6,000 to SR10,000 annually. There were also between 3,500 and 5,000 estates larger than ten hectares (around 7 percent of the total), whose owners were tribal leaders, royal family members, large merchants, and religious foundations.[24] The largest landowners lived in town, away from their land, renting it out and earning about SR100,000 annually. Abdullah al-Dabbagh, a former official in the Ministry of Agriculture and Water, claimed that, before the government intervened, "peasants increasingly became permanently indebted to merchants and big landlords" in the early 1960s and were forced to sell their land, which drove up the number of landless peasants and agricultural workers.[25]

The Saudi Agricultural Bank sought to relieve pressure on the midsize and smaller farmers, providing capital to entice peasants to stay on the land and help develop both cultivation and the agricultural base of the national economy, which central authorities hoped not only to expand but also to diversify. At its founding in 1964, the bank enjoyed a modest capital investment of just under 11 million riyals.[26] In its first year of operation, the bank distributed SR4.5 million in loans.[27] Both of those numbers rose considerably over the next decade. The bank's capital increased to SR30 million in 1967–68, and after five full years in operation it had risen to SR50 million, a 400-percent increase.[28] In 1974–75, ten years after the bank's founding and one year after the influx of revenue that followed the oil boom, it enjoyed SR150 million in capital, an increase of 93 million riyals over the previous year.[29] In the first five years of its operation, the bank loaned a total of SR52,486,218 to more than 13,102 borrowers.[30] The overwhelming majority of the loans went to small farmers, with the average loan running between 1,000 and 3,000 riyals. The bank's 1967–68 annual report remarked that the loans were made mostly to finance the purchase of irrigation and pumping equipment, with more than 58 percent going to that purpose.[31] From 1966 to 1969, 5,113 engines and 3,061 pumps were purchased with help from Agricultural Bank loans.[32] But by 1968 the loan program had achieved only mixed results. Although it had loaned out millions of riyals, it had not alleviated pressure on small and midsize peasant farms. In the hope that it might boost security and entice landless agricultural workers back to farming their own land, the king issued a royal decree on September 28, 1968, distributing uncultivated land in plots of up to ten hectares to any citizen who promised to farm it.[33]

It appears that the new land distribution program achieved very little. Not surprisingly, the 1974–75 loan data dwarfed the earlier totals, with SR145,505,437 going to more than 16,000 borrowers, who purchased 7,03 engines, 4,810 pumps, 501 tractors, 57 combines, 21 baling machines, and 506 vehicles.[34] But it is not clear from the data whether smaller cultivators were actually being served by the loan program. The Ministry of Agriculture and Water announced in 1975 that it had only recently established a program "for the expansion of agriculture by intensive means." According to a ministry report published in 1975, "This programme includes the introduction and development of farm machinery through the principles of farm self-help."[35] Given the 1968 decision to distribute land as a mechanism to promote agricultural expansion, the need to explore other means to achieve the same end in 1975 suggests that the government was struggling to meet its goals.

The results of the efforts by the Ministry of Agriculture and Water and the Agricultural Bank to contribute to and diversify the productive base of the national economy were mixed. There was economic growth in the 1960s and early 1970s, even in agriculture.[36] Although agriculture's share of total gross domestic product decreased during the 1960s, the sector did grow, albeit in limited fashion. Farming contributed around 10 percent of GDP in 1962–63 but fell to around 6 percent in 1970. It declined even further as a total contributor to GDP in 1975, to around 1 percent.[37] These numbers are not necessarily surprising, considering that oil revenues grew so spectacularly in the same period. In spite of growth, and although the available data are limited and not conclusive, there are additional indications that economic growth did not stimulate an expansion in the number of cultivators, nor did it serve the interest of smaller ones. The total area under cultivation expanded only from 200,000 to 300,000 hectares in the 1960s to 385,000 to 525,000 hectares in 1975. The Ministry of Agriculture and Water reported in 1975 that the small expansion represented a fraction of the country's potential, claiming that there were potentially 4.5 million hectares of arable land, of which 600,000 were good for cultivation and around 3.5 million were potentially good.[38] Even more revealing, over this same time period agriculture's share of per capita GNP failed to rise in relation to other sectors. From 1964–65 to 1974–75 the country's overall per capita income rose from US$460 to US$1,300, but the rates for cultivators rose only from US$85 to US$105, hardly an encouraging trend.[39] Also, by the 1970s, Saudi Arabia still relied on imports for around 55 percent of domestic agricultural consumption, indicating that not only had the kingdom fallen short in alleviating pressure on smaller farmers, but it also had yet to achieve its goals with respect to diversifying and strengthening the national economy.

In spite of its limited success, the operation and impressive expansion of the Agricultural Bank itself was consistent with the emphasis on building technocratic institutions as a way to strengthen central oversight. Over ten years the bank had expanded from five to ten branches and from fourteen to forty-one offices, offering services in every major city in the kingdom.[40] Its personnel increased from 95 employees in 1964 to 714 full-time staff members in 1975.[41] The education levels of the full-time bank staff demonstrated the government's increased inclination toward placing technocrats and experts in key bureaucratic posts. In 1964, 27 bank employees had university degrees in agriculture, agricultural economics, economics, or business. The highest level of achievement among the remaining employees ranged from secondary certificates to primary-school graduates, of which there were 20.[42] The number of full-time employees increased steadily each year, although the number of university-educated personnel remained around 30. In 1975, of the 714 staff members only 32 had university degrees, although all of these were in positions influencing bank and agricultural policy.[43] In addition to growing in size and placing technically educated personnel in decision-making positions, agricultural institutions also increasingly emphasized and incorporated the principles of scientific planning and development. In 1969, the Ministry of Agriculture and Water brought in the Menlo Park, California–based Stanford Research Institute (SRI) to help shape its short- and long-term thinking regarding not only the development of agriculture but also the operations and strategies of the ministry itself.[44] SRI's recommendations focused on developing expert in-house technical knowledge, promoting the use of science and technology in addressing production and development dilemmas, scientific management, and, especially, the need for continual "technical and economic" study of the country's natural resources and development goals. SRI called for the development of "in-job training and study activities in order to build stronger capacities within the Ministry for conducting economic and techno-economic studies related to biological and other technological developments."[45]

In conjunction with the newfound commitment to building the kingdom's institutional foundations, government leaders turned again to science, and especially geology, in their quest to expand their control. Identifying and integrating more fully the country's limited water and other natural resources once again became key objectives for central authorities. This broad approach was justified in terms of the need to develop the national economy and national productivity. In March 1964, King Faisal charged the Ministry of Agriculture and Water with the responsibility of "developing the land and water resources of the country and thereby increase[ing] agricultural production."[46] And, of course, the policy was cast as beneficial to Saudi citizens as well. The king and the ministry both claimed that the purpose of these efforts was to serve the people and improve the living conditions of the struggling farmers, including the Bedouin. But the program also had an underlying political purpose, most notably to get the central government more involved along the margins of the kingdom, where social discontent had first reared itself, lending a spatial logic to the government's domestic geopolitical strategy.

As was the case earlier in the century, command of nature and natural resources provided a context and a pretext for moving forward with the incorporation of the provinces into the orbit of central authority. Indeed, efforts to stimulate agriculture and, in particular, to enroll Saudi subjects who depended on the land for their livelihood, proved a key arena of state-building activity. To this end the Ministry of Agriculture and Water signed an agreement with the United Nations Food and Agriculture Organization in 1964 to create an advisory team that would oversee the operations of foreign firms contracted to carry out surveys of the kingdom's hydro-agricultural resources. The FAO and the ministry agreed to divide the kingdom into eight administrative zones based on existing knowledge about the country's hydro-geological and topographical features, a departure from Karl Twitchell's overlapping geologic and political-administrative zones. The creation of these eight agro-zones reflected the deepening of the Saudi leaders' increasingly technical approach to managing domestic affairs. Breaking up the kingdom's agricultural areas into smaller units justified the intensification of the government's presence and authority, with more offices and personnel operating in each. The expansion of state offices into these smaller regions around the kingdom not only integrated more places and spaces into the polity but also rendered them more easily monitored.[47] The resulting micromanagement reflected increased state capacity and will to operate at overlapping local and national levels. Moreover, such miniaturization and micromanagement made the political project of scientific and technological work easier. The purpose of surveying the zones was to measure the quality, quantity, and location of both surface and groundwater; to determine the prospects for expanding farmland and rangeland; and to suggest ways and opportunities to provide more water and increase productivity. The ministry reported that the object of the surveys was "not only to gather data on natural and human resources but also to establish a sound basis on which schemes for long term improvement could be made for the welfare of the people of Saudi Arabia."[48]

Foreign firms undertook the survey work at an estimated cost of around US$28 million. By 1970 they had surveyed six of the eight administrative areas, an area that spanned just over 800,000 square miles, or around 55 percent of the kingdom's total area.[49] The survey reports included a wide range of information, including data on water location, water salinity, soil conditions, estimates of both shallow and deepwater reserves, regional microclimates, and rainfall, as well as accounts of the kingdom's geologic and natural history. The survey teams wrote thousands of pages, covering in unprecedented detail the peninsula's geology. They also carried out social-scientific analyses of local communities, local economies, farming techniques, and water-usage patterns, conducted studies of Bedouin herding practices, and made estimations of the quality and usability of rangeland. The hundreds of reports composed and filed through the ministry provided a thorough index of knowledge on a vast array of technical, natural, and social issues. Although the sheer amount of data and the scope of the survey teams' ambitions vastly transcended the efforts of the first American geologists in Saudi Arabia, the efforts served the same basic purpose—mainly to provide information for the central government on where it could and needed to assert itself.

The key findings of the survey teams were also consistent with earlier efforts and would have hardly come as a shock to those who sought to expand agriculture. The Ministry of Agriculture and Water noted that "the soil surveys have indicated that availability of water is the limiting factor rather than the extent of arable lands."[50] This was especially true for surface water sources. But the survey teams reported a disturbing trend that was observed all over the kingdom. Shallow wells and underground water stores were reportedly being depleted at a pace greater than the recharge rate of the aquifers. In its review of agricultural development during the 1960s and early 1970s the ministry wrote that "the drying up of shallow aquifers and the continuous fall of the ground water will endanger not only agricultural production but also water for domestic use and become a risk for capital investment" and the expansion of agriculture itself.[51] The surveys further noted that agricultural production was low due to high soil salinity and alkalinity and a lack of nutrients, as well as the prevalence of damaging pests and weeds. The scientific approach to analyzing agriculture led to the formulation of scientific and technological solutions. In the 1960s, the ministry called for a water-management policy and even suggested that extraction should be limited and the sinking of water wells strictly controlled. More important, they urged the improvement of the traditional irrigation (and drainage) systems, which they blamed for wasting precious resources. In addition, agricultural policymakers outlined the need for the more systematic introduction of fertilization, improved seeds, animal management, and disease and pest control. They called for a commitment to continuous research and the creation of research stations that would explore alternative crop possibilities and more effective techniques of cultivation in specific areas. The government embraced many of the surveys' findings and would spend hundreds of millions of dollars pursuing schemes to put them into practice.

As in the 1940s and 1950s, providing the government with certain kinds of knowledge and enabling it to respond to potential threats played an important role in the geological survey work. The Saudi government continued to view water resources and agriculture as vital to its authority, and even in the 1960s this meant keeping potentially disruptive locals productively engaged and as prosperous as possible, in the hope of distracting and enticing them away from destructive or even politically subversive activities. The kingdom's leaders continued to be sensitive to regional divisiveness, restiveness in the country's outlying provinces, and the destabilizing tendencies of the Bedouin population, which still numbered around 600,000 by the end of the 1960s. Increasingly, the pursuit of political stability was framed in the context of building a national economy and diversifying the nation's economic base, steering it away from overdependence on oil.

Unlike during the 1940s and 1950s, in the 1960s the government also pursued large-scale projects to harness the kingdom's natural resources, made possible by the oil economy itself. The budget of the Ministry of Agriculture and Water increased from the equivalent of about US$69 million in 1965–66 to US$170 million in 1972–73. By 1975 the ministry had a budget of more than US$500 million. Between 1970 and 1976 around 80 percent of the budget was consistently allocated to ongoing agricultural and water projects.[52] Intensive efforts were undertaken, at great expense, during the 1960s to build irrigation and drainage networks in the large oases of al-Hasa in the Eastern Province as well as in the Jizan Valley along the Red Sea in Asir. A water development and conservation project was also carried out in Qatif, and the ministry financed the construction of a series of dams across the peninsula. It later stated that "the purpose of such dams is to retain sudden floods and prevent them from inundating wadis, oases and villages, to increase infiltration of shallow aquifers, and where appropriate to irrigate agricultural lands below the dam sites."[53] The largest of these was Jizan Valley Dam, completed by a West German company over a period from 1967 to 1970. The dam was designed to store water for irrigation, increase the recharging of groundwater, and help control seasonal floods. The dam measured over 100 feet tall, almost 1,000 feet long, and more than 100 wide at its base. It contained more than 145,000 cubic meters of concrete and had a storage capacity of more than 71 million cubic meters of water. The ministry paid over US$9 million for 700 workers and 50 technicians to build it.[54] At least ten other dams were also built between 1963 and 1974 in various locales. In addition to efforts to augment water resources for irrigation, the central planners labored to supplement drinking-water resources across the kingdom. Starting in 1969, the kingdom financed the construction of several massive desalination plants, with the largest ones in Jidda on the Red Sea coast and on the Persian Gulf coast at al-Khobar. The ministry hoped in 1975 that "desalinated water [would] become the main dependable source of fresh water for domestic purposes along the coastal zones," although the plants were also intended to serve Riyadh.

In one of the most ambitious projects imagined in the 1960s, the government once again initiated a Bedouin settlement program tied to agriculture. Historically, Saudi leaders viewed the Bedouin as particularly troubling, a perennial political threat. Their movements allowed them to evade central oversight. More important, they had previously proven capable of challenging Saudi leadership, especially in the 1920s when the Ikhwan, the religious militia that helped the Al Saud conquer much of the Arabian Peninsula, revolted against their political masters. The ruling family had attempted to subdue the Bedouin in the first part of the twentieth century by forcing them to live in agricultural settlements *(hujjar)* and take up farming. Saudi Arabia had abandoned its *hujjar* settlement policy in 1929 following the Battle of Sibilla, between government forces and those Ikhwan who had challenged Saudi authority. Some Bedouin had continued to settle voluntarily in the 1940s and 1950s, but there were no systematic efforts to direct them. One Saudi academic noted that the *hujjar* from the 1950s were "established by migrants from early hijar [*sic*] who left because of overcrowding or tribal conflicts, and by Bedouins who opted for sedentarization . . . [R]eligion played a minor role in motivating recent hijar to settle."[55] In the 1960s, the government's disinterest gave way to grand ambition and it once again sought to use agriculture and the management of nature to subordinate the Bedouin. Unlike in the 1910s and 1920s, however, rather than sending in missionaries and clergy to woo the Bedouin and assert its central authority, the government sent in engineers and technical experts. In 1963, the kingdom experimented with Bedouin settlement in response to environmental damage done to important nomad rangeland at Wadi Sirhan, north of Riyadh, as a result of heavy flooding. But that settlement scheme was hastily constructed and short-lived. Later in the decade the government agreed in principle to a program that would incrementally settle more than 400,000 Bedouin over the course of two decades, although it never implemented the plan.[56] The government did carry on with the planning and construction of at least one major agricultural settlement, the Faisal Settlement Project at Haradh, a small village located between Riyadh and Dammam.

The reasons for undertaking what turned out to be a time-consuming, costly, and frustrating project—one that failed to settle any Bedouin—were partly consistent with the aim of developing and diversifying the national economy. Until the 1960s the Bedouin were not seen as contributors to the productive base of the national economy. One account suggested that "from the government's point of view, nomadism is a constraint in the way of a complete and integrated economic development. The nomads' contribution to the national economy is not significant anymore and they can increase their share by participating in different production systems in stable localities" and that "most governments [in the Middle East], if not all, do believe that nomadism is a retardant factor to their development programs."[57] Saudi leaders also made the same claims about enlightening the Bedouin and aiding them materially. Most accounts of settlement and Bedouin-related agricultural programs claimed to have the best interest of the Bedouin themselves in mind, suggesting that the improvement of their lives and standard of living was the central impetus for all the effort being expended to settle them. The Ministry of Agriculture declared that "the prime objectives of the Harad [sic] Project were to enable the Bedouins of the region to participate in and enjoy the development and rising standard of living within the Kingdom, and thus a purely economic justification for the project though desirable was not essential when considering whether the project should or should not be implemented."[58] Setting aside the sincerity of such statements, there were other political and practical reasons for Bedouin settlement programs, particularly the one at Haradh.

Even though the Bedouin population had declined considerably over the course of the century, there were still hundreds of thousands of them moving about inside the kingdom, particularly in the northern, northeastern, and eastern provinces. Some estimates put their number as high as 600,000, or around 15 to 20 percent of the population in the 1960s.[59] In 1965, the Arab League said that the number was considerably higher, representing around 30 percent of the population.[60] Historically, the nomadic tribes had always threatened political stability. The scope of that threat had declined in the twentieth century, but it had not disappeared altogether. The Bedouin did not directly threaten the power of the royal family, but they were a disruptive force. Just as worrisome, by the 1950s they began to put a burden on the oil industry, raising concerns both at Aramco and within the government that they might undermine the country's ability to securely pump oil from the ground.

Near Haradh, a small outpost on the southern edge of the Ghawar oil field, and in the Eastern Province more generally, thousands of Bedouin from the al-Murra tribe continued to lead nomadic lives. Their home territory and traditional grazing areas *(dira)* included many of the kingdom's oil facilities, most notably those located around Ghawar. But it was not just the al-Murra tribe that was coming into contact with the oil field. Suddenly in 1956 tens of thousands of Bedouin from around the kingdom converged on Ghawar. The numbers were staggering. Many of those who set up tents in Ghawar had traveled thousands of miles from their traditional grazing grounds far from the oil field. And whereas Bedouin typically migrated and then decamped seasonally, many of those who had made their way to Ghawar in 1956 settled in for several years. Perhaps ironically, given the anxiety that their arrival produced, it was the oil industry and the nature of its operations that accounted for the arrival of the Bedouin, who regularly migrated with their sheep and camels in search of food and water. Oil-rich Ghawar provided plenty of the latter.

Most of the oil pumped from Ghawar has historically been "sour crude," oil mixed with large quantities of problematic gases, including hydrogen sulfide. Oil producers have preferred to separate hydrogen sulfide from oil before piping it from the field to refineries or shipping terminals. To do this Aramco built ten small installations called gas-oil separator plants (GSOPs) around Ghawar. The GSOPs removed the gases from the oil, after which they were either reinjected into the oil field or flared. The GSOP installations were a tangle of pipes and balloonlike storage tanks. Federico Vidal, an American anthropologist working for Aramco who was sent to Ghawar to study the Bedouin encampments, wrote that "in the Arabian deserts they stand out, unmistakeably [sic], for any traveler to see for miles around." The facilities burned the gases day and night. Vidal noted that "at night the light of the flared gasses makes their location equally unmistakeable [sic]."[61] The GSOPs required ample supplies of water. Vidal pointed out the obvious: "In the Arabian deserts the knowledge of an assured water supply at known locations is likely to attract massive concentrations of nomads, who are perennially in search of water sources."[62]

Anxiety set in for Aramco management and personnel with the arrival of thousands of Bedouin in 1956. According to Vidal, field crews who operated the GSOPs wanted to know "when are we supposed to expect an invasion of Bedouins asking for water, for themselves as well as their livestock?" Aramco management also grew increasingly concerned about the rapidly mounting number of Bedouin settlements popping up around Ghawar and their potential impact on the operations of facilities there. The Bedouins presented a security risk to the sensitive facilities. They also obstructed operations. In addition to drilling for water for operational needs, Aramco transported water by truck around the oil field to reach more remote locations. Flocks of sheep and herds of camels learned to associate the trucks with their payload and often rushed the transports, bleating for the drivers to open their spouts.

The oil company dispatched Vidal in the summer of 1956 to investigate the reasons for the Bedouin's arrival. He traveled more than 10,000 kilometers by truck and plane, carrying out reconnaissance and research. Vidal offered a number of explanations for why the Bedouin had flocked to Ghawar, including the ease of movement provided by its network of paved roads and its proximity to agricultural markets. While water remained the paramount reason for most of the settlement activity, many Bedouin also traveled to Ghawar to be close to family and tribal members who had taken up service with the Saudi Arabian National Guard, a "paramilitary organization" made up of trusted Bedouin who were charged with the protection of the king and his personal concerns. The National Guard was the legacy of the old Ikhwan militia that had served the royal family during the Saudi conquests several decades earlier. By the 1950s the National Guard was a paid branch of the military, providing personal security for the king as well as for essential facilities, including those around Ghawar. Vidal wrote that "membership in a National Guard contingent provides a means for a tribal group to receive regular subsidies."[63] The use of the National Guard for security in Ghawar produced the opposite effect, however, as those claiming even a distant relation to the guardsmen descended on the region in pursuit of the gains, material and environmental, that came with their relatives' service to the crown.

Vidal drew some interesting conclusions about the broader significance of the Ghawar Bedouin phenomenon. The anthropologist speculated that the unusual settlement pattern indicated an erosion of traditional notions of grazing rights, tribal membership, and allegiance. Vidal wrote that "in my field experience it is becoming more and more common that, when one tries to draw out some Bedouin on the question of tribal grazing limits, he gets answers such as *'dirathum wahidah'* or *'al-ardh kulluha dirat al-Sa'ud'* ('their grazing lands are one' or 'the entire country is the grazing land of the Al Sa'ud')."[64] He went on to write that "these remarks are very important," claiming that they indicated "that the nomads of Saudi Arabia are slowly shifting from considering themselves as members of a noble tribe at the top level of the social organization to being members of a nation-state, a *super-tribe,* which nevertheless remains defined with the help of the *dirah* concept." From the Bedouin's remarks Vidal concluded that "the entire country has become a *super-dirah,* a monumental grazing territory." Adopting the voice of the Bedouin, Vidal intoned, "As long as I, a member of one of this country's tribes, have sworn allegiance to the paramount *shaykh,* i.e. the king, I am not just a member of his entourage, but I can graze my livestock anywhere. My lord's *dirah* becomes my *dirah.* And the idea of a nation takes root."[65]

Vidal's was a difficult claim to substantiate. The Bedouin in Ghawar have left no known record of their own. It is certainly likely that the country's leaders would have been enthusiastic about the Bedouin's embrace of their leadership and deference to the king as the paramount sheikh. Bedouin deference was probably just as much the result of pragmatism and opportunism, however, using nationalism as a framework for justifying their claim on territories outside their traditional areas. Whatever the Bedouin justification for their migration to the oil field, Saudi Arabia's rulers did not agree with the idea of a super-*dira,* that the lord's *dira* became the Bedouin's *dira,* or that they could graze their livestock anywhere. There were clear limits to where the Bedouin would be tolerated. The oil fields and their facilities were too sensitive to allow open access.

Several years after Vidal's study of the phenomenon, the Saudi government set out to resolve the problem by attempting to resettle the Bedouin elsewhere and to convert them to a life of settled farming—despite the fact that the settlement of Arabia's nomads had been tried before, even in the area around Ghawar, and it was a policy the government had struggled to implement successfully. The local al-Murra tribe had foiled government settlement policies in the past, perhaps making the tribe an object of more determined policymakers by the 1960s. In the early twentieth century al-Murra tribal leaders had resisted Abd al-Aziz's *hujjar* policy. Karl Twitchell had observed during his travels with the U.S. Geological Survey in 1942 that the al-Murra had no interest in settled farming. He recorded that "listening to suggestions regarding improved living conditions, the local Amir said with unfeigned pride, 'We are Bedouins, not farmers. We tend our camels, sheep and goats, coming here, only when necessary, to pollinate and to harvest dates.'"[66]

In addition to its concerns about the oil facilities, the government also worried about an uptick in rural-to-urban migration and the abandonment by Bedouin of their traditional pastoralism for the kingdom's rapidly growing cities. And because of the large numbers of Bedouin still living in the kingdom's desert, the Saudis realized that they were not in a position to compel resettlement. Force was not an option. Instead, the kingdom used the incentive of government-subsidized farms and the provision of technical training to persuade nomads to take up permanent agriculture. They promised to construct and maintain the necessary infrastructure and to provide the necessary natural and material resources to make farming work, and claimed that farming would eliminate the uncertainty and harshness of Bedouin life. Once again, science and technology were brought in by the state to manage one of the government's most pressing sociopolitical dilemmas.

In 1964 a California-based company, the Farm Machinery Corporation (FMC), agreed to carry out studies of the area around Haradh and to prepare "recommendations justifying the development of some 4,000ha of land."[67] The FMC reported that underground water resources could easily be tapped. In 1965 the company followed up its hydrological surveys with comprehensive soil surveys and determined that although there was abundant gravelly and coarse soil, there was also enough fertile loamy soil to sustain a settlement project. In consultation with the FMC and other foreign experts, the Saudi government determined that Haradh was "favourable for agricultural development due to" the availability of water, comparatively favorable soil and topographic conditions, a nearby gas-oil separation plant that could provide a cost-effective source of power, a nearby railway line, and, of course, a community of Bedouin in the vicinity to settle.[68] In 1966 the Ministry of Agriculture and Water called for international bidders to submit final designs for the settlement and awarded the project to Wakuti, a Swiss engineering and construction firm that had considerable experience in Saudi Arabia.[69]

The scope of the Faisal Settlement Project was extensive, with an objective of permanently settling around a thousand Bedouin families living in the area, representing, according to one estimate, as many as 36,000 people.[70] The government announced, as its main enticement for the Bedouin, the promise of sustained technical investment at no cost to the settlers, as well as the guarantee that they would be sole owners of the land they farmed. The technical scope of the project was also ambitious. The Swiss firm Wakuti carried out all the grading of the 4,000 hectares of land projected as needed for the project. It also drilled fifty water wells and supplied and installed powerful pumps in each with a capacity of seventy-five cubic meters of water per second—which coursed through 180 miles of concrete irrigation canals, also built by Wakuti. The company constructed and equipped an electrical power station, built almost 200 miles of roads, and excavated more than one million cubic meters of earth and rock for concrete drainage canals.[71] Finally, it helped build facilities for a demonstration farm as well as housing and recreation and community centers.

Despite the abundance of planning and provision for the project, the settlement scheme ran into immediate difficulty. The Ministry of Agriculture and Water, which set up an internal board of directors to oversee the operation of the project, decided early on *not* to turn over ownership of the land to the Bedouin, many of whom had expressed an interest in taking up farming in exchange for property. The decision not to follow through on the landownership promise was a curious one, perhaps explained by corruption among the planners themselves, although this is uncertain. Instead, project managers decided to operate the demonstration farm on a commercial basis in the hope that they would recoup the expense of construction. A Saudi analyst of the project noted that they hoped to "provide job opportunities to the nomads, who in turn will gain skills and training before they are actually given farms to cultivate."[72] The decision not to follow through on the promise of landownership led many members of the al-Murra tribe to abandon the project. According to one survey carried out among tribe members, 68 percent said that they would not settle without tenure.[73] The reality of this was clearly reflected in the makeup of the laborers who staffed the project and worked the farms. By 1972, 56 percent of the project's wages were going to non-Saudis, mostly expatriate workers from South Asia, and 44 percent went to Saudi Arabians not from the area around Haradh.[74] By 1975, of the 778 laborers only 28 were from the al-Murra tribe, less than 4 percent of the group.[75] The project also failed to achieve its goal of stimulating cultivation and eventually shifted its efforts from growing crops to animal husbandry, especially the raising of sheep and fodder. The Ministry of Agriculture and Water cited two imperatives for doing so. It noted, without apparent embarrassment regarding its earlier position, that "the Bedouins are adaptable to this activity and the majority of them do not take to growing crops." Administration officials also cited economic reasons for the change in direction, determining that "sheep husbandry is more profitable at present than growing vegetables and fruits (the soils lack nutrients and are deficient in available phosphorous and nitrogen). Also sheep manure will improve the fertility of the land over the years. It is expected that the project will produce a great number of lambs per year which is about 5% of total imported meat."[76]

The shift to husbandry did little to change the facts on the ground, that the al-Murra tribe members saw little incentive to participate in the settlement without landownership. The project proved both a technical and a political failure. Yet in spite of the project's failure, and especially its inability to settle the Bedouin, its implementation reflected how broadly conceived modernization and development had become by the end of the 1960s and the mid-1970s. The rhetorical goal of uplifting the Bedouin hinted at the importance of development as an ideological program. Simultaneously with their commissioning of hydrological and soil surveys, dam construction projects, and Bedouin settlement schemes, Saudi leaders began talking about development as a key marker of state-society relations and as a substantial part of the Saudi identity.

THE MEANING OF DEVELOPMENT

Development did not replace or subordinate Islam as the ideological glue that bound ruler and ruled in Saudi Arabia. Saudi rulers continued to justify their rule and to demand political quiescence within a mostly religious framework. But as the 1962 ten-point program demonstrated, Islam was no longer viewed as sufficient to pacify restless citizens, a growing number of whom were in fact antagonistic to Wahhabi-Saudi rule. The government's claim that it was an Islamic power also was not effective in ameliorating the social ills that were giving rise to dissent. King Faisal outlined a more complex political contract in which the government would undermine hostility by giving priority to the provision of services and social welfare. He also made it clear that it was the government's burden to pursue national economic health, which modernization and development were supposed to help achieve. Development was formulated and framed as a means to engender social and political harmony.

Alongside Islamic law, which the royal family claimed granted its members special status, development became a substantive element in the government's efforts to carve out the state from society, to project its authority by making itself distinct.[77] Institution building, the construction of infrastructure, and the hundreds of development projects that took shape across the country all embodied Saudi authority in tangible, visible, and material forms. Citizens negotiated new and more elaborate physical and administrative systems, all of which further reinforced centralized power and strengthened the state's grip on their lives. While the government asserted greater central authority, it also formulated and disseminated a new narrative that detailed the significance of development and the government's role in bringing it about. Thus, in addition to being seen as a political, economic, and social practice, development was also ideological and was increasingly cast as a meaningful part of what it meant to be a citizen in Saudi Arabia. Development discourse, which took shape in various forms, including the glossy publications put out by various ministries in the late 1960s and 1970s, integrated Islam and modernity, attempted to make sense of the two together, and outlined how they made Saudi Arabia and its rulers exceptional. From the perspective of the rulers, while development continued to be mostly about strengthening their hold on the country, development discourse made an effort to mask this. The new narrative, a fundamental part of the development pose, deemphasized the actual processes of state building, the centralization of power, and the subordination of citizens to the Saudi authority.

Aspects of Saudi Arabia's development discourse were consistent with how authoritarian regimes have historically handled the challenge of nationalism and national ideologies.[78] With no real social base of support in the Arabian Peninsula in the 1960s, the Al Saud oversaw the invention of a discourse that claimed the kingdom was undergoing an awakening *(nahda)* and that it was the royal family that was steering it on a course to progress. In the 1960s and 1970s, the result was the birth of the cult of the kingdom's founder, Abd al-

Aziz, and its third monarch, Faisal. Routinely in government literature King Abd al-Aziz was lionized for his role in detribalizing the peninsula, "uniting" its disparate peoples under the banner of the Al Saud, and asserting much-needed central authority. Faisal received similar accolades, but he was singled out for initiating the country's rapid ascent to modernity.

In 1964 the Agricultural Bank honored the new monarch for coming to understand the importance of becoming modern, stating that "it is in the context of the complete renaissance [al-nahda al-shāmala] that brings civilization to life in the kingdom, thanks to the stewardship of the wise leader, His Highness King Faisal, whose government focused on paving the way for development of the agricultural sector in all its aspects, which ensures that it will develop and flourish."[79] Madawi al-Rasheed writes that Faisal embraced "a vision that Saudi Arabia can import technological expertise and modernize economically while remaining faithful to authentic Islam" and encouraged the adoption of a "discourse of modernization within an Islamic framework."[80] To be sure, the ten-point program Faisal outlined in 1962, and subsequent policy speeches, emphasized the interconnection between Islam and modernity. In Saudi Arabia's *Second Development Plan,* for the years 1975 to 1979, the government announced that its first goal was to "maintain and preserve the religious and moral values of Islam." Only after reaffirming its fidelity to Islam did the government outline the other goals to be achieved, including economic growth, reducing dependence on oil, developing human resources, promoting social stability, and developing the physical infrastructure.[81]

Development and progress became central themes in the cult of personality that emerged around the leaders of Saudi Arabia in the 1960s and afterward. But they involved additional layers of complexity, particularly in terms of how the kingdom's rulers deployed development as a tool for binding their citizens to them more completely. Not surprisingly, given the government's efforts since early in the twentieth century, agriculture and the environment more generally were important fields for fleshing much of this out. As late as the mid-1970s, more than half of Saudi citizens continued to earn most of their income from agriculture, either settled or pastoral. This was the main reason that the country's leaders had focused so much money and attention on agriculture. Ideologically, the kingdom's rulers made it clear that while they were part of a paternal order in which the government was responsible for caring for those in its charge, it was also a contractual relationship. Saudi leaders hoped their efforts would undercut antigovernment hostility by making the state appear more sympathetic to people's needs and committed to addressing them. They also engaged in a program to publicize those efforts, in effect marketing the kingdom and its development program to the citizens. The government's narrative showed that it expected something in return. Published materials were not so brash as to demand loyalty and political quiescence outright. Rather, they placed the burden of responsibility on those who benefited from state largesse to take advantage of the opportunity, help themselves, and thus strengthen the nation and especially the national economy.

Contrary to the conventional wisdom regarding how patronage worked in Saudi Arabia—that the kingdom simply delivered cash to citizens to ward off frustration—ideology mattered. Rather than displacing Islam and Wahhabi principles, the development discourse integrated modernity and religion and attempted to demonstrate that the two were not mutually exclusive; together, Islam and development would lead Saudi Arabia on the path to greatness. More than a decade later, in the first major academic study of Saudi development by a Saudi citizen, Minister of Information Fouad al-Farsy wrote on the cover of his book *Saudi Arabia: A Case Study in Development,* "Saudi Arabia, the only nation to use the Holy Qu'ran as a State Constitution, is adjusting well to the conditions of the twentieth century while sustaining its distinctive Islamic identity. This demonstrates, therefore, that neither is Islam an obstacle in the way of progress, nor is secularism a pre-requisite for development."[82]

Early in his tenure, on February 9, 1965, King Faisal delivered a set of prepared remarks to a group of citizens in Dammam, the administrative capital of the Eastern Province of Saudi Arabia, entitled "The Duties Incumbent upon Us," in which he outlined in detail the core themes of the development discourse. The king spoke about the various achievements that he, as "representative of the state [*dawla*]," claimed had been undertaken in the service of "our religion, our *umma* and our nation."[83] While he noted that "all our hopes have not been realized," he used his address to discuss recent accomplishments and his vision for future progress. Not unexpectedly, Faisal trumpeted the strides made in areas related to oil. In coordination with European companies, Saudi Arabia was continuing to probe the earth for petroleum reserves. He also pointed to the developments made in the processing of petroleum products, including recent efforts to build a petrochemical plant that would produce enough derivative products for export. The expansion of oil production beyond simple extraction was meant to convey the notion that Saudi Arabia was diversifying its industrial capacity and, as a result, empowering itself by becoming more self-reliant, more independent. The king featured other industrial efforts, including the construction of various chemical plants and mining facilities across the Arabian Peninsula. In addition to the oil and industrial efforts already mentioned, the king discussed two other fields in which the kingdom hoped to make advances. One, related to energy, was extraordinary, and, at least publicly, has never been acknowledged as having succeeded. The other, related to agriculture, was more mundane, but also more central to both the kingdom's ambition and its identity.

King Faisal stated that although it was not the first time he had committed publicly to becoming a nuclear power, he wanted to repeat "our resolve to establish atomic reactors [*afrān dharriyya*]."[84] For reasons he did not elaborate, although they were presumably understood by all those present, he confided that "of course, we are not able to import this energy from the outside world." Instead, he called for Saudis to undertake the project themselves, remarking, "We prefer to send groups of our citizens [*abnā' al-watan*] to obtain the science from foreign institutes and return to their country and concentrate on this project to enlighten it [*liyunahidū bihī*] in a manner that honors the *umma* and humanity and to serve the people." The theme of service—in this case, a nuclear-energy program to be carried out by citizens for the state—dominated Faisal's remarks. His comments during most of the day focused on what the government had done for its citizens. His comments regarding Saudi Arabia's goal of becoming an atomic nation, perhaps a peculiar wish for a place that sat atop the largest known oil reserves in the world, also embodied a second important message: large-scale technology was fundamental to Saudi Arabia's vision for its future and for its place in the global community.

In his comments on agriculture, Faisal argued that the kingdom needed a strong farming foundation in order to feed itself and occupy the productive energies of many citizens. And the king also argued that the government expected farmer-citizens to act responsibly and work diligently toward the goal of improving not just their lives but the nation's as well. Agitated by the apparent failure of some farmers to understand that they were responsible for doing more than just accepting handouts, the king stated that no longer would the government support the unproductive, profligate few who abused the government's generosity, threatening that there "may come a time when the government is unable to pay subsidies" to farmers struggling to make their way.[85] It is unlikely that Faisal was serious about the threat, but the fact that he felt the need to make it is instructive. Rarely before had a Saudi official, let alone a king, appealed directly to Saudi citizens to bear some responsibility for the direction of future development. Faisal left little doubt that productivity was to become a measure of service to the state and the community. The government would happily continue to finance farming, for it needed its citizens to be successful, but it would do so with an eye toward results, implying that future expenditures would be based on past performance.

By the late 1970s Saudi Arabia's experiment in development had achieved only partial success. Although the national economy remained dependent on oil revenue and the patronage that it generated, the kingdom's efforts did lead to the construction of a large and integrated infrastructure that included roads, waterworks, and planned cities. Agricultural and water projects were a major part of this expansion. As important, the steady accumulation of scientific data about the country's natural resources had provided the government and its growing body of experts with massive quantities of information that enabled it to know the space it ruled, mark it as "Saudi" territory, and, by extension, assert authority over the people who lived within it. Agriculture, although its contribution to the country's GDP declined steadily, remained important to hundreds of thousands of small settled farmers as well as nomadic herders. However, because efforts to reverse the power of large landowners had failed, most cultivators remained dependent on the government's support. Indeed, Saudi Arabian development came up well short of its economic objectives. As a political strategy, though, development was much more successful, at least for a time. The state grew in size and in power largely as a result of its efforts to build institutions, and it was increasingly able to assert its authority through them. The founding and expansion of bureaucratic institutions such as the Agricultural Bank and the Ministry of Agriculture and Water brought millions of Saudis into direct contact with representatives of the government and compelled them to participate in a dependent relationship for their livelihood. The kingdom's large and sometimes sprawling technological projects produced visible manifestations of Saudi authority, material markers of the state and its presence.

4

In 1913, a little more than ten years after their dramatic conquest of the Arabian heartland, Saudi leaders turned their imperial gaze to the east. From central Arabia a small but formidable army marched nearly three hundred miles through inhospitable desert and laid siege to the lush villages and farmland perched near the warm waters of the Persian Gulf. The invaders vanquished a small Ottoman garrison and annexed the region in the name of their leader, Abd al-Aziz ibn Saud. It was not the first time a Saudi army had stormed the shores of the Gulf. Twice before, once in 1795 and again in 1830, Saudi forces had occupied al-Hasa, a region that drew its name from its large southern oasis. Those early efforts at imperial rule had proved cursory. On both occasions the Saudis quickly crumbled against a superior foreign power. In 1913 the Saudis reversed their past misfortunes. This time the advancing army defeated a beleaguered Ottoman Empire, which on the eve of global war lacked the energy to defend a remote imperial outpost.

The relentless endeavor to control al-Hasa was driven by myriad considerations. Successive rulers viewed conquest as a means to check the ambition of various enemies, from the Ottomans to local rivals, and as the most direct way to expand imperial power. Political ambition was also cloaked in moral and religious righteousness. Claiming divine inspiration, the Saudis were driven as much by spiritual as political deliberation. Supportive clergy sanctioned Saudi militarism. Religious scholars enjoined the Saudis to conquer and urged them on as doing Allah's will. But although conquest had a religious imprimatur, perhaps the most important impulse driving expansion was material desire: the quest to expand the Saudi purse. Like all imperial powers, the Saudis coveted the prizes that attended conquest. And what prizes the oases in al-Hasa were. In stark contrast to hardscrabble central Arabia, al-Hasa's oases were verdant gardens, overflowing with water, dense with date-bearing palm groves and other vegetation, and filled with what must have seemed to the raiders to be wondrous natural bounty. Given the seemingly endless desert all around them, the oases were Arabian miracles. Their azure waters and bubbling springs had long provided relief for desert travelers, including regional merchants. But they were not merely way stations for caravans. Their copious water supplies made possible a vibrant agricultural and settled commercial life, providing a livelihood for hundreds of thousands of residents. For the Saudis and their closest allies, who were forced to eke out a meager living in the much harsher climate of central Arabia, al-Hasa must have appeared as something of a paradise. Over time the coastal communities had evolved a complex regional trade and emerged as among the most important of Arabia's and the Persian Gulf's commercial entrepôts. Residents exported dates and other commodities around the Gulf and to places as distant as South Asia and East Africa. Merchants trekked from afar to trade their wares and procure new merchandise. For the Saudis, the combination of natural and commercial wealth was tantalizing, an invitation to conquest. Shortly after putting the oases to the sword, Abd al-Aziz ibn Saud appointed one of his most trusted cousins to administer the region, establishing the first territorial possession in what would become a permanent Saudi empire.

Al-Hasa soon became Saudi Arabia's most important possession, arguably even more valuable than Islam's two holiest cities, Mecca and Medina, which the Saudis seized in the 1920s. By the late 1930s it was clear that al-Hasa would be the wellspring of Saudi political authority and economic wealth. Already valued for its natural resources, the discovery of massive oil reserves in the region proved the greatest prize of all. Al-Hasa held virtually all of the kingdom's vast oil reserves, with veritable oceans of black gold trapped in thick lime-stone rock beneath its sands and gardens. Initially, oil and the fabu-lous wealth it generated obviated earlier concerns about securing the region's other natural and economic resources. Oil rendered them something of an afterthought, at least for a time. More pressing mat-ters were at hand, such as building institutions of governance and shoring up alliances elsewhere. In fact, Saudi concerns about the ad-ministrative fate of what they eventually renamed the Eastern Prov-ince were diminished with the discovery of oil. This was mostly the result of the arrival of the large American oil conglomerate that would become known as the Arabian American Oil Company. With a short interruption during World War II, Aramco acted as some-thing of a surrogate for Saudi political leaders, administering the re-gion's affairs, building its infrastructure, employing its residents, and carefully looking after many of Riyadh's interests. Aramco adminis-tered the Eastern Province with two goals in mind: to get rich and to safeguard the stability of a still-vulnerable regime.

Even with the support of a powerful surrogate such as Aramco, Saudi authority in the Eastern Province remained tenuous at mid-century. Several rounds of labor unrest at Aramco in the 1950s made it clear that the stability of the region was far from certain. Given the Eastern Province's great importance, uncertainty would not do, and the government quickly refocused its attention on the east. A more attentive Saudi government discovered that deep resentment ran through the ranks of Aramco's mostly Arab workforce. Thou-sands of Aramco's Arab employees, including those from Saudi Ara-bia as well as others from around the region, suffered consider-able indignities at the hands of the oil company. Poorly paid and forced to live in wretched conditions, Arab workers endured the worst of American racial segregation and animus.[1] Weary of their second-class status they staged a series of strikes in the 1950s that sought to paralyze company operations, in an effort to gain im-proved working and living conditions and to attract the govern-ment's attention, in the hope that the kingdom's leaders would support their cause. They won few friends in Riyadh and achieved few concessions to relieve their suffering. Saudi officials determined that protecting Aramco and their oil served their interests better than protecting labor and their subjects.

Labor agitation raised other alarms in Riyadh about the perils of instability in the oil-producing province, sparking concerns about the possibility for further unrest in the Eastern Province. Many of Aramco's Saudi workers hailed from nearby oases, and both the company and the government worried that agitation might pour out of the labor camps into surrounding communities, whipping up frustration across the oil frontier. There was a solid foundation for concern. Not only did local workers at Aramco suffer hardship, but many faced pressure because they were from a hated and persecuted religious minority in Saudi Arabia. The population of the Eastern Province, which numbered several hundred thousand in the early 1950s, was mixed religiously, home to large numbers of Sunnis and Shiites, with the latter making up the majority.[2] The presence of large numbers of Shiites in the region was a particular concern for Saudi leaders. Their political credibility depended on their support for an interpretation of Islam first outlined by the eighteenth-century cleric Muhammad ibn Abd al-Wahhab that held Shiites in special disregard. During the 1920s, when the Saudis were consolidating their empire, some of the family's most ardent and zealous supporters rebelled against Saudi leadership because Abd al-Aziz ibn Saud hesitated to carry out mass murder against the Shiites. Shiite enmity against the Saudis was equally fervent. The Shiites in the Eastern Province bristled against Saudi-Wahhabi rule. And potential Shiite resistance to Saudi rule at midcentury was doubly disturbing because of the region's massive oil reserves.[3]

Anxiety about potential unrest converged with other concerns—concerns about political authority more generally and how to put oil to work to shore it up—and led to a more hands-on approach to the Eastern Province. Among the emerging and most pressing concerns for Saudi planners and leaders in the middle decades of the century was the country's ability to feed itself. While oil wealth enabled the kingdom to import goods to fill most of its agricultural and nutritional needs, dependence on foreign sources of food and water generated anxiety among Saudi officials, who fretted over the vulnerability caused by such dependency. While Saudi Arabia faced especially daunting environmental challenges in producing enough food and water to meet domestic needs, food security and self-sufficiency became two of the government's most important political and economic objectives. The desire to overcome food scarcity, together with the abundance of oil, helped lead the Saudis back to the Eastern Province for its nonpetroleum natural resources, and especially its water and fertile soil. Of particular interest was the oasis of al-Hasa, the largest oasis in the region. Because of its size and its vast water resources, al-Hasa occupied a central place in the government's effort to become agriculturally self-sufficient.

It is hardly surprising that planners would work to expand the productivity of the kingdom's limited natural resources and to grow more food. The country's harsh conditions provided a compelling imperative to expand agriculture where possible. But environmental austerity and the presumption of need are not sufficient to explain Saudi efforts to harness al-Hasa's resources and boost agricultural output there. Ultimately, Saudi efforts to control and then remake al-Hasa's environment were linked to the expansion of their central authority and the projection of governmental power onto a restless province, one that was home to two of the country's most valuable resources, oil and water. Increasingly, Saudi rulers and their supporters sought to assert their authority along the country's periphery and to secure their imperial reach. Oil, then, led back to water.

Efforts to harness and reengineer al-Hasa's water resources took final shape with the completion of the massive al-Hasa Irrigation and Drainage Project (IDP), which opened to great acclaim in December 1971, bringing to a close seven years of intense engineering work in the heart of Saudi Arabia's Eastern Province. On the day of its commissioning, following a short introduction from the minister

of agriculture and water and the recitation of poetry commemo-
rating the moment, a throng of enthusiastic supporters cheered as
Saudi Arabia's King Faisal cut a ribbon launching the operation of
one of the country's most ambitious development projects.[4] The
scope of the IDP was grand. Upon its completion, the project collected freshwater from dozens of underground springs and distributed it via almost two thousand miles of concrete canals, through
mechanized pumping stations, over and adjacent to freshly paved
roads, to provide life-sustaining nourishment for al-Hasa's two million date-palm trees.[5] Massive by any measure, the new system transformed the oasis physically and forced the government into the lives
of its residents in material ways.

The completion of the IDP marked the culmination of more
than two decades of efforts aimed at understanding and remaking the oasis environment. Saudi engineering at al-Hasa reflected
broader trends that had taken shape in the Arabian Peninsula since
the early twentieth century, in which the pursuit of mastery over nature was bound up with the political and imperial ambitions of the
ruling family. Across the kingdom, and especially after midcentury,
Saudi leaders had turned to science and technology to maximize agricultural productivity, to control water and other natural resources
and the people who depended on them.[6]

But even though the IDP succeeded in establishing the presence
of the central government in the oasis, and even though it was Saudi
funded and initiated, the projection of centralized political power
was not a straightforward affair. The Saudi government lacked the
technical and human resources to engineer the oasis on its own. Furthermore, government leaders, officials, and planners did not openly
justify efforts to harness and engineer al-Hasa as a means to shore up
political authority. Rather, they used the language of progress, development, technical management, and modernization—all apolitical
vocabularies that emphasized what was taken to be the self-evident
logic of science and expertise over the political language of interests
and power. The result was that the surveying, design, and engineer-

ing work that went into remaking al-Hasa masked the political stakes involved, and also masked the political connections between state power, oil, global capitalism, and expertise. The actual work of engineering al-Hasa was the result of collaboration between the government, social scientists at Aramco, and a handful of European engineering and design firms. It was through transnational networks of expertise, science, and technical management that both the IDP and its impact on Saudi political authority were achieved. The expense and scope of the project first imagined by an Aramco anthropologist in the early 1950s was finally constructed in the late 1960s and early 1970s by German and Swiss firms. The transnational and seemingly unconnected character of these networks had the effect of concealing the efforts' political objectives and consequences.

For oasis residents, however, the political nature of the IDP was clear—although many held out hope that it would also achieve the stated goal of expanding production and increasing incomes. It did not. More important for them, the project ended up intensifying political tensions between al-Hasa residents and the government, laying the material foundations for decades of unrest. While reining in the potentially restive Shiite population of al-Hasa was almost certainly one of the government's principal unspoken objectives, the IDP led to exactly the opposite outcome. The effect was that Shiites became increasingly polarized and disaffected. And they increasingly came to see the environment in political terms, terms they would use to rally government opposition once tensions boiled over in 1979.

ARAMCO, ENTOMOLOGY, AND ANTHROPOLOGY

The Irrigation and Drainage Project in 1971 clearly represented the ambition of the central state to tame nature in al-Hasa. The completion of the IDP followed years of scientific study, engineering planning, and various other developmental efforts carried out by the state itself or by foreign firms contracted specifically for those purposes. More than a decade before the central government enthusiastically took up the charge of developing al-Hasa's agricultural resources, it had cooperated with the Arabian American Oil Company on other scientific efforts in the region.

From 1948 through 1955, Aramco—collaborating in name with the government, although acting mostly on its own—undertook to eradicate malaria in al-Hasa as well as in Qatif, a second oasis located around 150 kilometers to the north. The antimalaria campaign was launched following a particularly virulent outbreak in 1947. Richard H. Daggy, an entomologist who was recruited from the University of Minnesota to head up Aramco's malaria-eradication team, told the company's English-language magazine *Aramco World* that "so many were stricken that Aramco didn't have enough hospital beds for even its own employees. Beds had to be allocated arbitrarily to those with fevers of 102 or higher."[7] At the height of the epidemic, the rate of infection was astonishing. According to early field analyses carried out by Daggy and his staff, 70 to 98 percent of the children who lived in al-Hasa and Qatif were infected. All infants were afflicted; only those able to develop immunity survived into adolescence.[8] The conditions at both oases proved idyllic for the thriving mosquito population. Water gushed year round from large underground aquifers and much of the runoff from the date groves pooled at the edges of the oases, incubating millions of the *Anopheles stephensi* mosquitoes that bore the malaria parasite. Aramco scientists referred to the pest as "Steffie," as only the female mosquito transmitted the disease. Malaria outbreaks peaked in the fall, when lower temperatures set in and relative humidity remained high. But even during the grueling summer months, when temperatures regularly reached levels that would normally kill mosquitoes (in al-Hasa temperatures can climb to a sweltering 120 degrees Fahrenheit), the pests found ways to survive. Most often they took shelter near their human victims, on the walls inside the cooler environs of local residences.

Aramco used several methods to control the mosquito population and to fight off the malaria threat. Initially, scientists sprayed families' homes with DDT, coating the walls and ceilings with the poison. The initial results were spectacular. Within two years, the infection rate in Qatif dropped to 14 percent for children and 3 percent for infants. But malaria rates jumped again several years later, when, Daggy and his team determined, the mosquitoes had developed immunity to the DDT. In 1954 Aramco switched to another insecticide, dieldrin, which drove down infection rates once again.[9] By 1957 the infection rate among infants had dropped to zero, and among others, to a rate of 6 percent. The rate was even lower in al-Hasa.[10]

Although malaria killed more people than any other affliction in the eastern oases, other diseases took lives as well. Aramco scientists and physicians documented various medical problems, including tuberculosis, trachoma, and smallpox, although none was as prevalent as malaria. Aramco's attempts to deal with threats beyond malaria reveal something of the extent of its cooperation with the Saudi Arabian government and its representatives. The head of Aramco's malaria team recalled an outbreak of smallpox in which Abdullah ibn Jiluwi, a cousin of the king and the regional governor, initially obstructed efforts to contain the problem. Shortly after Daggy had carried out a malaria survey in the Shia village of Safwa in the late 1940s, word reached him that pilgrims returning from Iraq were manifesting signs of smallpox. Although local residents had not approached Aramco for help—Daggy expressed alarm at their apparent disinterest, exclaiming later that he "couldn't imagine that they wouldn't have asked for help from the government or from somebody for a smallpox epidemic!"—Aramco sent an investigation team anyway.[11] Fearful that the epidemic would spread, Daggy's team provided help, and also sought to launch an education campaign to teach local residents the most effective ways to combat the spread of smallpox in the future. Daggy set out to show a scientific film in the hope that it would serve to enlighten the residents of Qatif as well. The determined entomologist ran into several levels of resistance, however. Aramco's Government Relations Department, which was in charge of all communication with the central and local governments, instructed Daggy that he would have to obtain permission from ibn

Jiluwi before showing the film, and even discouraged him from trying. In spite of the dissuasion, Daggy appealed to ibn Jiluwi, who initially refused to allow the film to be shown. The governor eventually relented, for reasons that are not clear.

Daggy's recollection of the governor's reasons for forbidding the film at first are revealing, signaling his belief that the governor's interest in supporting Aramco's scientific efforts was hardly based on benevolence or concern for local residents. As the American recalled it, ibn Jiluwi said, "No, there will be no health education films shown on smallpox. If God had not wanted smallpox visited on the population, he would not have sent it to the population. All these educational films were verboten; he didn't want just any kinds of films. The amir enjoyed war pictures and battleship pictures. No entertainment film and no educational film, nothing of this sort. I said, 'Oh my God, I can't believe this!'"[12] Ibn Jiluwi did eventually relent, permitting Daggy to show old Walt Disney–produced health films made for South American communities, which the entomologist doubted would work because they were filmed in wooded, green areas with flowing streams—an environment to which he believed residents of Safwa would have difficulty relating. In spite of his doubts, his team did rein in the smallpox outbreak in Safwa, although the disease appeared again intermittently. As for ibn Jiluwi's striking initial refusal to allow the films to be shown, there are several possible motives. Perhaps most important was his desire to protect his own authority in the region. The Saudi state had little institutional or administrative presence in the region other than the governor, who had wide latitude in shaping regional policy and relation. In addition, ibn Jiluwi was strident in his anti-Shiism, having little sympathy for their fate at the hands of deadly disease.[13]

Although the individual scientists who toiled to survey and then eradicate the malaria threat no doubt were concerned about the toll the epidemic took on individuals and families in the oases, it is unlikely that Aramco's executives had humanitarian interests in mind when they dispatched the teams of entomologists and public health scientists. Rather, their motives were primarily commercial and driven by the bottom line, although the company also had a political interest in eradicating the disease. Aramco would become less dependent on labor much later on, but in the late 1940s its work was still labor intensive, especially the construction of oil facilities and supporting infrastructure.[14] Foreign workers from Palestine, Egypt, and elsewhere in the region filled some of the need, but most of the company's labor hailed from al-Hasa's towns and villages, especially the nearby oases. Between 1945 and 1959 Aramco hired more than 56,000 local residents for work in various aspects of the oil industry.[15] The malaria threat in those places thus represented a perennial problem for the health of Aramco's labor force. As Daggy noted, illnesses among workers put a tremendous strain on the company's limited health facilities. Compounding the toll, workers' families also attempted to use the same facilities whenever they fell ill.[16] Aramco's main offices and residential compounds were far enough removed from the infested villages that malaria did not represent a direct threat to company officials. But outbreaks of smallpox did, justifying the expense of what would become ongoing public health efforts through the 1950s and 1960s. Aramco did none of its public health work for free. The partnership between the government and the oil company was entirely contractual, with the state hiring Aramco to carry out "research" and treat disease in the local communities.

The Saudi government had its own reasons for supporting public health measures. While the regional governor ibn Jiluwi may have cared little about the health of the local residents, especially the Shiites, the state likely understood that having relatively healthy and productive communities in the rich agricultural zones served its interests, especially its desire to see local farmers produce food for domestic consumption. The government also made it clear that it wanted Aramco to honor its wishes and that it retained some semblance of control over the oil company's operations. In the original oil concession agreement drawn up in 1933, the state had stipulated that it wanted the company to train and support workers from within the kingdom, in the hope that doing so would facilitate the development of a professional and commercial class.[17] It is unclear how hard government officials actually worked to stimulate such development. But it was important at midcentury for the state to be able to dictate terms to the company and to maintain its authority over the Eastern Province. The government also understood that by appearing to cooperate with Aramco on local projects it was achieving two additional objectives. First, Aramco was laying an institutional and operational foundation that the government would eventually be able to take over (as it did with the malaria program), one that bound local communities to an authority that would be located both inside the community and outside it. Second, through public health institutions and the networks that they tapped into, and even created, state officials were better able to understand local society, to be in contact with it, and to attempt to control it. Aramco's scientific and public health work in the oases created a fountain of knowledge for the state to tap into. In fact, it was from within the malaria program that Aramco, and eventually the government, discovered what appeared to be even more serious long-term threats to al-Hasa's potential productivity.

Among the team of entomologists working in al-Hasa, it was an anthropologist who first noted that the oasis was shrinking. In 1955 Federico Vidal, a Harvard Ph.D. who worked directly for Aramco's Arabian Research Division, wrote a comprehensive 216-page report for the oil company titled *The Oasis of Al-Hasa*.[18] The report was based on fieldwork he carried out in 1951 while acting as field supervisor for the Malaria Control Program in al-Hasa. The report contained extensive data on social relations, the local economy, the local geography, and a precise accounting of the oasis's demographic and sectarian breakdown, including all fifty-two of the Shiite and Sunni villages. The author documented the varieties of structures and homes found in the small villages as well as in the oasis's two main cities, Hofuf and al-Mubarraz. In addition, Vidal thoroughly described the intricacies of al-Hasa's hydrological features and agricultural practices, including discussions of each of the oasis's fifty springs, the existing irrigation and drainage system, water use, a breakdown of land tenure, and a rich description of dates and date farming, which constituted al-Hasa's main cash crop and consumed the energies of the vast majority of Hasawi farmers.

SOCIETY AND SECT IN AL-HASA

At midcentury, the al-Hasa oasis measured approximately 25 kilometers long and around 18 kilometers wide, with a total area of around 160 square kilometers. Between 60,000 and 100,000 acres were under cultivation.[19] The district was in fact two oases that were separated by a swath of sand. Together they formed an L-shaped region in the heart of the eastern desert. The largest component, known as the eastern oasis, was home to 35,000 inhabitants in the early 1950s. It stretched across 16 kilometers west to east at al-Hasa's southern edge, with a maximum width of 10 kilometers. The northern oasis was considerably smaller—about 60 percent of the size of its more fecund neighbor. Along the eastern border of the entire oasis area lay thick sand, which was interrupted by mesas as well as boggy catchment basins that collected irrigation runoff from the fields.[20]

Vidal's description of the oasis's geography was his least significant contribution to the body of company and state knowledge about al-Hasa, as Aramco geologists and previous travelers had already surveyed the region's physical features. More important, *The Oasis of Al-Hasa* offered a thorough accounting of social and economic life in al-Hasa and the nature of Shia-Sunni relations, the details of which keenly interested the brain trust of Aramco's Arabian Affairs Division (AAD). The AAD, located within Aramco's Government Relations Department, was set up in 1946 as a direct outcome of a series of worker strikes in 1945.[21] The AAD existed as an intelligence-gathering operation. It was literally modeled on the Cairo branch of the Office of Strategic Services (OSS) of World

War II—the precursor to the CIA—and even served as a home for several CIA operatives in later years. Aramco's interest in having "intelligence" operatives working in al-Hasa is consistent with its interest in understanding the motives and ambitions of its workers, who carried out additional work stoppages throughout the 1950s, posing a threat to Aramco's bottom line. Vidal wrote other reports on tribes in the Eastern Province, on archaeology in the oasis of al-Hasa, and on other aspects of the region's society and history.[22]

In the Arabian Affairs Division, Vidal worked alongside others carrying out social scientific research in local communities, such as George Rentz, who would later work at Stanford University's Hoover Institution, and Phebe Marr, a Harvard doctoral student who had been undertaking research in Iraq up until the revolution in 1958. After fleeing Iraq, she signed up to work for Aramco but stayed for only a short time in Saudi Arabia.[23] While Aramco's use of social scientists to carry out ethnographic and sociological analysis was consistent with the company's efforts to manage the health of its labor force, it also revealed the extent to which Aramco acted like a state, dispatching "intelligence" operatives into local communities in order to "know" more about the native culture, of which the company took a dim view. Much of Vidal's work turned out to be politically sensitive, especially his treatment of sectarian relations. It is unclear if Aramco was fully aware of the scope and importance of Shiite-Sunni relations before the publication of *The Oasis of al-Hasa*. It is also unclear what the government's response was to the report. What is clear is that surveys carried out by foreign firms just a decade after Vidal's report mostly omitted any substantive discussion of religion or potentially fraught religious differences, suggesting that they were either disinterested in the issue, viewing it as unconnected to what they considered a set of environmental and technical issues, or they were ignoring it as a result of their keener understanding of what the central Saudi government did or did not want to hear.

It is possible that Vidal produced the account that he did because neither he nor Aramco knew where the political redlines were in Saudi Arabia. It is also possible that Aramco was simply not concerned with the central government's response, considering that the state relied heavily on the oil company for a great deal of work in the region. A third and more intriguing possibility exists as well. While the central government was well aware of the religious makeup of al-Hasa, it is unclear what it knew of the actual nature of the relations that bound Shiites and Sunnis there. There is no available evidence that suggests the government requested that Aramco undertake a study of the social and natural order of the oasis of al-Hasa. But the state did not possess the capacity to carry out a similar survey on its own. Considering that the government had increasingly sought information about society and nature more generally through the lens of scientific surveys, it is reasonable to assume that Vidal's report added to a growing reservoir of such knowledge gathered by the central government. If this is true, then Aramco not only provided details about society and social relations to its state hosts, but also imparted a specific way of understanding society based on social-scientific models, which were part of a broader set of beliefs connected to the ideas of modernity, progress, and modernization being embraced by Saudi officials. That an American oil company, presumably in pursuit only of expanding its bottom line, engaged in a pedagogical project that "instructed" the Saudi state how to understand society, and therefore how to better manage it, demonstrates the extent to which the construction of knowledge was connected to capital and to the social, economic, and political world of oil.

The Oasis of al-Hasa remains among the most comprehensive ethnographic and sociological studies of the oasis today and is the single most exhaustive source on the oasis as it was at midcentury. Vidal put the oasis's population at around 160,000 in the early 1950s, although other estimates offer both higher and lower figures.[24] Just over half of all Hasawis lived in the oasis's two main cities, with around 60,000 residents in Hofuf and 28,000 in al-Mubarraz.[25] The remaining 70,000 or more were spread throughout the oasis itself, living in villages located mostly along the perimeter of al-Hasa's date gardens. The fifty-two villages varied from as few as 30 inhabitants (al-Sidawiyyah) to as many as 3,700 (Taraf).[26] The residents of Hofuf and al-Mubarraz engaged in a variety of economic pursuits, including crafts and trade.[27] Each town held weekly markets that sold prepared food and fresh produce, meat, agricultural utensils, livestock, clothes, jewelry, metalwork, and other wares.[28] Hofuf was particularly well known for the manufacture of woolen or camel-hair *bishts* (cloaks), which sold in markets in Riyadh and even in the Hejaz.[29]

The overwhelming majority of those who lived in the oasis's villages tended the date groves and grew a small number of additional crops, most notably alfalfa for fodder, rice, and assorted vegetables. Vidal wrote that "first in importance among all the items of al-Hasa's agricultural complex is the date grove, called *nakhil*, which here occupies as prominent a place in life as does the camel among the desert Bedouins."[30] Farming in al-Hasa demanded considerable energy. Because space was at a premium in the crowded oasis, agriculture was intensive. Hasawi farmers relied almost exclusively on hand tools. Vidal wrote that "everything is done by hand, even the spading and breaking of the soil, and there is little room for labor-saving machinery. The plow is not used in al-Hasa at all, in spite of the availability of animal power."[31] Date groves occupied as much as 27,000 of the 30,000 acres under cultivation, with farmers harvesting as many as forty varieties of dates.[32] Date gardening was seasonal. Farmers pollinated the palm trees in early spring. The harvest season occurred late in the summer and during the early fall. After harvesting, farmers heaped the dates in piles on top of reed mats, which they then wrapped around the dates and sewed shut, finally transporting them to merchants in Hofuf and al-Mubarraz who sold them at market.[33] The local date market suffered a severe depression in the post–World War II era. After the war, the tough market conditions forced many farmers to abandon their work for employment with Aramco in the oil fields, thus explaining the company's interest in knowing something about their background, particularly as the specter of labor unrest reared itself after 1945.

Most important, Vidal's work also exposed, for the first time, the nature of the socioreligious and hierarchical system that dominated in al-Hasa, perhaps the oasis's most unique feature. The population was mixed Sunni-Shiite, the only one of its kind in Saudi Arabia, with the Shiites probably enjoying a slight overall advantage.[34] There are few reports of open conflict before the arrival of the Saudis and their proxies. But that does not mean al-Hasa was free from communal tension or that there were no imbalances between the Shiite and Sunni communities. The social hierarchies and social power overlapped with religious difference. *The Oasis of al-Hasa* is remarkable for its open discussion of the nature of sectarian relations, which even then were a source of sensitivity in public discourse. Both before and after Vidal composed his report, Saudi officials and authors in various media avoided writing and talking about the Shiites. Covering up the existence of any religious differences served Saudi leaders, who claimed that their political legitimacy derived from Wahhabi (anti-Shia) thinking. Ignoring the Shiites and keeping them outside the public record served a practical political aim by allowing the Saudis to frame Saudi Arabia as homogeneous and free from any source of ideological—let alone theological—difference. Rubbing out the Shiites from the record helped them overcome the problem that a "heretical" community existed inside the kingdom. Acknowledging their existence could have easily led to pressure to remove them, as it had in the past. In the interest of stability, Saudi leaders preferred to avoid widespread violence in the Eastern Province, which would threaten not only their grip on the region but also their hold on the rest of the Arabian Peninsula. Nevertheless, the erasure of the Shia from state narratives was itself an act of violence. It was also fundamental to the Saudi colonial strategy, which pivoted on the need to impose Al Saud's own version of history on its subjects while erasing theirs.[35] Vidal ignored these conventions and documented the social foundations of religious difference, providing perhaps the only thorough account of its kind in Saudi Arabian history.[36]

Both Hofuf and al-Mubarraz were mixed cities at midcentury and their demographic makeup was reasonably balanced. Vidal noted that, although it was difficult to document for certain, "There is a Sunnite majority in the town of Hofuf, but certainly not overwhelming, hovering perhaps around 60 percent." He pointed out, however, that the pattern of balance appeared to be in flux and that the Sunni community was growing as a result of the rapid settlement of Bedouin there.[37] The Shiites may have outnumbered the Sunnis, with a slight majority in the smaller al-Mubarraz.[38] Although both cities included sizable numbers of each, Sunnis and Shiites mostly lived in separate residential quarters. Vidal observed that "religious differences in everyday life become mainly apparent in the division of labor (a majority of traders being Sunnites; a majority of craftsmen being Shiites) and in education." Public schools were available to both Sunni and Shiite children and while some Shia children apparently did attend the main schools, "[Shiite] parents prefer to send them to receive a less formal type of education in one of the unofficial schools operated by Shiite divines in the *husainiyah* [*sic*] of Abu-Khamsin."[39]

Differences assumed a more hierarchical nature outside the two towns, most notably when it came to land tenure and who actually did the work inside the date gardens. The village was the most important social unit in the al-Hasa gardens. Vidal attributed this to a systemic sense of insecurity given the past raiding practices of the Bedouin. He wrote that "an isolated house in the gardens was too great a risk, and safety could only be expected within the confines of one's own village."[40] There were very few mixed villages. "By and large," Vidal observed, "the villages of the garden area contain people of only one denomination. Villages with mixed Sunnite and Shiite populations are rare and, where they exist, the Shiites are usually in the minority and live in one particular corner of the community."[41] More often than not, Shiites in mixed villages abandoned them to establish their own smaller villages.

The village structure was not equal. While many Hasawis owned their own land, thousands of others worked as day laborers, tending the private date gardens of large landowners. The most successful gardens belonged to absentee landowners who resided in Hofuf or al-Mubarraz.[42] Overwhelmingly, landowners were Sunni. Vidal commented that "only a few of the most important Shiite families of al-Hasa can be considered landowners . . . The bulk of the Shiites, although perhaps owning small garden plots, are either craftsmen or laborers working the gardens for wages. In many of the smaller villages and hamlets this is true of the entire population, including the village headman."[43] For the most part, then, Shiites living in the gardens constituted the oasis's working class, filling the ranks of agricultural laborers and dependent on their Sunni neighbors for their daily wages. The system worked, at least until midcentury, but given that the two communities did not mix frequently and did experience some enmity, as evidenced by the flight of Shiites from predominantly Sunni villages, it hardly seemed harmonious. Further underscoring the hierarchical nature of oasis society, those Shia villages where local residents did own their own land were far removed from the best sources of water, a fact that undermined the productive capacity of their farms.

Historically, Hasawi farmers and merchants produced and marketed dates and date products for local, regional, and global consumption, although intrapeninsular trade was paramount. Until midcentury, dates constituted the single most important component of the diet of not only the average oasis resident but also the neighboring Bedouin tribes. The typical Hasawi derived enough vitamin and nutritional sustenance by eating around 1.5 kilograms of dates per day (three *artāl* per day).[44] Meat and vegetables replaced dates as the main source of nutrition in the 1950s. The profitability of date agriculture depended on a number of interrelated factors, and in particular on a complex regional commercial system. Until the 1940s dates trade was profitable, enjoying high demand and fetching high prices. The key to commercial success rested with the relationship between al-Hasa and Qatif, the oasis to the north that also produced dates, although in smaller quantities. Although they grew enough dates for local consumption, Qatifis preferred to convert almost all of their harvest into a sweet candy called *saluq,* which they then sold to traders from around the Persian Gulf.[45] With insufficient product to consume locally, Qatif imported dates from al-Hasa to make up the shortfall. This balanced system promised profits for merchants in both communities—at least it did until Saudi officials quashed it.[46]

The local and regional date economy suffered a sharp setback in the years shortly after World War II, leading to a domestic agricultural depression that hit al-Hasa's Shia community hard. One reason larger farmers and merchants could operate successfully in the regional trade—and why smaller Shia farmers proved unable to compete—was their reliance on large caravans to transport dates from south to north. The large caravans provided much-needed security against Bedouin raiders, who plundered smaller, poorly protected groups moving between the oases. After their conquest of the east in 1913, Saudi leaders strove to rein in the tribes and their raiding practices, partly by settling them in agricultural villages as well as in the two main cities in al-Hasa. Saudi efforts to control the Bedouin were not carried out in the interest of local residents. Rather, Saudi leaders considered the nomadic tribes to be a security problem, although they also viewed them as martial allies. In addition to sedentarization efforts, the Al Saud enacted economic measures to accommodate the Bedouin. Most important, the government took steps to drive down the price of dates, making them more affordable for the Bedouin. The government accomplished this by setting a quota on the amount of *saluq* that Qatifi farmers and merchants could produce, keeping it between 20 and 25 percent of the crop, and by placing an embargo on date exports. The drop in prices proved dramatic and devastating. From 1948 to 1951 the price of 140 pounds of dates (one *qullah* in local measure) dropped from forty-eight Saudi riyals to ten.[47] The government lifted the export embargo in the spring of 1952, raising prices back to an improved but still low seventeen Saudi riyals per *qullah.*[48]

The drop hit small farmers particularly hard. Larger farmers and merchants who were not entirely dependent on dates for their income did not suffer as much.[49] As the value of dates and date gardens fell, many small farmers who owned their land were forced either to join the ranks of day laborers or to look for work in local industries or, more likely, outside the oasis. Those who depended exclusively on labor for their wages were pushed to the brink, and thousands left al-Hasa to find work with Aramco and in the Eastern Province's rapidly growing metropolis Dammam, located around 100 kilometers to the north. A second blow to small farmers and landless laborers was the rise in real estate prices, which locked the lower and working classes into their subordinate status. Vidal wrote that "although the rise [is] in part attributable to inflation, [it] is mainly due to the highly increased prestige value of a date garden as a luxury item. At present there is a clear tendency among some of the upper classes of al-Hasa society to accumulate properties."[50]

DIAGNOSING AL-HASA

Vidal saw little hope that the economic situation in the oasis would improve, even going so far as to suggest that "the date agriculture and the farmers of al-Hasa are now at a crossroads."[51] He sounded an ominous warning about the future of agriculture in the region. But his—and what would become the government's—primary concern was not the deleterious effects of the drive to suppress the price of dates. The most pressing set of problems had to do with the slow but steady decline of al-Hasa's cultivable area; the oasis was, according to the Aramco ethnographer, "slowly drying out."[52] Vidal drew on a number of available sources to document the diminution of fertile land. Aerial photographs taken by Aramco in 1950 revealed where local residents had periodically abandoned villages and old water wells, many of which were now in the desert. Little was left of the abandoned sites except for the rubble of old houses and irrigation ditches. It was clear that the desert had gradually overtaken them, burying them in the suffocating and desiccating sands that rode the backs of migrating dunes. Based on the patterns of settlement that Vidal had observed while working in the oasis, he surmised that the sites of the ruined villages marked the former outermost perimeter of the date gardens.

It was unclear to Vidal exactly how much of the oasis had given way to the encroaching desert, and he did not hazard a guess. Several years later the Saudi Arabian Ministry of Agriculture sent in a team of scientists to investigate the scope of the problem. They determined that, along the entire eastern edge of the oasis, "a great mass of sand was advancing on the oasis at an estimated average rate of 30 feet annually. Each year some 230,000 cubic yards of sand were ebbing into the oasis, and near 14 villages [in the southeastern corner of al-Hasa], the dunes were looming over the very roofs of the houses . . . The dunes that were moving . . . measured five and [a] half miles by 100 miles [and were] advancing so fast that it would bury the [closest] village . . . within seven years if immediate action was not taken."[53] In addition to the invasion of the massive desert dunes, the al-Hasa water table appeared to be in decline. Underground springs that once needed no assistance in bringing water to the surface required mechanical pumps and human help by midcentury.

Vidal believed that the problem was partly environmental, although he had little tangible geological data to work from in the early 1950s. The intruding desert dunes demonstrated the awesome power of nature and its fickle ways. Vidal noted that the underground water that had fed al-Hasa's lush gardens for centuries was a finite source, partially renewable but not indefinitely so. Al-Hasa's water resources would not last forever. But he argued that it was humans who were most to blame for the decline of the oasis's water level and the approaching demise of Hasawi agriculture. Considering his detailed analysis of the region's social relations, along with his discussion of how social inequalities overlapped with religious identity, Vidal's diagnosis of al-Hasa's unfolding "environmental" crisis took an odd turn. The anthropologist observed that the decline in the oasis's water table had "been helped along by agricultural malpractice," but he ignored his own findings as to the social and hierarchical foundations of the problem—and the connection between water and power.[54] Ultimately, Vidal determined that the "malpractices" responsible for the problem were technical and managerial in nature rather than bound up with the hierarchical and religious network that his work had helped unravel in the first place. This way of thinking would become the foundation for all future scientific, technical, and developmental efforts in al-Hasa, including the construction of the Irrigation and Drainage Project a decade later.

Date farming requires significant quantities of water, which the oasis historically had in abundance. It was the use and management of that water that most concerned Vidal. There were between fifty and sixty underground springs spaced throughout the oasis, which still provided bountiful, if declining, amounts of water for the area under cultivation at midcentury. In spite of the large number of springs, however, the use of water for irrigation purposes was tightly controlled and hardly egalitarian. Two types of irrigation were in use in al-Hasa as late as the 1950s. The first type, called *mugharraf*, was the least important. In *mugharraf* irrigation, farmers lifted water from springs located near their gardens (either by hand or with the aid of animal power). The second type of irrigation, known as *saih*, dominated in al-Hasa and proved considerably more problematic.

Water in the *saih* system flowed from large springs and passed through an elaborate irrigation canal, called a *masqa*, and a network of secondary ditches, from which it was diverted to the various farms. The physical network was complex, with canals and ditches crisscrossing and traversing the length and breadth of al-Hasa. Its complexity, however, was not the product of need but of social power. The *saih* irrigation system involved the timed distribution of water from spring to canal to farm. Farmers abided by a rigid system that determined who enjoyed early access to water fresh from the spring—access that made all the difference in the quality of the water received and, not surprisingly, the quality of the crop eventually harvested.[55] Typically, the right of first access went to landowners and farmers who held the largest plots of land. Distance from the spring did not affect the system of privilege. Water that flowed directly from the spring (called *hurr,* or pure, water) passed through a *masqa* and was then diverted directly into the plots of those who had first access. Those farmers lifted floodgates located along the masonry or stone-lined *masqa* adjacent to their land for specified periods of time, often measured by the changing lengths of the shadows of the palm trees or by the location of the evening stars, allowing the water to flow over and saturate their fields.[56] In almost all instances, farmers who received *hurr* water took more than they needed from the *masqa,* resulting in a surplus of unused water that pooled on the ground. Because al-Hasa sloped gradually from west to east, the leftover water (called *tawayih,* or forfeited, twice-used water) then ran off the land and was redirected through a second gate, called a *munajja,* where it passed "into a common channel, usually referred to as *thabr,* which conducts [it] over longer distances and from which smaller canals branch out into other gardens."[57] *Tawayih* water passed in this way repeatedly—from farm to *thabr* to farm and so on—until it arrived at the perimeter of the gardens and either ran off into the desert or pooled in bogs that lined the oasis.

Cultivators and landowners who owned rights to *hurr* water took great pride in that fact. Conversely, those who relied on *tawayih* were held in some disdain. Vidal wrote that it was common for local farmers to malign those lowest in the irrigation hierarchy: "Gardens at the very end of this redistributing and regathering system are spoken of with disdain as 'drinking' *tawayih al-tawayih,* twice-used or twice-forfeited water."[58] Because of the symbolic significance attributed to the superiority of *hurr* water, the local system took measures to guarantee that *tawayih* water was never mixed with the pure. Vidal reported, "Thus long and complicated channels must be built and maintained, once a farmer is assigned a place in the irrigation order and schedule, even though his garden may be closer to a second source of water."[59]

The cultural ridicule directed at those who lacked the clout to command water from further up the chain was hardly the most serious problem those farmers faced. Forfeited or twice-used water was of poorer quality, and its nourishing power was diminished based on the number of farms through which it passed. As water passed from field to field, it rapidly accumulated salts by leaching them from the soil. The longer that water was exposed to the sun, evaporation exacerbated the problem by concentrating the mixture. Vidal ran a series of tests to determine the salinity of water as it ran from specified points along one *saih* network originating from the al-Haql and al-Khudud springs just east of Hofuf.[60] At its origin, the water collected from the two springs had an average salinity of around 1,275.5 parts per million, a quality good enough for drinking and irrigation. As it passed through the large palm gardens and the predominantly Sunni and mixed Shiite-Sunni villages of the eastern oasis, it became more saline. At the end of its route, at the edge of the oasis in the Shiite village of Abu Thawr, it contained more than 4,000 parts per million, "thereby making the water almost useless for anything but date agriculture of mediocre results," wrote Vidal.[61] The small Shiite farmers were not the only ones hard hit by the irrigation system; Sunni owners of small farms also suffered by being at the end of the irrigation order. But in terms of overall impact, there is little doubt that al-Hasa's Shiites bore the brunt of the system's imbalance.

Vidal's discussion of the deficiencies of the irrigation system directed attention to the human source of the problem, but he either decided against or overlooked the extent to which the "environmental" crisis was directly attributable to social and Shia-Sunni relations. It is unclear why he did this. After all, his report hardly shied away from discussing the sensitive issue of sectarian relations in al-Hasa. Perhaps he believed that a close reading of the text would make clear that agricultural "malpractices" and the declining health of the oasis were connected to sect and society. More likely, based on the brief summary at the end of his report on the scope of the challenges facing the oasis, Vidal lapsed into a mode of analysis that would have been familiar to other social scientists, engineers, and technocrats operating in the postwar era—one that framed and understood the world in terms of technology and modernization theory. His recommendations, which called for an overhaul of the techniques of irrigation instead of the hierarchical nature of the system, represented not a willful erasure of society and sect but rather their incorporation into the technologies that resulted from them. Where Vidal rearticulated the link between society and system when it came to the oasis's impending "environmental" crisis, those that followed him overlooked society altogether, emphasizing the technical and the managerial issues exclusively. Most notably, the Saudi Arabian government picked up on the technical and managerial approach as the preferred solution. In the case of the government, however, the decision to emphasize technology over society and sect constituted a political act.

ENTER THE STATE

The Saudi Arabian government took Aramco's warnings about the declining health of the oasis seriously, although it did not immediately move to confront the threats facing the area.[62] It took six years for the state to finally mobilize its resources in al-Hasa; it launched its initial investigations there in 1961. The government was aware of the problems and continued to contract with Aramco for help in researching and understanding the environmental aspects of the challenge. Agronomists and engineers in the employ of the oil company stayed particularly busy in the oasis of Qatif during the late 1950s, carrying out agricultural research and promoting its development. This made sense. Qatif was considerably closer to Aramco's headquarters in Dhahran than al-Hasa was, and the company's American employees were often among the first to benefit from the company's efforts there. The much smaller Qatif suffered salinity problems similar to al-Hasa's. Under the guidance of Grover Brown, head of the agricultural division of Aramco's Arab Development Department, and with financial support from the Saudi Arabian government, as early as 1955 the oil company had established an experimental farm to determine what varieties of vegetables would survive in the tough climate. In addition to the experimental work, Brown also suggested that an improved drainage system be employed in order to mitigate the crop-killing effects produced by waterlogged soil, a move that the company guessed would expand the area under cultivation by more than 9,000 acres, and even suggested that over twenty years the return on the investment would be seventy times the cost of the project. By the end of the decade Qatifi farmers began supplying fresh produce to nearby markets patronized by company employees and local residents. According to a report in the company magazine published in 1960, Qatifi farmers sold over 650,000 pounds of produce in 1959. In 1960 Aramco alone contracted to purchase 580,000 pounds of vegetables grown in Qatif.[63]

In 1961, villagers in al-Hasa reportedly pressed an appeal for assistance upon the Ministry of Agriculture to help resolve their various problems.[64] Ten years after Vidal carried out the fieldwork for his report, the government answered the call. It was in the early 1960s and the decade that followed that the government's will to develop al-Hasa fully materialized. From 1961 to 1971 the Ministry of Agriculture and Water spent tens of millions of Saudi riyals addressing the twin environmental threats, sand encroachment and water, first outlined in detail by Federico Vidal and Aramco. Much like the Aramco anthropologist, in the end the government fully embraced the belief that the oasis's ills, and the future of agriculture in Saudi Arabia, rested with the construction of large irrigation systems and the implementation of new managerial practices. It would make little effort to address the underlying social and sectarian relations that helped produce al-Hasa's environmental crisis. In fact, it became clear over time that the government had little interest in overturning the social elements of the crisis. Considering that it was al-Hasa's Shiites who were locked into the subordinate role, it is likely that the government had no desire to empower them.

In 1962 the government established the Sand Control Project within the Ministry of Agriculture to determine the best way to protect al-Hasa from the encroaching desert. Migrating dunes threat-ened the oasis on three sides. Two giant deserts and one smaller one loomed on the southern, northern, and eastern borders. To the south, the shadows of the 365,000-square-mile Rub al-Khali (the Empty Quarter) hung over the oasis's perimeter.[65] In spite of its mas-sive size and movement—in the Rub al-Khali, sand dunes literally migrated on top of other sand dunes—the southern desert posed the least dangerous threat. More serious were the sands that were mov-ing in from the north and the east. Winds from the Mediterranean swept in sand from the great northern desert, the 265,000-square-mile al-Nafud (roughly the size of West Virginia) that sits on the Saudi Arabian-Jordanian border, where they accumulated with those of the dunes of the Jafura, located between al-Hasa and the Persian Gulf.[66] Aramco carried out a study in the early 1960s to determine precisely how the dunes moved. Company researchers observed that the sands migrated in a number of ways, including by surface creep and through the suspension of small grains of sand in the air. Most troublesome was a process called saltation, in which windswept sand bounces off the surface of the desert. With saltation, which was re-sponsible for transporting the largest amount of sand, the bouncing sand dislodges more particles, steadily expanding the total amount of sand being moved. Aramco determined that dunes moved an average eighteen meters per year. According to one Saudi Arabian scientist, in the twentieth century alone more than half of the cultivable area in al-Hasa had been lost to the desert.[67] The dunes ranged between four and twenty meters in height.[68] They gobbled up more than 75,000 square meters of territory every year, covering the consumed area with a layer of sand ten meters deep.[69] Northern winds (the *shamal*) blew at a brisk rate throughout the year, carrying sands in all seasons. But April to July proved the most blustery time of year, when wind speeds well exceeded the twenty-two kilometers per hour needed to bear sand. During Saudi Arabia's late spring and early summer, high-speed winds, sometimes in excess of ninety kilometers per hour, gusted for more than nine hours a day during daylight.[70]

The Ministry of Agriculture experimented with several potential fixes.[71] Among those abandoned because they were too expensive or too inefficient, given al-Hasa's size, were several mechanical and physical approaches, including covering the dunes in various hardening materials such as asphalt, high-gravity oil, rubble, mud, cement, and combinations of all of them. None worked particularly well. With the exception of oil, all the other hardening methods cracked under the weight of vehicles and work animals, and oil proved too costly to use on a sustained basis. For a time, the Ministry of Agriculture tried to relocate the dunes physically, using dump trucks and hand labor to transport the sand from one location to another. When that failed to address the scope of the problem, teams of bulldozers were brought in to demolish, level, and break up the symmetry of the dunes in the hope that the sand would then follow new patterns. It did not. The government also briefly attempted to plant high grass, in the hope it would act as a windbreak, but that also proved too expensive. State officials finally came upon an effective technique in 1963, when they planted a 150-foot-wide grove of tamarisk trees along a nine-mile stretch of the eastern border of the oasis.[72]

The process was not complicated, although it was labor intensive (requiring 500 local workers). Workers first constructed fences to provide temporary shelter for the trees. They then leveled the closest dunes and covered them with saline soil from nearby *sabkhas* in order to weigh down the sand. The protected areas were then divided into four- to five-meter basins, which were flooded by newly dug irrigation canals. In the flooded basins, the workers planted 3 million tree seedlings.[73] The process was very slow because it required the trees to grow to maturity. By 1974 more than 645 hectares of trees had taken firm root, a not inconsiderable number. By the end of the 1970s, Saudi scientists applauded the efficacy of the afforestation project, but criticized its limited implementation. Yahya Albokhair wrote in 1982 that the problem worked in the small areas where it was undertaken, but that the problem of sand encroachment still existed for much of the rest of the oasis.[74]

The very local implementation of the project in reality stood in contrast to Aramco's applause for its own efforts, as well as those of the government, when it claimed the great relief of al-Hasa villagers. *Aramco World* magazine reported in 1965 that "for villagers who faced destruction just four years ago this is a startling change and they are as grateful as they are hopeful."[75] It is likely true that those in the area adjacent to the nine-mile grove were thrilled with the relief. But as later observers noted, the results were in fact localized within the oasis. Not surprisingly, the Ministry of Agriculture claimed to be serving everyone. It attributed lofty aims to its efforts, some of which were earnest and entirely consistent with its interests. Aside from halting the dunes and protecting land from being absorbed by the desert, the ministry outlined several additional reasons for its sand-stabilization efforts. Among them, it hoped to protect water resources and to achieve balance in the oasis's humidity ratio. It sought to accomplish this by reducing the size of the dunes around the drainage fields, in the belief that doing so would keep water from pooling excessively. In reducing the marshy bogs, the ministry also aimed to exterminate diseases that festered because of the mosquitoes and other pests that thrived there. By cutting back on sand infiltration, the state also supposed it would be improving soil quality. The most revealing objective may be seen in the ministry's statement that it sought "to improve the status of the urban people and encourage them to increase their agricultural land."[76] This statement would have been cryptic to most readers—and there were likely few readers of the report—had it not been for Vidal's social and ethnographic survey of the oasis. By 1963 the most stable and successful residents of the oasis were large Sunni landowners who lived in al-Hasa's two main cities. Smaller Sunni farmers along the edge of the oasis struggled to compete. But by far it was the Shiite farmers and day laborers who had lost the most. Given the Ministry of Agriculture's statement, it was clear that the Saudi government's sand-stabilization scheme was not intended to serve them.

Efforts to retard sand encroachment proceeded apace throughout the 1960s and continued to be a subject of scientific inquiry into the late 1970s and early 1980s, as the work of a handful of Saudi Arabian graduate students cited here attests.[77] But the Ministry of Agriculture expended considerably more energy in addressing problems associated with water and water usage. In 1962 the ministry hired the Swiss engineering firm Wakuti to investigate the condition of al-Hasa's cultivation practices as well as its water and soil resources, and to propose a solution to the challenge of improving the oasis's irrigation and drainage system.[78] Wakuti operated in the oasis from 1963 to 1971. For the first three years the firm's consultants collaborated with agronomists and scientists from the German Leichtweiss Institute of the Technical University of Braunshweg in a reexamination of Federico Vidal's findings. On the basis of the findings and proposals submitted by Wakuti to the government, the Ministry of Agriculture hired the West German construction company Philipp Holzmann to build what would become the al-Hasa Irrigation and Drainage Project.[79] Philipp Holzmann's construction operations took place from 1967 to December 1971, when the IDP officially opened.

One other consulting firm carried out geological, hydrological, and agricultural studies in al-Hasa in the 1960s. In 1968, Italconsult, an Italian engineering firm that undertook studies in other parts of the kingdom as well, included an analysis of al-Hasa as part of its examination of the water and agricultural resources of the entire Eastern Province. Italconsult maintained no connection to the efforts surrounding the Irrigation and Drainage Project, but it is instructive to consider its findings and commentary on agriculture and society in the region alongside those filed by Wakuti during the same period.

Wakuti's vision for what the completed project would look like and what it would accomplish was grand—and expensive. In 1964 Wakuti estimated that it would cost the Saudi Arabian government a total of 339,865,850 Saudi riyals for all civil and mechanical engineering work to build a new irrigation and drainage system. The Swiss company averred that the cost was worth it, claiming that a well-constructed project that followed specific scientific and technical managerial practices would more than double the area under cultivation. Drawing on data the firm collected in 1963, it claimed that the area then put to productive agricultural use measured around 8,000 hectares.[80] The company projected that with proper techniques, equipment, and the growing of new crops, the area would be expanded to more than 20,000 hectares.[81] It wrote confidently and at that point somewhat obviously that "the conditions shall be established for an increase of the agricultural area and the [sic] general economic productivity. This can be achieved by an improvement of the yields on the present agricultural acreage and by an extension of the irrigation area."[82] The Saudi Ministry of Agriculture was duly impressed and laid out 245 million Saudi riyals (US$51 million) to bring Philipp Holzmann in to carry out the construction work.[83]

The technical and scientific data recorded by Wakuti and Italconsult largely confirmed Federico Vidal's finding that the oasis faced an uncertain future unless something was done to rescue it. They also showed that a few of the oasis's basic features had changed. One major change was that Hofuf and al-Mubarraz had grown noticeably, with the former home to more than 76,000 inhabitants, and the latter 36,000, by 1968.[84] Italconsult observed that the number of villages had declined from more than fifty in 1951 to thirty-six. Urbanization had clearly intensified in the late 1950s and early 1960s.[85] The number of Hasawis engaged in agriculture dropped consistently, with only 21,900 individuals working in the gardens by 1968.

Most important, however, the firms confirmed Vidal's findings about the effects of the present irrigation system on the quality of water. Wakuti carried out tests on forty-two of the oasis's springs and found that the water's average salinity close to the springs measured 1,530 milligrams per liter, a level that was fine for irrigation. But by the time that water reached the edge of the oasis, its salt level rose to between 4,000 and 6,000 milligrams per liter.[86] The company reported that "especially the irrigation areas far away from the springs have been affected by unfavour[able] conditions of oversalting while the gardens adjacent to the springs are not so much subjected to the danger of . . . oversalting due to their better water supply."[87] The effects of the water's high salt content was dramatic: "A high content of soluble salt directly affects the plants like a toxin. The trees die when detrimental chloride or sodium concentrations occur . . . The soil silts up. Water and air [can no] longer infiltrate unchecked. The soil becomes partly gelatinous and impermeable for water and air. In a dry state it forms crusts. It is hard to cultivate. The spring up of the seed is bindered or stopped."[88]

The effects of highly saline water on plant life were noticeable. By 1968 the number of palm trees actively producing dates had dropped from around 2 million in 1951 to just over 1.1 million.[89] Almost all of al-Hasa's water was considered "good to detrimental," based on a water-classification system that considered salt levels between 700 and 2,000 milligrams per liter (60 to 75 percent) to be barely acceptable. Excellent water—water that contained less than 700 milligrams per liter—was virtually nonexistent in the oasis.[90] The company was not able to explain why al-Hasa's water had such a high salt content, although it did provide new insight into the region's sources of water. Most of the water came from two different subterranean strata. Most commonly, water came from the Neogene formation, which lay 100–180 meters below the surface and bubbled up into aquifers that fed the oasis's springs. Additional water was located at a depth of 250 meters, in the Khobar strata.[91] The water was ancient, between 13,000 and 17,000 years old.[92] By the early 1960s these two water strata, which were separated by a thick impermeable limestone layer, were under pressure from heavy usage. Between 1951 and 1963, Hasawi farmers bored more than 330 wells, drilling into both the Neogene and the Khobar formation in an attempt to overcome the oasis's salinity problem, an effort that was mostly futile.[93]

Using its research findings, Wakuti designed and planned what would become the basic blueprint for the Irrigation and Drainage Project. The firm made it clear that while the new irrigation system was vital for reducing the level of salt in the water, proper drainage was no less important. Because al-Hasa had a high water table—water was often just a few meters below the surface in many areas—the soil was constantly susceptible to waterlogging, which led to greater levels of salt being leached from the soil. In addition to plans for managing water resources, Wakuti advanced several proposals for adding new varieties of crops. The firm pressed the need to dedicate more agricultural space to the growing of alfalfa in order to sustain a larger livestock community, which it and the Saudi Arabian government believed would be more profitable than agriculture. But it also advocated using much of the 12,000 hectares to be added by the IDP for growing grains, corn, lettuce, beans, cantaloupes, and peas.[94] It was inconceivable that dates would diminish in importance, but Wakuti seemed to be responding to pressure from the Ministry of Agriculture to explore a more diverse crop-growing pattern, to answer what would presumably have been increasing national demand for new kinds of produce.

The construction of the IDP transformed the oasis as well as its irrigation system. By the time it completed construction work in 1971, Philipp Holzmann had built more than 1,500 kilometers of concrete canals that carried water from thirty-four local springs to al-Hasa's farms, as well as an additional 1,300 kilometers of canals that carried it away.[95] The new irrigation area measured more than 16,000 hectares. Most of the area relied on gravity to transport water from the springs through the network of canals. But 4,000 hectares of farmland sat above the main springs, requiring the construction of three pumping stations and elevated reservoirs, each with a capacity of 15,000 cubic meters. Sections of the main 155-kilometer irrigation canal and 140-kilometer drainage canal were either rectangular or trapezoidal in shape, varying from 1.6 to 9.26 meters wide and 8 to 10 meters long, and weighing around 20 tons each.[96] All of the 3,185 kilometers of secondary canals were parabolic in shape, measuring from just less than half a meter to 1 meter in width.[97] In the course of building the network, Holzmann excavated more than 9 million cubic meters of earth and used over 450,000 cubic meters of reinforced concrete.[98] To carry through the construction of the project,

Holzmann engineers had to organize and build factories for the production of cement as well as a separate massive complex that included various workshops, laboratories, storage areas, offices, a power station, and housing for employees.[99] Two hundred German engineers, as well as 2,000 locals, worked on the project. Holzmann's housing camp for the engineers and their families included a swimming pool and a bowling alley, as well as a nursery and an elementary school for the more than 100 children of the German employees.[100]

All of the production took place on site in al-Hasa. Planning and organizing for the construction of the operations facilities took almost one full year.[101] The transport from Europe of prefabricated concrete canal sections and the necessary steel (more than 15,000 tons) to reinforce them would have been prohibitively expensive. Because of this, the differently shaped canals were all produced in factories in al-Hasa, each requiring considerable space and resources. Ironically, making concrete proved an unexpected challenge. Concrete production requires the use of mineral aggregates typically found in sandy environments, something Saudi Arabia has in abundant supply. Much to the surprise of Holzmann's engineers, however, appropriately sized aggregates were initially found only in one area ten to fifteen kilometers from the concrete-mixing plant. While the distance was not necessarily a problem, the methods used to collect them were. The company noted that the "course aggregate was collected by Bedouins raking stones together in the desert, a most improbable procedure."[102] Eventually the company located a large deposit that, although farther away, allowed for easier collection methods. Once completed, the lengths of concrete and other materials were transported by truck to the oasis for installation.

The movement of millions of tons of earth and the construction of thousands of kilometers of canals represented an impressive engineering accomplishment. In the years after the project opened, it became a source of media and public interest, the subject of articles in a variety of professional and popular magazines and journals in Saudi

Arabia and around the Gulf.[103] Indeed, in the 1970s the al-Hasa Irrigation and Drainage Project became a spectacle, a symbol of the power of oil and the progress it helped bring about in Saudi Arabia. It was a source of national and regional pride. Its completion represented the kingdom's will to conquer nature, its technical acumen— even though it was European firms that had done the work, the Saudi Ministry of Agriculture had imagined it first—and its commitment to developing the necessary resources to escape from its dependency on foreign providers of food. In the early 1970s the IDP lent substance to claims being made by Saudi Arabia's leaders that it saw the country's future in the application of science and technology in everyday life. For its part, the al-Hasa oasis assumed even greater significance nationally because it was home to the IDP. In various writings published after 1971, the IDP and al-Hasa were cast as one and the same: the irrigation project subsumed the oasis itself. It would be an overstatement to suggest that the blending of al-Hasa with the IDP was the intent of the Saudi Arabian government in the early 1960s. But it did serve the government's political ends, especially the erasure of Hasawi society—particularly its religious complexity— from all public discourse. After the project's completion the state continued to emphasize the oasis's scientific and technological importance, most notably by providing space and resources for Germany's Leicthweiss Institute (which had collaborated with Wakuti in the studies conducted in the early 1960s) to carry out experimental work in al-Hasa throughout the 1970s. At least in state records and academic studies, al-Hasa's geology, agriculture, soil characteristics, and water resources overrode the complicated social networks that Vidal had described in the 1950s.

The brushing aside of place and society by science and technology was the result of a decade of work carried out by Wakuti and Italconsult in the 1960s. While Wakuti's most important role during that period was its sketching of the plans that would become the IDP, it also contributed greatly to the production of knowledge about al-Hasa and Hasawi society. With some notable exceptions, Italconsult, which worked in the oasis only in 1968, helped in this process. The two European firms provided the only systematic data on al-Hasa in the 1960s. Their departure from the work of Vidal was complete, as they almost totally ignored the socioreligious dimensions of life in the oasis. Although the two companies did note and write about society, they mostly relied on negative assumptions based on race and culture. None of this comes as much of a surprise. Wakuti and Italconsult were driven by capital interests and the goal of successfully completing an expensive business transaction. They were even more focused on the bottom line than Aramco. Those who authored the various company surveys and technical reports were not social scientists but engineers. Neither Wakuti nor Italconsult maintained a large enough staff to carry out the kind of work that Aramco had been capable of the decade before.

Company officials had little interest in the political dimensions of their work. Accounting for the political and social causes of al-Hasa's impending crisis might even have jeopardized the millions of riyals in revenue to be made by simply overlooking them. But there was more behind their ignoring the complexities of al-Hasa's social life, and especially how social relations contributed to the environmental woes, than business interests. Overlooking those features of Hasawi society was entirely consistent with the extent to which science and technology informed the worldview of those who carried out the surveys and subsequent work, and of their main audience: the Saudi Arabian government. To them, technological backwardness was the product of primitive racial and cultural factors and basic social structures such as the traditional family unit, which in Saudi Arabia worked only to obstruct the march of modernity. The companies' research studies effectively black-boxed the religious and social-hierarchical dimensions of life in al-Hasa, subordinating important social details to thousands of pages of technical data and commentary on methods.

The firms did not ignore Hasawi society, but their accounting of it was framed in such a way as to justify imposing technical fixes rather than attending to many of the underlying social inequalities that caused the problems in the first place. Wakuti addressed only the most basic social data, preferring, when it talked about actual people at all, to focus on the techniques employed by local farmers under the old irrigation system. The firm did take note of the land-tenure system, pointing out that the government was involved to various degrees in ownership. Absentee owners living in Riyadh laid claim to large sections of the oasis, although the extent of their holdings is unclear. In addition, local "statesmen"—civil servants and higher-ranking officials—owned land, and the state also retained a large share of the oasis as government property. There continued to be private ownership, although the company made no mention of specific patterns. It did note that smaller farmers were engaged in two kinds of collective farming, in which cultivators irrigated their land in common and harvested it either together or separately.[104] As for the existing irrigation system, Wakuti lifted most of its details directly from Vidal's report. The company did not connect land-tenure practices with the irrigation system in any detail, let alone mention the oasis's religious makeup. Clyde, Criddle, Woodward, a Utah-based consulting firm contracted by the Saudi Arabian Ministry of Agriculture to comment on Wakuti's findings as well as on the feasibility of its proposal for the IDP, noted that there was a gap in the Swiss company's reporting on property. In comments it sent to the Saudi Arabian government, it called for a complete cadastral survey of the project area, stating that the sketching "of maps showing ownership is of first priority." But the American consultants were not concerned about the political or hierarchical dimensions of property. They were solely interested in the potential impact of property ownership on the construction phase of the project and vice versa: "It will be necessary to establish land ownership and property boundaries since rights-of-way will be needed."[105] The Saudi government was not then and has not subsequently been interested in conducting any kind of cadastral survey or census, at least not one that has been made part of the public record, although it did pay indemnities to landowners whose harvests were interrupted by the construction of the IDP. By 1970 the Ministry of Agriculture had paid out 7.5 million Saudi riyals to affected farmers.[106]

The Italian firm Italconsult made much more extensive remarks on the society and culture of al-Hasa. On a much broader scale than Wakuti, it invoked social and cultural relations as justifications for major technical works and for the implementation of better management practices. There was no relationship between Italconsult and the construction of the IDP, although the firm carried out its survey of the oasis in 1967–68, when major engineering works were well under way. While its work proceeded independently of the building of the IDP, it was no less important to the overall remaking of the oasis. The company's surveys and reports contributed important technical information about geology and agriculture to the growing reservoir of knowledge being accumulated by the Saudi government. But whereas Wakuti's studies closely scrutinized technical and natural data related to the construction of the irrigation project itself, Italconsult not only confirmed the justifications for the IDP but also argued that there were broad social and cultural reasons to proceed with the development scheme.

Unlike Wakuti, Italconsult did briefly observe the nature of sectarian relations in al-Hasa, noting that in contrast to nomadic communities, distinctions in the settled oasis were based on religious and not tribal differences. The company's final report on al-Hasa noted the presence of the large Shia community but paid little more than cursory attention to it. Completely missing was any discussion of Shiite-Sunni relations or the scope of their interaction. The report's authors did offer up a bit of analysis regarding intra-Shiite relations that, while not inaccurate on a limited scale, overlooked the fact that the same system even better characterized Shiite-Sunni relations: "Instead of lineage, village and class relationships are the rule [in the Shia community] . . . Class stratification is related to wealth— the city merchants, land-lords and jurists representing the upper layer—and to alleged [descent] from the caliph Hussein."[107] The firm's reluctance to draw broader conclusions, or at least to state them directly, about land tenure patterns and class relations did not mean company analysts did not understand them. The firm's final report noted that absentee ownership was widespread, that it was rare to find an owner-farmer, and that much of "the property does not belong to the farmers, but to non-agricultural classes. In sample villages 80 percent of the plots area is rented."[108]

Nevertheless, after offering up class analysis as one way of approaching an understanding of al-Hasa, Italconsult then abandoned it as an explanatory framework. Of more interest were other sets of social relations that Italconsult analysts believed played a direct role in inhibiting development. Foremost among these was the family, which it considered the basic economic unit, especially among agriculturalists, and saw as particularly powerful in undermining development. Farmers clung to their familiar family structures and practices, which meant maintaining small primary residences in increasingly impoverished remote villages and directing the vast majority of their income toward farming expenses—in spite of the fact that "a large majority of [farm] holdings are too small to ensure family subsistence."[109] This trend baffled the Italian observers, as the reward for investment was typically very low. Farming offered little opportunity for growth, which observers thought should be the primary motive of small farmers.

Moreover, by 1967 more and more of a family's income was generated by work undertaken in industries other than agriculture. That is, more and more members of families engaged in work in the region's major cities, and especially in the oil industry, without breaking up the power of the family in society. Italconsult reported the existence of "new strata that are being moulded by the migratory streams in the urban centers, where, under the thrust of the oil economy, thousands of people from every tribe of the country mingle with the original settlers of the Eastern Province."[110] In spite of the movement of people to and from the rapidly growing and "modernizing" cities, there appeared to be little impact on the economic life of the oasis's rural outposts: "Despite their geographical proximity, the modern economic structures are strictly confined to industry and urban services have not so far appreciably modified agricultural structures."[111] Compounding the apparent economic limits of family-operated farms, the nature of such enterprises was "technically backward" and lacking any entrepreneurial spirit, Italconsult claimed.[112] There was no apparent investment in improving agricultural methods. This led, according to Italconsult, to farming families wasting money on their own labor.

But more important, it was the conjuncture of the social and the technological that Italconsult determined to be the core of the problem, arguing that social and cultural norms were manifested in technological "backwardness." Together, social and technical backwardness worked to retard progress, and the company made the sweeping claim that this was tantamount to being inhuman, Italconsult's code language for uncivilized. The final Italconsult report remarked that

> the persistence of the traditional farm, with all its implications, i.e. low technological level, subsistence production, absence of enterprise with regard to stocking and to the market, seem to be due both to the "clinging nature" of the traditions and to the insufficient transformation of the human element prevailing there. The modern structures and infrastructure have so far modified a number of external conditions . . . but they have not radically modified either the human element or the farm structures.[113]

The company clearly believed that the most important obstacle to achieving agricultural development was cultural. Italconsult pressed for the modification of the "human environment through extensive training of adults, both at the level of personal maturity and of awareness of the real conditions of the economic and social environment in which they will work and at that of technological and professional modernization."[114] It was through technology, scientific education, and management that the entirety of al-Hasa's social and cultural makeup would be transformed and that Hasawis would apparently be humanized. The company made it clear that technology was more than merely a set of implements and practices; it also constituted a set of values that demanded the acculturation of the typical Hasawi farmer. There was nothing surprising in such a belief. The blending of technology and culture, and especially the elitist and hierarchical view of the world that technological difference seemed to support, had been central to European and Western understandings of the non-West for centuries.[115] Italconsult's apparent unwillingness or inability to depict the *real* social and economic conditions that had dominated in the oasis up to that point was entirely consistent with the kind of knowledge and work the state sought to produce.

SUCCESS IN FAILURE

For their part, Hasawi farmers remained skeptical about the Irrigation and Drainage Project even as it neared completion. In late 1970, one year before the IDP officially opened, local cultivators were equivocal about what the project would deliver. One farmer told an *Aramco World* journalist, "We are happy about the drainage because we were almost swimming in the fields here." The magazine went on to write that "then he scratched his head and added thoughtfully 'but we haven't seen any water yet.'" Another, whom the journalist likened to the "notoriously taciturn New England farmers," agreed, remarking that "it's too early to tell" if the project would deliver on its promises. It may have been too early to tell for the two farmers interviewed for the *Aramco* piece, but it is noteworthy that parts of the IDP had already been operating for several months without altering what the magazine generally labeled the "skepticism of the al-Hasa farmers." Heinrich Hopp, Philipp Holzmann's manager in Saudi Arabia, attributed the uncertainty of the farmers to the intrusion caused by the construction of the project itself. He stated that "farmers here, as everywhere, are conservative by nature, and since there has been a certain amount of disruption to their old canals and roads, there have been complaints."[116] Hopp's assumption—indeed his hope—that the community's cynicism was the product of the construction process was not unreasonable, given the scale of the effort. Reasonable or not, time would prove Hopp wrong and confirm the skepticism of the farmers.

By the end of the 1970s, the IDP had failed to achieve almost all of its technical objectives. Within three years of its completion the project had helped expand the area under cultivation by more than 2,000 hectares, a promising start.[117] But by the end of the decade it had added little more, falling well short of its goal of expanding the total area from 8,000 to 20,000 hectares.[118] More alarmingly, tests carried out after the construction of the irrigation and drainage network determined that al-Hasa's water resources were declining rapidly in spite of the IDP's goal of managing and conserving them. Within the network, some of the main springs performed better than others, leading to higher levels of water in some canals and lower levels in others. The water level proved so low along some canals that the area under cultivation actually declined by a third or more. The total area committed to date cultivation also declined throughout the decade, from 4,750 hectares in 1967 to 4,547 in 1980.[119] Some agricultural land was simply not put to use. In 1977–78 more than 43 percent of the land alongside one of the major irrigation canals lay fallow.[120] Those farmers who did continue cultivating made up the date shortfall by growing more vegetables, but their farms still constituted only 14 percent of the total area. In the new oasis, rice, which had been the second most important crop after dates before the IDP, became too expensive to grow. The area committed to rice cultivation dropped from 880 hectares to 120 and the price rose to over ten times its 1960s levels.[121] Even with the expansion of vegetable harvesting, the oasis did not produce any more for domestic consumption than it had previously.

Old social patterns also endured in the oasis. Labor patterns remained mostly unchanged, with large numbers of residents leaving the oasis to find work. The majority of families who continued to engage in agriculture, especially those who lived in the garden villages, remained poor and essentially indentured to large landowners in the urban areas. While some owned small plots of land, these were often too minuscule to be profitable, forcing the residents to work as wage laborers. One post-IDP study found that, together, more than 380 farmers owned 1.1 square kilometers out of the 3.5 square kilometers of land adjacent to one of the main irrigation canals. Of those farmers, 215 owned less than 1,000 square meters of land (.1 hectare) while the rest owned between 1,000 and 2,000 square meters (.1 to .2 hectare), which represented a drop from the 1960s when the average holding was closer to 1 hectare.[122] Large landowners not only continued to dominate holdings and the social and political power that came with ownership, but also seemed to have expanded their grip on land tenure in the period after the IDP was built.

The decline of the area under cultivation as well as the decline in the size of the average holding for smaller farmers after the completion of the IDP underscores what the engineers and planners failed to see: that in addition to soil salinity and sand-encroachment issues, land tenure and social patterns were also important. The project did help stabilize salinity levels, making it possible for farmers throughout the oasis to farm more productively. But there was little incentive for cultivators with steadily declining acreage to invest their labor in their own fields.

Among the most enigmatic outcomes of the Irrigation and Drainage Project was the drop in the oasis's once overabundant water supply. There are several possible explanations for this decline. Wakuti carried out extensive tests on the oasis's water supplies in 1963–64 and confidently attested to their long-term availability as well as to the viability of the thirty-four springs ultimately used to feed the irrigation system. The boring of private wells, over three hundred of them by the mid-1960s, by small farmers certainly had some effect, although the flow rate of the wells was too low to have dramatically diminished reserves. It was most likely true that the reserves from both the Neogene and al-Khobar water formations were finite and that once exhausted they would no longer sustain agriculture. But it would have been remarkable for the water level to have declined significantly in the middle decades of the twentieth century, considering that the oasis demanded less water during that period, when it had proved bountiful for centuries.

Local residents offered up a much more cynical interpretation thirty years later, one that is not supported by any evidence but is nevertheless plausible. Area residents interviewed in 2003 suggested that Aramco was responsible for the disappearing water in the 1960s and 1970s.[123] Saudi Arabia's underground oil reservoirs are not pressurized, meaning that oil has to be pushed to the surface somehow. Aramco resolved the challenge by pumping water into the subterranean fields to force the oil out. One group of Shiite landowners claimed it was widely believed that the oil company relied heavily on the same freshwater sources that Hasawi farmers used to pump oil from the Ghawar field, which lay less than twenty kilometers from al-Hasa but over eighty kilometers from the Persian Gulf, the next closest source of water. The IDP, they suggest, was an attempt by the government to cover up Aramco's destructive practice. Even if Aramco did not use the water from underground reservoirs to pump out oil, the company, along with the state, likely did put pressure on those reserves in other ways. In addition to al-Hasa the growing cities of Dammam, Dhahran, and al-Khobar north of the oasis also relied on water from the Neogene and Khobar formations. As the cities expanded under the weight of intrapeninsular migration and the addition of Aramco facilities after midcentury, especially housing and structural facilities built to accommodate the company's American workers, they no doubt strained the entire region's water supply. Diminishing water in the region led to the expensive efforts to build two massive desalinization plants along the Persian Gulf near Dammam.

The skepticism articulated by farmers in the 1960s and 1970s to journalists and project engineers about whether the project would ultimately serve their interests proved prescient. The expressions of frustration after the IDP indeed failed to produce results, and the belief that the project was built as a cover for oil company practices, reveal the extent to which Hasawis came to view technology and politics as connected. The disillusionment and suspicion connected to Saudi and foreign engineering practices led to the entrenchment of antistate and anticompany feeling throughout much of the local and regional population; even as early as the late 1970s, it helped politicize and galvanize Shiite dissent.

Although the IDP failed to achieve the goals imagined for it by both the Saudi state and the European firms that designed and built it, the project lived on in Saudi Arabia's national narrative as a wondrous achievement, a testament to the kingdom's modernizing impulse and its will to conquer nature. And because the IDP was an agricultural development project in the heart of a harsh desert environment, it was held in particularly high regard. Even critics of the project muted their censure by heaping plenty of glowing praise on the IDP, and on the state for helping imagine it in the first place. Despite the shortcomings of the IDP, and especially its technical failures, it was a political success. The project represented the culmination of several decades of "development" work in al-Hasa carried out variously by Aramco, the Saudi Arabian government, and those contractors brought in on its behalf. Since the late 1940s, when the Saudi state's grip on al-Hasa was tenuous, scientific and technical projects, such as malaria eradication as well as irrigation and drainage works, have resulted in the expansion of the power of the central state. Foreign actors operating in al-Hasa, from entomologists to anthropologists to engineers, were not always complicit in the act of projecting Saudi authority. Yet unwitting or not, they helped produce knowledge about the oasis that was useful to the expanding central state as well as the literal technologies of political power. From the 1950s to the early 1970s the efforts of foreign engineers and scientists overlapped with a sharpening Saudi state strategy of using science and technology as mechanisms in the expansion of state control. While those Americans and Europeans projected themselves as both apolitical and as engines of progress, they made clear political choices in how they characterized al-Hasa, its people, and its problems.

It was in the choice and nature of their characterizations that the political interests of the central government were served. The work of the European firms that designed the IDP systematically ignored the complicated sociosectarian relations that dominated in al-Hasa and that contributed to the scope of the oasis's environmental woes. Society and culture played important roles in the various studies that helped achieve the IDP. But the trajectory of the narrative that emerged around the oasis reimagined al-Hasa, looked past the power of religious identity and how it overlapped with land tenure and irrigation rights, and introduced the notion that traditional culture that was a source of the region's threats. Even though culture was pointed to as a justification for massive technological intervention, the discussion of society and social practices remained broadly conceived and overly generalized. This inattention to detail served a purpose, which was to focus not on people but on science itself. In various texts, discussions of geology, sand, water, wind, and climate took precedence over people, an approach that served the Saudi state's vision. Since it first asserted its political power in al-Hasa in 1913, the central state had been uncomfortable with the large Shiite presence there, not only because the Shiites themselves represented a potential threat, but also because state leaders worried that their presence would invite hostility from hard-line Sunnis elsewhere in the kingdom. "Erasing" the Shiites and replacing them with science helped achieve an important political objective.

Development work in al-Hasa, especially the IDP, served to bring the state directly into the Shiite community in al-Hasa. The malaria-eradication program initiated by Aramco in the 1940s helped expand the power of the central government beyond the administrative posts it had created, such as the governorship and the local municipal councils. Those offices remained urban phenomena, largely failing to have much contact with the Shiite villages of al-Hasa. Efforts to wipe out malaria, and then the decade-long project of reinventing the oasis's irrigation and drainage system, brought the central government in. This was especially true with the IDP, which introduced not only the massive state-managed physical presence that controlled the oasis's water resources but also the administrative and bureaucratic apparatus that attended it. Alongside the IDP the state opened the al-Hasa Irrigation and Drainage Project Authority, which came to be a major force in the oasis economically and politically by way of its control over the region's water. The IDP Authority also became al-Hasa's largest employer, taking in thousands of would-be day laborers and making them directly dependent on the state for continued work in agriculture. There is little information available on the IDP Authority and its hiring practices, but if labor patterns were similar to those elsewhere in the kingdom—and there is no reason to believe they were not—then the poor Shiites who took up work for the IDP would have remained in the lowest-paying jobs, perpetuating the cycle of their subordination.

5

The expansion of development work, particularly projects that targeted the Eastern Province's rich oil and water resources, worked to extend the power of Saudi Arabia's central authorities. It also heightened both the expectations and the frustrations of those Saudi subjects who made their home in the region. The completion of the Irrigation and Drainage Project in al-Hasa in 1971 marked a major achievement for the government, although it came at a considerable cost politically. The failure of the IDP and similar projects in the region would ultimately transform local politics. By the end of the 1970s, the environmental and social consequences generated by development work and by the failure of the state to ameliorate environmental problems would help radicalize some elements of the Eastern Province's Shia community, turning some of them into militants.

The embrace of radicalism by the Shiites was not inevitable, however. In the 1950s and 1960s, when F. S. Vidal carried out his ethnography of al-Hasa and the Saudi government launched the project to remake the oasis, residents throughout the Eastern Province had begun to express considerable frustration about state development policy, environmental neglect, and the uneven distribution of oil wealth. The 1950s and 1960s did not prove to be violent decades, although Shiites in the east did become increasingly critical of the government. They used their frustration with the state's emerging environmental policies and development agenda to push not for a rollback of central authority but for Saudi Arabia's rulers to govern their communities and their region more equitably. While they embraced the principles of development work in general, they lamented its uneven execution. For the most part, at least publicly, anxieties about the failures of development projects took priority over those about their status as a large religious minority. Privately, though, community fears about religious discrimination were acute. Shiites had historically faced various kinds of discrimination, at various levels. The Saudi state placed severe restrictions on their religious observances, refused to hire or represent Shiites in local and national government, and allowed Sunni extremists to promote the view that Shiites were guilty of a grave form of apostasy, a sin that justified their subordination and even their death. Many in the Eastern Province privately expressed their worry about sectarian discrimination and even spoke of it to Aramco researchers. But in public they focused on development and environmental work as a means to overcome sectarian enmity and as an avenue for the Shiites' inclusion in Saudi society.

In the late summer of 1948, Salah al-Zakir, an assistant secretary serving in the Ministry of Finance, accompanied the Saudi finance minister, Abdullah Sulaiman, on a trip to Dhahran, the corporate heart of the kingdom's petroleum industry. Al-Zakir recorded his impressions of the trip for the Medina-based journal *Al-Manhal* (The Spring).[1] Oil and the changes it brought about inspired the secretary. The sheer scope of the oil industry's infrastructure left him awestruck. Facilities sprawled across the region, providing tangible evidence of the country's bounty. Al-Zakir relished what it all meant, applauding Aramco's seemingly tireless efforts to probe the earth for more oil, including the construction of new oil wells, pipelines, refineries, and production facilities. Every bit of energy put out by the company confirmed al-Zakir's hope that crude oil would continue to bestow fabulous wealth on the kingdom for years to come. Aramco's good works, al-Zakir assured his readers, went beyond exploring, drilling, and the endless quest for more. He believed the company was committed to helping the country itself achieve new heights. He took particular notice of the fact that Aramco had worked to improve public facilities, singling out its role in building a new hospital in Dhahran, a new airport, and improved trade and shipping facilities. Favorably impressed, he declared spiritedly that "Dhahran just gets better and bigger every year."[2] Almost eight years later, in the spring of 1956, the magazine's founder and editor, Abd al-Qadus al-Ansari, trekked across the Arabian Peninsula in order to consider again the dramatic changes unfolding in the oil province. Al-Ansari reveled in the rapid changes that had taken place. "Is it real or is it a dream?" he wondered. "Seeing the Eastern Province," he wrote, "transported me back twenty years to when *Al-Manhal* was first published. It is not the same world." Just two decades earlier, al-Ansari suggested, the province had been poor, languishing in isolation. "Now," he attested, "it is striking": "as if all I knew of the Eastern Province had been taken by thieves and cut up," replaced with what he reckoned was a thriving, bustling center of business and industry.[3]

Oil company executives and Aramco's public relations department were no less enthusiastic about their efforts in Saudi Arabia, routinely engaging in self-promotion and self-congratulation. Company leaders heralded the company as a powerful force for progress, not only a beacon but also an engine for improving the fate of the country and its citizens.[4] In its annual reports to the Saudi government Aramco reviewed and celebrated its various activities to assist local communities, including efforts to develop vocational skills, improve education and health care, and stimulate agricultural growth.[5] Aramco claimed its benevolence was widespread. The company also disseminated this message in its public relations material. The same year that al-Zakir toured Aramco's facilities, the company's executives began to characterize their work in Arabia as a "junior Marshall Plan" and even a "private Point Four program."[6] In 1953 Aramco published the first issue of *Qafilat al-Zayt* (The Oil Caravan), its monthly journal in Arabic, a companion to the English-language *Aramco World,* in which it took every opportunity to play up its commitment to outreach. There were deeper implications in all the talk of progress, development, and service. Together, the Saudi government, its supporters, and the oil company were in effect suggesting that not only had their efforts heralded a new progressive age for the region, but also that time itself had begun with their arrival. The Eastern Province had no history before oil.

While visions of progress and legends of development in the east began to appear in company publications and pro-government periodicals, many in the Eastern Province took a much dimmer view. In the inaugural issue of *Akhbar al-Dhahran* (The Dhahran News), a local newspaper first published in December 1954, Abdullah bin Khamis, a local intellectual, wrote a long essay titled "My Impressions of al-Hasa."[7] In florid prose, bin Khamis refuted the company's and the government's claim that oil had breathed life into the region, that history had started with the arrival of outsiders. Bin Khamis narrated the rich cultural and literary history of the al-Hasa oasis, highlighting its central role in regional trade, its beauty, and its once-abundant natural resources. In the not too distant past, he claimed, water had flowed copiously and date palms, whose fruit dominated not only the local residents' diet but also their social and cultural lives, had grown in abundance. By 1954 bin Khamis was lamenting that it was all lost. Market pressures, particularly the importation of food by Aramco, and direct state manipulation of date prices had crushed the value of the sweet fruit, plunging the fragile local economy into a deep depression.[8] More than three-quarters of the water resources had mysteriously disappeared, and what was left was often foul and virtually unusable in the palm groves. Worse, bin Khamis argued, the old customs and ways were dying. Thousands of young men had flocked from the oasis to the oil fields, draining the agricultural sector of vital labor power. As a result, the once-rich groves stood on the edge of ruin. Al-Hasa, the author declared, "needs a better future."[9] Although he stopped short of stating so outright, there was little doubt about what and who were to blame: oil and the Saudis. Indeed, bin Khamis would almost certainly have agreed with Abd al-Qadus al-Ansari's impression that the region had been cut up and taken by thieves.

Challenging the oil company or the pro-government narrative

came with significant risks. Bin Khamis avoided reprimand. Others were less fortunate. Muhammad Said al-Muslim, a prolific author and a member of *Akhbar al-Dhahran*'s editorial board, wrote passionately about the Eastern Province's pre-oil history, pushing back firmly against the Aramco and pro-government narratives. In *Sāhil al-dhahab al-aswad* (The Black Gold Coast), a book-length history first published in 1960, al-Muslim detailed the long social and cultural history of communities in eastern Arabia before the Saudi conquest. He also discussed frankly the region's struggle with outsiders such as the Al Saud. Al-Muslim paid a steep price. Saudi authorities imprisoned the author for ten years, starting in 1964, even though he had published a second edition in 1962 that omitted all references and materials critical of the ruling regime.[10] Prison proved a common destination for more than a few authors and journalists in the 1950s and after.

The combination of Saudi political power and the discovery of oil had brought sweeping and uneven change to the Eastern Province. The region had in fact become among the most developed and, at the same time, most neglected and imperiled regions in the kingdom. The key to understanding this apparent paradox is found in the two published accounts by al-Zakir and al-Ansari.[11] The authors of the two *Al-Manhal* articles focused on transformations in the metropolitan center of the region—the three interconnected cities of Dhahran, al-Khobar, and Dammam. These modern cities popped up where only small fishing villages had previously existed and transformed the Persian Gulf coast into a thriving commercial and urban landscape. Perhaps no other region of the kingdom underwent such rapid social, economic, and political change. The Eastern Province also saw the influx of thousands of Saudi Arabian and migrant workers from around the Arab Middle East, South Asia, and the United States. The movement and migration of people, goods, oil, and ideas accelerated in the 1950s as the oil industry and the cities of Dammam, Dhahran, and al-Khobar rose from the desert.

What al-Zakir and al-Ansari failed or chose not to comment

upon were the challenges and troubles that dominated on the region's periphery—in al-Hasa, Qatif, and the other communities that sat on the edges of the new oil metropolis.[12] There, the misfortunes were twofold. By the middle of the twentieth century, communities that had once been the heart and soul of commercial and cultural life on Arabia's Persian Gulf coast became marginalized politically and socially. They languished in virtual isolation, overlooked by local and central authorities in favor of their fast-growing neighbors. Bin Khamis, in his essay, poignantly captured what turned out to be a growing sense of disillusionment with the impact of oil and the uneven manner in which it was used to help some and not others.[13] Residents watched ruefully, and then angrily, as the administrative and oil-producing centers grew and prospered while frustration and despair mounted around them. In addition to neglect, residents in the marginalized villages and towns in the Eastern Province, some of which were thousands of years old, were also feeling the negative effects of oil directly. Water was disappearing, widely believed to be the result of environmental abuse by Aramco. And oil operations caused other kinds of environmental problems, including the fouling of available water and increased pollution and congestion, and produced negative pressures on the local economy as well.

But while bin Khamis and al-Muslim expressed deep dismay over the negative impact of oil, they were not repudiating what oil *could* do. Observers disagreed about how good or bad things were and whether the effects of the process were "better and bigger" or demanded "a better future." But many remained enthusiastic, even hopeful, about the potential for positive change that oil represented. Fueled by their frustration over the uneven impact of oil wealth, residents in the east took to the pages of the local press in the 1950s to air their grievances and, more important, to outline various visions for how to remedy the imbalance. They demanded that oil revenues be put to broader use, that the interests of all citizens be addressed. And they challenged the close relationship between the American oil company and the Saudi Arabian government, arguing that Aramco did not and could not have the country's best interests at heart. More fundamentally, critics of the Saudi Arabian oil order were also demanding a new social and political contract with the government. Not only should oil serve more people, but the resource and the fabulous wealth it produced, they implored, should serve the interests of a nation in which ruler and ruled enjoyed equal access.

It was the latter demand—a call for a new nation in which oil was used to strengthen the position and status of Saudi Arabia's residents—that was most controversial and dangerous. Critics were, in effect, challenging the political authority of local and central government, straddling the fine line between criticism and political dissent. Oil and the changes it brought were at the heart of their frustration, and they offered pointed and focused critiques of how exactly oil was being put to use. Just as important, writers and editorialists offered sharp criticisms of the ways that the oil industry was being used to strengthen Saudi political authority. At midcentury, this meant they were taking on the government's environmental policies and the uneven impact of the government's efforts to control nature.

Critics were very aware that the central government had specifically sought to control nature as part of a broader program to bind society to its central authority. Indeed, frustration in the Eastern Province in the 1950s was linked directly to the government's own national governing strategy with regard to nature and the environment in other parts of the kingdom. Much of the anxiety expressed in print in the 1950s was directly related to the state's apparent disregard for environmental problems in the Eastern Province's oldest villages. Demanding that more attention be paid to the area, critics called specifically for more technology, for a more pronounced role for technocrats in their communities, and for the application of scientific management methods to solve environmental problems. Moreover, the environment and its degradation became not only a reason for concern about public health—as writers honestly fretted about dangers posed, for example, by piled-up garbage not removed by the local government, standing sewage, and other problems—but also a symbol for rallying national unity.

THE POLITICAL PRESS

From midcentury, talking about and criticizing the oil industry and the government was popularized in Saudi Arabia in print media in the Eastern Province, where the uneven effects of rapid change were often stark. The alienation generated by the uneven distribution of oil wealth served as a catalyst for the expression of disillusionment with what many local residents considered to be inattentive government institutions and neglectful officials. Critics of local government, and by implication of the central government in Riyadh, took aim at lagging material and social conditions in specific communities. In the outlying regions of the east, particularly in the communities of al-Hasa, Qatif, and the small villages that surrounded them, residents lamented their marginalization by the newly emergent cities of Dhahran, al-Khobar, and Dammam. In addition, editorialists and letter writers discussed and argued over questions of authority and who was responsible for the contrast between center and periphery. While they did not directly criticize the royal family or the regime in Riyadh, various citizens did engage in debates about local aspects of the burgeoning state, including local councils and their failings, controversies about corruption, and other concerns. They lamented, already in the 1950s, the shortcomings of oil, underscoring the growing importance of such discourse even at that early moment, as well as the volatility that would ensue from heightened and unmet expectations.

While criticisms reflected disappointment in the unequal levels of material gain enjoyed by citizens, the anxieties expressed in the regional press also reflected concerns and emerging ideas about a broader set of political issues and the ways that people were coming to terms with them. Most important, critics used the dislocations

brought about by change to articulate their expectations about what
the relationship of government should be to its citizens. At the heart
of their grievances, then, were political concerns about the obligations of the state to society and about the marginalization of some
communities at the expense of others. The relationship between government institutions and the officials who presided over them and
the residents of the Eastern Province remained unclear in the 1950s.
This relationship was complicated in part because the state itself remained immature. Earlier in the century, King Abd al-Aziz had appointed a powerful cousin, Abdullah ibn Jiluwi, to rule the Eastern
Province on behalf of the royal family. While the Al Saud were rulers
in name, ibn Jiluwi enjoyed considerable power in his own right to
rule the east according to his own interests.[14] This relationship began
to change in the 1950s, when state institutions, such as regional and
local municipal councils, were organized to oversee local affairs, including public health, road building, environmental issues, and so
on; at that point the media criticism of those agencies also began to
appear.

The frustration that emerged early with the failures of oil did not
go away easily. The intensity and specific character of many of the
complaints first vocalized in the 1950s endured for decades, leading
ultimately to more direct and violent opposition to the state. The
government never seriously addressed the root causes of the emerging frustration. Worse, the efforts it undertook to quickly establish its
control over regional resources and peoples exacerbated deteriorating conditions, all of which set the terms for the politicization of oil
and the environment. Indeed, those roots, nourished over a half century of anger, disillusionment, and political ferment, materialize in
print in the 1950s for all Saudi citizens to read, when they were expressed in the pages of the Eastern Province's local newspapers.

Journalism turned out to be a risky enterprise. Publishers and
editorialists were routinely imprisoned, and the newspapers themselves enjoyed short lives before being shuttered by the government.
Saudi authorities tolerated the young media for a few years, partly

because they had limited experience with a critical press. But as the government grew increasingly authoritarian, Saudi Arabia learned quickly. Papers were closed, journalists were imprisoned, and censorship became a central fact of the country's publishing industry, all in a few short years.

Part of the government's rush to clamp down on the critical press had to do with the prospect of a growing indigenous radicalism. By the middle of the 1950s the regime was threatened by activism and the specter of more broadly politicized communities. The Saudi dynasty witnessed several challenges to its power during the decade, including its own internal struggles between rival princely factions bent on wrenching away political control for themselves.[15] A group of military officers, inspired by the example of the Free Officers in Egypt, attempted an unsuccessful coup in 1955. In the Eastern Province, two major labor strikes at the Aramco compound in 1953 and 1956, which were sparked by grievances over low wages, poor working and living conditions, and racism, prompted a stern response from both the regime and the oil company.[16] As a result, the government clamped down on dissent by closing newspapers, constraining opportunities for speech, and restricting activities it considered threatening. In the Eastern Province, such measures to control local dissent in the communities coincided with more extreme efforts by the state, as well as Aramco, to choke off direct political action coming from Saudis working and living in the oil camps.[17]

For the most part, analysis of politics in Saudi Arabia outside the royal family and in the Eastern Province has tended to focus on life and labor unrest inside the Aramco labor camps. Popular politics—that is, subversive dissent or the questioning of state power from below—has rarely been regarded as serious and has been viewed instead as anomalous.[18] But in fact the middle decade of the century saw the politicization of citizens both inside and *outside* the labor camps in the Eastern Province. Omission of this fact stems from the challenge of locating and identifying what constituted political activity. The absence of organized political parties or an openly confrontational opposition does not signal the absence of political will or even activity. Political parties, public functions, and political activity were outlawed. The regime's hard-line and often violent suppression of such behavior mandated more subtle forms of the expression of disillusion. One observer has noted that "political opposition to the royal family and monarchical rule is forbidden . . . trade union organization is illegal and severe prison penalties are imposed on any worker who organizes or participates in a strike or any other form of collective industrial action . . . Civil liberties are non-existent and overt political activity is rewarded with imprisonment without trial."[19] In March 1961, the Saudi regime "created new instruments" to crush any opposition. That year it passed the State Security Law, "which prescribes the death penalty or 25 years imprisonment for any person convicted of an aggressive act against the royal family or the state."[20] Although they were unable to organize or operate in an official or formal political context, Saudi subjects did pursue the available means to articulate their concerns, interests, and dissent—in the press—before the state shut them down.

A second challenge in identifying and discussing politics in the Eastern Province in the 1950s has been that of religious difference and discrimination. Most of those outraged by the changes brought by oil in the 1950s were likely Shiites, although they did not identify themselves in that way. Sectarianism, while an important concern for Shiites, could not become an issue of public discussion. Citizens in communities all over the east expressed sectarian grievances in private—in particular their despair over sectarian discrimination—through personal letters to local officials and community petitions, as well as in interviews with researchers working for Aramco.[21] In public, however, due to state censorship and control, the focus was on problems that cut across tribal and sectarian issues.

The press, much to the surprise and chagrin of an initially supportive government, did give voice to local frustration, offering space to visionary intellectuals, and, most important, revealing the wide range of feelings on a number of topics and challenges that would later be deemed too sensitive for public discussion. Among the major papers in the Eastern Province were *Akhbar al-Dhahran* (The Dhahran News), the region's first weekly paper, published between 1954 and 1956; *Al-Isha'ā'* (The Shining Light), a literary and political journal published between 1955 and 1957; and the weekly *Al-Fajr al-Jadīd* (The New Dawn).[22] Articles in each of these publications are rich in details about local life and struggles, yielding short-lived but intense glimpses into the outrage over oil and the politicization of the environment.[23]

It was in the pages of *Akhbar al-Dhahran* that the most incendiary and provocative writing appeared, eventually leading to the forced closure of the paper and the arrest of its controversial editor, Abd al-Karim al-Juhayman. Al-Juhayman had moved to Dammam and found employment with a publishing and translation company in the early 1950s, after graduating from school in the Hejaz. In 1953 he and his colleagues received permission from then Crown Prince Saud, soon to be king, to begin publishing the new periodical. Because of poor facilities, the initial issues of *Akhbar al-Dhahran* were printed in Beirut, shipped to Dammam, and distributed from there. Reflecting on the early days of the paper, al-Juhayman remarked in his memoirs that "in the beginning [the paper] was very weak like any seed just planted in the earth, like any work started anew. Then, it was the first newspaper published in the region that reached many cities and villages."[24] First published on December 26, 1954, the paper initially came out every two weeks. After several months the four-page periodical began to appear every Thursday.

Akhbar al-Dhahran did not survive for long. Immediately political in content, the paper took a polemical tone on a number of subjects, and its intrepid editor boldly, if recklessly, pursued his own agenda. In November 1956, al-Juhayman ran an article by Muhammad bin Abdullah calling for the education of girls. The following spring, moved to action by a group of angry readers who were outraged by the prospect of girls attending school, regime officials ordered the closure of the radical periodical, after only forty-four issues. The last edition was published April 29, 1957. The paper's closure was only part of the fallout. Al-Juhayman found himself imprisoned, alongside Ahmad al-Sheikh Yaqub, the editor of *Al-Fajr al-Jadīd,* as well as that editor's brother, Yusuf al-Sheikh Yaqub. Although al-Juhayman subsequently denied it, he was reportedly beaten while in custody.[25]

Al-Juhayman later wrote, "I sifted through the musings and writings that came to the paper and I only published what was moderate and was directed in the national interest."[26] But it was precisely his determination of the national interest, and that he believed himself entitled to define it, that landed the editor in trouble, and that also makes *Akhbar al-Dhahran* such a rich historical record. In an editorial in the paper, al-Juhayman revealed in more detail the specific beliefs that ultimately proved threatening to the government: "We took upon ourselves the assignment that when we published this newspaper we would make of it an effective instrument [*adā faʿāla*] in taking part in the blessed awakening [*al-nahda al-mubaraka*] that has dawned on our beloved country and a free pulpit [*minbar hurra*] for the sons of our nation, to control its press as they wish in the service of their country, to educate them and to direct them to the desired current of Arab nationalism."[27]

The problem for al-Juhayman, as he would come to discover, was that the regime held altogether different views regarding the role of the press, the interests of the nation, and the appeal of Arab nationalism—or at least whether or not its appeal should be disseminated to Saudi readers. The regime's move to quash public discussion, which can only be read as a move both to control the content of the media and to head off the further politicization of communities in the Eastern Province, could not unwrite what had already been recorded. While it was the outcry over the call for girls' education that prompted the fatal blow to *Akhbar al-Dhahran,* the paper had from its beginning taken on the government and its failure to properly care for the residents of an increasingly polarized and depressed Eastern Province.

OIL AND THE SEARCH FOR A NATION

Much of the outrage over the uneven development brought about by oil took shape in the language of Arab nationalism and cries for Arab unity. While writers expressed concerns over various regional issues, they also used Arab nationalism as a framework for criticizing what they viewed as shortcomings in the kingdom's national development strategy. Saudi leaders perceived the local embrace of Arab nationalism in the kingdom's oil-rich Eastern Province as threatening. The turn to Arab nationalism suggested that some Saudi Arabians were looking outside the kingdom for political and ideological guidance. While Saudi leaders were critical of Israel and sympathetic to various anticolonial movements in the Middle East, they were leery of Arab nationalism because it seemed to call for, rhetorically at least, a more populist form of government as well as unity and close cooperation between Arab states. More concerned with sustaining their own perch atop the political system in the Arabian Peninsula, as well as direct access to the massive oil wealth hidden beneath its soil, the Al Saud had little interest in any kind of political association with neighboring states, let alone in the establishment of a political system that conceded the family's power to its citizens.[28] The blending of Arab-nationalist sentiment with the disparagement of domestic development policy made the threat even more serious, as the eastern region was home to the entirety of Saudi Arabia's oil wealth. Criticism of how the state handled the wealth that derived from that resource hit a little too close to home. State officials grew increasingly concerned, over the course of the 1950s, that radicalization in the region could threaten Saudi authority over the Eastern Province, or the operations of its cash cow, Aramco.

It is difficult to gauge the power of Arab nationalism in Saudi Arabia during the 1950s and early 1960s, when aspirations of regional unity reached their high-water mark.[29] Yet it is clear that such ideas were being expressed to a public audience, as outspoken journalists and newspaper editors pushed their writing into new communities.

As the intensity of letters to the editor in various periodicals demonstrate, residents across the Eastern Province both expressed and embraced such views. More important, as the press detailed and public participation confirmed, there was indeed a social foundation for political grievance and a justification for supporting ideologies that sought to provide services and assistance to those neglected. The complaints were real, as were the social and political problems that animated them.

What is remarkable about the role of Arab nationalism in the press and its impact on the intellectual and political lives of those who expressed support for it was not that Saudis were engaged in the affairs and ideologies swirling around them. Arab nationalism found widespread support across the region, including in Saudi Arabia, in the tumult of the 1950s and 1960s. Proponents of Arab unity were connected through their frustration with European and American imperialism as well as the excesses of monarchical regimes that dominated at home. For these same reasons, the call of Arab unity resonated powerfully in the Saudi kingdom. However, more important were the various ways in which some Saudi subjects actively imagined their relationship to the government and its policies. Support for Arab unity resulted in calls for united Arab governments, working together to repel foreign domination, to lift the standards of social and economic life for Arabs across the region, and to ensure equal political opportunity in existing states. In Saudi Arabia, this meant demanding equal access to oil revenue, the use of oil to improve the lives of ordinary people, and better governance when it came to local concerns. By embracing the causes and language of Arab unity, contributors to the critical press in the 1950s were outlining what might be considered terms for a new Saudi citizenship and a new Saudi nation, one in which they were not just residents in a polity dominated by the Saudi family, but partners in a nation of level opportunity.

In voicing these hopes, editorialists, journalists, and letter writers sought to fill what they considered an ideological political vacuum at home. In spite of limited efforts by some Saudi leaders to promote national belonging, Saudi rulers spoke primarily of their own rule and their service to the people. They emphasized what they intended to provide, from material to spiritual comfort. But they failed to make a compelling ideological or rhetorical case for why the residents of Saudi Arabia should share a sense of belonging to the Saudi nation or to outline what the terms of citizenship might be. There were many reasons why the Saudis failed to do so, but foremost was the rulers' lack of concern with promoting an ideological bond with those over whom they ruled. Saudi authority was rooted in violence and conquest, and while many in the Eastern Province had accepted the fact of Saudi political hegemony, they had done so reluctantly. Many continued to see the Saudis as an occupying power that ruled through force alone. Through midcentury Saudi rulers had ruled as though they were administering an empire rather than building a nation. The ruling family was also unequipped administratively to develop deeper ties with local communities across Arabia. Although the government had begun the process of building and staffing national institutions, the state remained immature, unstable, and insecure well into the mid-1960s. Within this vacuum citizens, and particularly those contributing to the press in the Eastern Province, attempted to work out for themselves the values and goals that a contract between rulers and ruled should be predicated upon. They wrote about their own expectations of the state and the burdens they believed the state should shoulder on their behalf. It was Saudi Arabian citizens, not state officials, who reflected on and wrote about the nature of state-society relations, what the nation should aspire to, and how it was falling short of expectations.

Public talk of the "Arab nation" was not uncommon in Saudi Arabia in the 1950s and even after. But open discussion of Arab nationalism fell out of favor among the kingdom's rulers in the early 1960s. Perhaps the most famous nonroyal Saudi Arab nationalist in this period was Abdullah al-Tariqi, an American-trained engineer from central Arabia who rose to favor and assumed a cabinet-level

position as the kingdom's first minister of petroleum and mineral resources in 1960. Observers have often used his example as a vehicle
for discussing the place of Arab nationalism and even dissent in the
history of Saudi Arabia. Al-Tariqi was certainly a controversial figure.
He advocated an aggressive program with respect to oil, arguing that
Saudi Arabia, along with the other Arab and third world oil producers, should pursue a much more self-interested set of policies and
assume command of their natural resources, taking control from
the foreign companies that had dominated them. In 1962, then engaged in a power struggle with King Saud, Crown Prince Faisal dis-
missed al-Tariqi from his post as minister of petroleum and pressed
him into exile.[30] Al-Tariqi was a foundational figure in Saudi and
Arab history. As well as being an early proponent of nationalizing
the kingdom's oil resources and a critic of Aramco, al-Tariqi was a
founding member of the Organization of the Petroleum Exporting
Countries (OPEC). His radicalism, particularly his embrace of Arab
nationalism, unnerved Saudi rulers, and particularly Prince Faisal,
who became king in 1964. Throughout the 1960s al-Tariqi continued
to act as a thorn in the side of Saudi rulers, from exile writing on oil
and its potential role in strengthening the cause of Arab unity, fend-
ing off foreign manipulation of Arab interests, and empowering the
citizens of various Arab nations.[31]

The peculiar career of al-Tariqi, his rise to prominence in the late
1950s, his appointment to the Council of Ministers, and his subsequent dismissal from that position two years later reflect the complexity and uncertainty that characterized the national political scene
in Saudi Arabia in the 1950s and 1960s. Acceptable ideologies went in
and out of fashion very quickly in the middle decades of the century,
largely as a result of the erratic interests of and power struggles
within the royal family. King Saud, who succeeded his father in 1953,
was not a unifying ruler. More important, he proved a political cha-
meleon. In 1955 he signed a mutual defense pact with the Egyptian
president Gamal Abd al-Nasser, largely because both he and Nasser
distrusted the intentions of Iraq, which had just joined the Baghdad

Pact, "a coalition of Britain, Iraq and Pakistan, the main purpose of which was to transfer military assistance to countries vital for Western interests."[32] The high point of the Saudi-Egyptian relationship came in 1956, when Nasser visited Dhahran and Riyadh in September, drawing huge crowds and support in the kingdom. The mutual friendship proved short-lived, however. In Egypt, Nasser was working to eliminate the Muslim Brotherhood in an internal campaign to cleanse the country of political rivals. This campaign was unpopular in Saudi Arabia, where many of the Brotherhood's ideas enjoyed state and popular support, and thus represented a threat to King Saud's credibility as a religious leader.

In 1958 it was revealed that King Saud, anxious about Nasser's rise in popularity, had actually financed a failed attempt to assassinate the Egyptian premier, which proved both a domestic and an international scandal. The one-time allies became bitter rivals, leading to the rupture of diplomatic relations in 1962 and their involvement in a protracted proxy war in Yemen in the 1960s.[33] King Saud was deposed before the conflict was concluded. It is important to note that Saud did not embrace Nasser because of his political message. Rather, out of fear, Saud sought alliances that would strengthen his own hand and security. Saud's erratic and self-serving maneuvers helped create an ideological vacuum in his own state about what and whom it represented. This vacuum made possible the rise to prominence of men like Abdullah al-Tariqi, even though his political message was unpopular among the ruling family. In those years of fleeting uncertainty, al-Tariqi took advantage of the opportunity to elaborate his vision.

Although he has become a symbolic figure among both Arab and Western observers, al-Tariqi was not alone in his public advocacy for Arab unity in Saudi Arabia. In the mid-1950s the press, and specifically the newspapers being published in the Eastern Province, was thick with talk of regional issues and infused with an ideology that called urgently for regional leaders, including the Al Saud, to deal more effectively with various challenges abroad and at home. Arab nationalism helped animate dissent among Saudi Arabian Aramco employees, particularly during the strikes of 1953 and 1956.[34] And the prominence of Arab nationalist sentiment in the local press demonstrated the appeal of the unifying ideology in the eastern communities outside the Aramco compounds as well.

Many issues provoked talk of, and support for, Arab nationalism in the kingdom. They included the Arab-Israeli conflict and the war in Algeria between French colonialists and Algerian nationalists, as well as continued British colonialism in the Gulf (which pitted the British against the Saudis in a border dispute in southern Arabia). Foremost was the question of oil: its revenues and whether the industry should be nationalized. The newspapers of the Eastern Province hosted impassioned discussions of these issues. Even journals that had the support of the regime, such as *Al-Isha'ā'*, ran articles embracing Arab nationalism and criticizing colonialism. *Al-Isha'ā'* published articles regularly on issues of regional concern and clearly advocated an Arab-nationalist position. In April 1956, in its ninth issue, the journal published an editorial titled "Oh Arabs, Rescue Algeria," exhorting Arab regimes to stand in unity against French aggression.[35] The same issue contained an interview with a Syrian visitor about his views on the perils facing Arabs around the region.[36] In subsequent issues the journal published articles on Islamic economics as a rescue from economic imperialism, public appeals for unity among Arab youth, and calls for struggle *(jihad)* on behalf of all Arabs.[37] The author of one impassioned letter, calling himself "one among you," appealed for the realization of social justice for the Arab *umma* (nation) and the achievement of freedom and Arab unity even through death, proclaiming that "we die and the nation lives [*namūt wa yahay al-watan*]."[38] Most of the articles published in *Al-Isha'ā'* were concerned with issues beyond the borders of Saudi Arabia and so likely did not overly trouble the country's rulers and also ensured that some talk of Arab nationalism remained permissible. But clear limits to acceptable discourse did crystallize, particularly when "foreign" affairs blended with domestic concerns on the pages of other periodicals.

There were red lines, and taking on oil and Aramco, even tangentially, proved to be more than Saudi authorities were willing to tolerate. Among the most provocative articles to address the cause of Arab nationalism and some of the more heated issues bound up with pan-Arab thought, including the Palestine-Israel crisis, appeared in *Al-Fajr al-Jadīd* in the spring of 1955. Like al-Juhayman at *Akhbar al-Dhahran,* the editor of *Al-Fajr al-Jadīd* viewed the paper as a sounding board on the local community's social and political problems. Noting that the Eastern Province was "plunged in a deep sleep isolated from the world and its events," Ahmad Yaqub wrote in the journal's first issue that "this paper will be a platform for the expression of the sentiment of our society and its various problems. It is for writers, employees, workers, merchants, and for every individual among our great people."[39]

In an article titled "An Impostor from across the Atlantic" ("Dijāl min warāʾ al-Atlasī"), Muhammad Hawshan described an experience he underwent as an interview subject for a visiting American scholar at Aramco.[40] The visiting author, Alfred M. Lilienthal, who was both Jewish and an invited guest of King Saud, met with Hawshan and three of his colleagues, all employees of the oil company, in August 1954 at the Department of Labor Relations for Aramco.[41] According to Hawshan, Lilienthal was interested in speaking with "a group of sons of a conservative country."[42] Because of Lilienthal's religion, of which Hawshan was aware, the Saudi writer anticipated a conversation about Israel and Palestine. He was wrong. Instead, Lilienthal asked a series of questions related to education in the kingdom, labor problems, and assorted other nonpolitical issues. Dissatisfied with the American's apparent disinterest in the Palestine-Israel issue, Hawshan broached the subject directly, questioning the visitor on his thoughts regarding a solution to the crisis. Lilienthal relented and outlined a solution calling for the creation of two states, Israel's renunciation of Zionism, the creation of a military and economic alliance between the two countries, and American and British protection for both nations.[43] Flustered and frustrated by what he interpreted to be a bit of hand-wringing on the part of Lilienthal,

Hawshan remarked candidly that if the United States sought to retain its friendship with the Arabs, it should cut off support for Israel "even if it increased [Israel's] financial straits." He also called for all those who had recently arrived in Palestine from foreign lands to return "to their homelands" and to allow "the Muslims, the Christians and the small number of Jews who know no other land than Palestine . . . to create a state, to name it and choose for it a system of government that pleases them."[44] For Hawshan, there was no other solution. Critiques of Israel and Western aggression were common in the press in the Eastern Province. Stories, poetry, and reporting on the crisis in Palestine appeared in all of the newspapers in the region. Hawshan's confrontation with Lilienthal, a guest of Aramco, produced a particularly dramatic effect, however: the closing of the paper and the arrest of its editor, not for his criticism of Israel but for his criticism of Aramco.[45]

The editors of *Al-Fajr al-Jadīd* crossed an important line when they ran an article indirectly criticizing Aramco. The government seemed content to indulge discussion of issues around the region and world, but not those that directly addressed its source of wealth and power, for several reasons. Aramco was, no matter how tangential the criticism, off-limits. A year earlier, in October 1953, thousands of Saudi and other Arab workers at the oil company had gone on strike for better wages and better living conditions. During the work stoppage, Aramco's Arab workforce staged demonstrations, held rallies, organized speeches denouncing unfair labor practices at the oil company. The oil company refused to negotiate with labor leaders, preferring instead to work closely with Saudi intelligence and military authorities to end the strike, aiding in the arrest of at least a thousand workers. The Saudi army ratcheted up the temperature by storming local villages, beating strikers, and seeking to uproot strike leaders and "troublemakers."[46] The heavy-handed response effectively ended the strike. But it also served to heighten anxiety about future criticism of and potential radicalism directed at Aramco. The oil workers' strike shocked and outraged the regime and the oil company, both for its intensity and for its tone. Because of the government's brutal intervention on behalf of the oil company, the laborers became as critical of the Saudi government as they were of Aramco. The strike's leaders were influenced by and then appropriated Arab nationalist language, which had the effect of further heightening the government's concern. In addition to appearing too soon after the events of 1953, *Al-Fajr al-Jadīd*'s 1955 article expanded the terms in which citizens began to protest against Aramco, suggesting that the company was quickly losing credibility in the province. As would become clear less than a year later, it was a short leap from criticizing Aramco to turning against the Saudi government itself.

In 1956, just before its own forced closure, the editor of *Akhbar al-Dhahran* went even further than *Al-Fajr al-Jadīd* and published a three-part series on Saudi Arabian oil, the failures of Saudi oil policy, and recommendations to ameliorate them. The essays, although discussing oil for the first time in such a way, underscored what had been commonplace in *Akhbar al-Dhahran* for over a year: the application of Arab nationalist ideas to local issues, which did not sit well with state officials. On January 27, Muhammad Bakir Atiyya wrote part one of the series, entitled "Our Oil Wealth," in which he criticized the Saudi royal family's handling of oil revenues, particularly its wastefulness and unwillingness to use the funds to build national institutions.[47] Fearful that the regime was overly dependent on the United States, Atiyya said that the regime should pursue a more independent line and cut ties with its imperialist Western benefactor, although he did not mention Aramco by name. In the subsequent articles, he expressed his frustration that oil wealth was leaving the country and wrote that the kingdom would languish unless it harnessed that wealth in the construction of a diverse industrialized economy. There was no reason not to rush in, he argued, urging the kingdom's rulers to move quickly. Atiyya did not stop at urging the kingdom's rulers to sever ties with the West and to quicken the pace of industrialization and diversification. He also called for a program to eliminate dependence on foreign experts and to prepare the

Saudi nation for competitive involvement in the global oil market. To achieve self-sufficiency, he suggested the building of scientific institutes to train citizens, including Saudi youth, for careers in technical positions. His vision was much more elaborate than a program for strengthening merely the oil sector. Atiyya outlined a vision for Saudi Arabia in which engineering and technical capacity were connected with the essence of the nation. He wrote that only through technical preparedness and the ability to operate and manage Saudi natural resources and industries would the nation become a powerful and truly independent international actor.[48]

Ironically, Atiyya's suggestions regarding the need for industrial and technical development fell squarely in line with Saudi policy, although he connected development work directly to notions of Saudi nationalism and identity, whereas the state did not. Indeed, his vision embraced the need for progress, much as did those who wrote for *Al-Manhal*, as well as many state officials. His call for independence from the West, however, and particularly for the replacement of expatriate workers (a clear reference to the American employees at Aramco) with Saudis, did not line up with state views. Similarly, Atiyya's demand for greater commitment to scientific and technical training was also a critique of Saudi government policy. He was not critical of what the government was saying; rather, he chided the regime for not carrying through on its commitment to the program and values of development—a line of critique common in the pages of *Akhbar al-Dhahran*. The newspaper operated for only a few more months before local officials decided to shut down its operations and arrest its editor. While Abd al-Karim al-Juhayman would later write that he believed it was the uproar surrounding an article calling for the education of girls in state schools that led to the shutdown, it is likely that his paper's role in questioning state policy and advertising local grievances helped determine both his own and the paper's fate, an issue that remained sensitive enough that years later he decided against commenting on it.

As writers expressed outrage about local and regional problems, they were also outlining their respective visions of what the character of the nation, both Saudi and Arab, should be based upon. The passion with which contributors and editors fleshed out and contested the principles of the nation, the oil business, and their place as citizens reveals the complexity and depth of political sensibilities in communities around the Eastern Province. Perhaps more important, the hostility in much of the writing about local issues and officials reflects the power of unmet expectations in rousing civic action—in this case, writing for public consumption in the local press.

ENVIRONMENTAL POLITICS

In addition to the issue of oil, more specific concerns about environmental neglect emerged as matters of local contention, and local environmental politics began to take shape. For example, throughout 1955 and in 1956 *Akhbar al-Dhahran* regularly ran articles on topics ranging from railroad schedules to school openings. The paper also reported on regional, national, and international news, much like any other newspaper. It even published a short item about the opening of the massive Intercontinental Hotel in Hofuf, the capital city of al-Hasa, in 1955. That story would have been unremarkable except that the hotel was built on land owned by the Saudi finance minister, Abdullah Sulaiman—land he obtained through conquest and at the expense of residents of the Eastern Province when the Al Saud arrived in 1913, a source of enduring irritation among local residents. The paper's role as a community sounding board about environmental problems crystallized very early. Articles and letters on problems varying from water pollution and disease, to the shortage of doctors and mosquito epidemics, dominated the paper. Skepticism about the competence and political will of local and national authorities was always a feature of political commentary as residents vented their frustration with a failing local government.

One of the most powerful, spirited, and protracted dramas to unfold in the pages of the newspaper was sparked by the publication of a letter to the editor by an anonymous author on August 19, 1955. The letter incited a heated exchange between readers of the paper and other residents from around the region who disagreed about a multitude of issues and problems confronting them and their communities. A close reading of the feud offers an intimate glimpse into the complicated character of politics and community life in the Eastern Province, and the powerful role of development and its failures in framing the expectations and political discourse of Saudi citizens. Although oil featured only in the background of these debates, discussions of public service and environmental crises were very much the product of the structural changes set in motion by oil and the work it brought about in the kingdom.

The letter of August 19, signed "Qatifi in Dhahran" and titled "Rid the Municipality of Qatif of This Administration," captured the depth of the anger felt by some readers. It opened the door to a polemical debate about marginalized communities, the responsibility of authorities, and the shortcomings of development planning and activity in Saudi communities.[49] Frustration over the neglected status of Qatif, situated less than forty kilometers north of the capital city of Dammam on the Persian Gulf coast, prompted the angry missive. Citing his admiration for the growth of Dammam and al-Khobar, the author lamented that while Qatif's neighbors moved forward, his northern community "remains plunged in a deep sleep and it does not feel this new spirit [of progress] which has entered into the life of this young nation."[50] Directing his opprobrium at local government, the author launched into a vague but acrimonious tirade directed against Qatif's municipal council, a body of elected officials who oversaw various services in local communities.[51] He wrote, "We put the blame on the Municipality. National and state duty was incumbent upon them to do more than necessary and in the happiest manner to overcome difficulties and to surmount hardship of their nation, and to restore it."

In his opening salvo against the municipality, the anonymous writer made clear that his ire derived from the local council's inability to fulfill its commitment to meeting community needs. He wrote that the council members were "leftovers from the last century, the residue of a departed age, and are accustomed to a life of mosquitoes, swamps, narrow roads, dark corners and caves that strangle breathing. They have become accustomed to darkness and have lost the ability to see the light . . . they do not feel the psychological push that drives [others] toward effective work and essential reform." More than being merely incompetent, the author believed the local officials were guilty of willful neglect. He remarked:

> Qatif is an old country erected on an old model and founded on a pattern not congruent with the modern age. Reforming it demands great effort and the most careful thought. It requires from all those undertaking development to know where, when, and how to value the spending of the resources of the Municipality and how to undertake development planning. They need to be able to distinguish between what is important, the most important, what is necessary and what is not. Then, in addition to all of that, it is necessary that in them are abundant nationalist sentiment, the spirit of work, and an appreciation for the welfare of their country. Abundant in them should be honesty and morals, and [they should be] free from personal desire, to the extent possible. And all of these characteristics are not abundant in our Municipality.[52]

The author's charge that local government officials were obstacles to rather than agents of modernity, were accustomed to "dark" rather than "light," and represented the interests of a bygone age attest to the embracing—at least by the intellectual elite and community leaders—of the need for modernization. Indeed, the accusation that government officials had arrested the march of progress in Qatif was intended to be particularly hard-hitting and to underscore that the municipal councils were failing in their basic mission. In a rare public move in Saudi Arabia, the irate author charged the municipal council members directly with corruption. He elaborated: "The reasons for corruption are deeply rooted and penetrate far in this Municipality. If I want beneficial reform [development] and it is what the heart of every citizen is starved for, then it is necessary to do away with this administration."

The author's proposed solution was no less radical than his tone. He concluded his letter by demanding that the government create "the opportunity for all citizens to [re]make the Municipality in their areas through new elections. It is necessary to create the full opportunity for the youth to participate in selecting the members, because he is most knowledgeable of the competencies and abilities and because it is he who feels more than any other the necessity of development. If the freely elected members are not stirred to undertake their duty, then they will be held responsible."[53]

A remarkable document, the letter captured the depth of this Qatifi's ire at the marginalization of communities located on the edge of the political, administrative, and corporate heart of the province. Noting the languid attitude toward the state of affairs in Qatif, without going into any particular detail the author called for the equal distribution of effort—that is, the even distribution of spending and public works across all communities. The failure of state organizations to handle this burden generated intense frustration.[54] The writer's call for fairer elections and an end to corruption were exceptional in the Saudi press, and no doubt contributed to what would become the newspaper's reputation as a repository of threatening ideas.

The first response followed on October 3, when a letter sent in by a resident of Dammam, writing under the pen name Ibn Rashid, blasted the claims of the anonymous author from Qatif. Expressing thanks for the role that *Akhbar al-Dhahran* played in the community, particularly for its efforts to bring attention to social problems, Ibn Rashid nonetheless proclaimed that "what I read about Qatif stunned me [*dahashatni*]." The author, he exclaimed, "presented an article full of shameful mistakes and he obliterated and deformed the obvious truth."[55] The Qatifi, Ibn Rashid suggested, sought political advantage by criticizing the then-current municipal council and calling for elections to usher them from government. He charged that the unknown author was "a member of a well-known group [fi'a] that does not have any value in society. The goal of this group is shameful commentary. Every member is preoccupied with gaining membership on the Municipal council. Perhaps they . . . possess vulgar goals. They do not hesitate to walk on the shattered remnants of consciousness, the path of lies and shadow, [to] wallow in the muck."[56]

"The lies of this group," he insisted, "do not apply to the [current] officials, who are only concerned with the interests of the city." Citing the efforts of the council, Ibn Rashid claimed that its members were committed to community services and development efforts, including "the cleaning of sewers whose waters stream into the streets. [The council] also removed the rubble that surrounded the houses. It improved and removed places that constituted a danger . . . The Municipality of Qatif has achieved great progress and is moving along with more projects with all seriousness and interest."[57]

Ibn Rashid's retort to Qatifi letter writer, and his spirited defense of the municipal council, quickly gave way to a vicious assault on the character and culture of the people of Qatif. Amid the allegedly modern facilities constructed under the auspices of the municipality, Ibn Rashid directed attention to the continued presence of crumbling homes and widespread dilapidation. The fault for the wretched state of things, he concluded, could reside only with the citizens of Qatif itself and not those who oversaw its administration. He wrote:

> Whereas many of its homes are demolished, threatening collapse, no measure is taken to restore them. How is it possible to change the planning of the interior streets when all of them are so old? How true is the comparison between the two Municipalities of Dammam and al-Khobar [with] that of Qatif? There is a big difference in the people of these two modern cities [Dammam and al-Khobar], whose people carry a good-natured frame of mind and a real love of renewal. The modern facilities are the result of the solidarity between the people of these two cities.[58]

The implication was clear. The residents of Qatif lacked the appropriate "nature" or "frame of mind" to understand progress, let alone to bring it about.

Ibn Rashid closed his letter by stating that "they destroy their homes by their own hands." The overt turn to using culture and geography, and by default the religious difference that marked the residents of Qatif from those in Dammam and the other new cities in the east, indicates the clear animosity of the author toward denizens of the communities to the north.[59] Ibn Rashid's critique can be seen as an implicit condemnation of rural communities as compared with the more "civilized" new cities like Dammam and its environs, although Qatif was itself a city in ancient times.[60] In addition, his strident comments suggest that an imperial mentality, one that viewed "natives" with disdain and that justified the presence of outside actors who would lead the way to a new and better future for the region, was settling in among some residents of the Eastern Province. Although it is impossible to know where Ibn Rashid was from originally, it was not likely that it was Dammam. The city of Dammam developed later than even Dhahran, which Aramco built after 1933. While some residents of Dammam were from the surrounding area—they resided in the city while working for Aramco—it also became home to a large community of people from elsewhere in the Arabian Peninsula. Outsiders from central Arabia were likely close supporters of the Al Saud and even dependent on them for patrimony and for rights to commercial contracts with the oil company. It was no secret to outsiders that the region's original residents had been forcibly incorporated into the kingdom in 1913 and that they were for the most part Shiites and thus held in particular disregard. It was a short leap from cultural and religious intolerance to arguing that not only were the Shiites racially incapable of achieving modernity on their own, but also that they would probably be better served by being excluded from development altogether and left on their own.

The Qatifi writer fired back with a second and even more contentious piece in early November. Two weeks before his rejoinder, however, a third interlocutor entered the fray. On October 18 another letter writer from Qatif, writing under the name Ibn al-Asima, challenged Ibn Rashid and added further credence to the frustration disclosed by the first Qatifi.[61] Citing "shameful contradictions and failures" as well as the "childlike prerogative" evident in Ibn Rashid's response to the August missive, Ibn al-Asima set out to refute him. He noted that Ibn Rashid, by arguing that Qatifis themselves were responsible for the poor conditions that surrounded them, reaffirmed that the situation in the coastal city was grim. Ibn al-Asima remarked that "in fact, Ibn Rashid proves the existence of standing pools of water and mud. But he does not know what he wants to say about them. Perhaps he wants to say that it is not the responsibility of the Municipality to take care of [such problems]. If that was the case, then who among us is not right if we wonder what the duties of the Municipality are?" Mentioning several specific problems, Ibn al-Asima wrote that Ibn Rashid "claims not to know of any" efforts undertaken by the Municipality to ameliorate difficulties. Furthermore, he said, Ibn Rashid

> noticed the sewers whose waters flow even in front of the door of the director of the Municipality himself and the homes of the members. And likewise the garbage that greets their homes. There were other people for whom it is worse: what are the important decisions realized by the Municipality? What of the garbage that is piled along the coast close to the schools and fouls the air for the students, who are struck by the terrible odor? Or what about the mud in the main streets? Are these the development projects in the view of Ibn Rashid?[62]

Ibn al-Asima, like the Qatifi in the earlier letter, made much of the poor environmental conditions that had come to dominate in the poorer communities of the region. Garbage, clogged sewers, and foul odors not only threatened the health of local citizens but also symbolized their dehumanization at the hands of state institutions. The environment was a measure of standing in the nation.

On November 1 *Akhbar al-Dhahran* published the Qatifi's response to Ibn Rashid, in which the author remarked, "We were waiting for a response, a defense of the Municipality." Silence, he offered, "would have meant failure."[63] Attempting to distract from the possibility that he harbored personal political ambitions, Qatifi denied accusations that he simply sought a seat on the local council. In fact, he responded that he had never served "one day" and had no ambition to do so. In response to his original charges against the council, he claimed that Ibn Rashid failed to make a compelling case for the municipality. "The previous article," he stated, "did not mention any work undertaken by the Municipality . . . [Ibn Rashid] says that the Municipality of Qatif achieved a key aim [*shawtān kabīrān*] of its reclamation projects and that it is moving toward subsequent aims with all seriousness and interest. We request that the author clarify for us those projects that the Municipality has realized and when this occurred. As for the land that we live on, we see no evidence of these projects."[64] Noting that it had been a year since the new council took office, Qatifi wondered, "What has the [new] council done? What are the important decisions that it has taken? What year is it? They will not answer any of these questions." In fact, he argues, "The key development projects, such as the decision to build fruit, meat, and fish markets, and the decision to build a modern butchery, the emphasis on cleanliness and health, the decision to purchase DDT [to fight mosquitoes and flies], as well as other decisions—all of them were the product of the [previous] councils and . . . not the product of this council." Other problems included rubbish in the streets and flowing sewage, which he argued the municipality had failed to do anything about. He also blasted the head of the 1955 council, arguing that even its efforts were less than satisfactory. For example, the council's purchase of tractors, to be used in expanding and modernizing the road network, was met with derision. "[The tractors] were taken from the wreckage of Aramco, [who] throws dust in [our] eyes." A similar decision was made to purchase cranes and other heavy equipment for public works. These items too, he alleged, were purchased "from the leftovers of the company" and were in such bad condition that "they were transported [back] to Aramco for repair, where they remain."

The Qatifi made clear that he did not think the institution of the municipality itself was corrupt. Rather, he faulted those serving, for their lack of political will. He noted that "if the people found the Municipality carrying out its precise duties in rigorously overseeing its orders, then that would force its supporters or critics to concede to it and obey when it [demonstrates] that the public interest is its guiding principle." But he did not believe the council members had any concern for the general public, and he said so, remarking that "the Municipality lost the respect of the citizens and lost its values and importance before the people. They know that it is merely an asylum" that some individuals "control" and "take comfort in."[65]

On November 16 the editor, al-Juhayman, declared that the issue was closed, refusing to publish "the many responses," including a second letter from Ibn Rashid. It was a statement he had to reiterate on January 20, 1956, because the deluge of letters from Qatif continued.[66] In addition to the eventual forced closing of the widely circulated paper, al-Juhayman's repeated declaration that the issue was no longer open for discussion is a powerful indication that the issues being discussed were both controversial and at least familiar, if not widely shared, in eastern Saudi Arabia. The debate between residents of Qatif and those in Dammam leaves little doubt that the contributors accurately described the squalid conditions that dominated in various places around the east. The communities on the geographic margins of the Eastern Province had clearly been left behind. The contributors' letters underscored the acrimony that pitted residents in the peripheral towns and villages against the new center. The failure and even the absolute unwillingness of municipal council members in Qatif to attend to basic services and honor expectations about development generated intense emotion. They also underscored the extent to which the central government's politicization of the environment and the linkage of political authority to nature had been achieved. Citizens in the Eastern Province were so frustrated in part because they had come to understand that taking care of public health issues, and the environment more generally, was the responsibility of local and central authorities. These controversies were not unique to Qatif.

Al-Juhayman's decision to terminate the dispute in his paper between Dammam and Qatif did not end the larger debate involving the environment, government services, and the tension between the new oil center and the periphery. Letter writers continued to probe these issues. Remarkably, the initial exchange even generated debate and confrontations within the periphery itself. On December 1, 1955, *Akhbar al-Dhahran* published a short letter from Muhammad al-Sulayman al-Shiha, a resident of Jubail, a coastal city 100 kilometers north of Dammam. The letter, titled "The Municipality of Jubail Is in a Deep Slumber," echoed similar themes to those outlined in the debate between the antagonists from Qatif and Dammam only a month before. Like the anonymous author from Qatif, al-Shiha gave voice to specific grievances that the municipality appeared disinterested in addressing. Also like the letter writers from Qatif, al-Shiha's frustration was compounded because similar problems, and more, were being overcome in Dammam and al-Khobar. As an example, al-Shiha noted that the municipality of Dammam purchased land on the perimeter of the city, reclaimed it, and constructed shelters that were available free of charge to poorer residents of the city. Al-Shiha directed glowing praise toward the city council and administrators of Dammam, while simultaneously condemning their counterparts in Jubail for failing to consider similar policies—"which" he wrote, "all societies deserve."[67] Then, listing a series of grievances in common with his neighbors in Qatif and the smaller villages surrounding the old city, al-Shiha noted that a host of additional problems afflicted Jubail, including piles of garbage and foul odors in public areas, water pollution, standing pools of stagnant water in the city's streets, and heavy infestations of mosquitoes and flies as well as the diseases that accompanied them.

On December 31 the paper ran a follow-up letter titled "Which of the Two Is more Asleep?! The Municipality of al-Hasa or the Municipality of Jubail."[68] The writer had "read and agreed with the writer from Jubail in issue 21 that the Municipalities today are not doing enough and they deserve the criticisms when we fix our gaze on what they are doing." He challenged al-Shiha, saying that if he visited al-Hasa, several hundred kilometers to the south, he would "see with his eyes great calamity [*adhān*]" and who is "more asleep. Yes, he will see the total coma [*al-ghaybūba al-kāmila*] that no doubt is a state of death [in al-Hasa]." Like the other letter writers, he held the municipal council responsible for persistent problems in the oasis. He remarked that the municipality's "lexicon" was devoid of the terms for basic services such as street lighting, road paving, and sanitation. The writer, Abu Farawis, conceded that the municipality had accomplished the construction of one main road, King Saud Road. Yet, he chided facetiously, "This is all the work that the Municipality can acknowledge in over 30 years and this in 20 cities and villages. The Municipality of al-Hasa does not want to admit this. Nothing but absolute silence." Skeptical of the municipality's intention to do anything about the poor conditions that abounded in the oasis, he remarked that "nothing can break [the silence] except the sound of the Municipality's tractors, and they are doing today what they did yesterday in the Hofuf market . . . sitting in a deep slumber undisturbed by the masses."[69]

More letters followed—one on January 15 critical of Abu Farawis, and a second on February 10 in support of him.[70] The letter writers rehashed themes similar to those of other contributors elsewhere in the region, debating the forces behind the stagnation plaguing the old communities on the edge of the Eastern Province. Even the more moderate magazine *Al-Ishaʿāʿ* published materials critical of the municipal government in al-Hasa. Ibrahim bin Abd al-Aziz al-Masiri wrote an article in *Al-Ishaʿāʿ*, more than a year after the closure of *Akhbar al-Dhahran*, entitled "Who Will Awaken the Municipality of al-Hasa from Its Slumber?"[71] Al-Masiri paid a brief visit to al-Hasa from his home in Unayza, in Najd (Central Province). He was struck by the wretched conditions in the oasis, including its residents' poor appearance, which a friend of his and long-time Hasawi attributed to their drinking contaminated water. He remarked that choked and narrow streets were marred with dirt and filth and that various markets, including a local butchery and a vegetable market, were disease ridden. He slammed the municipality, criticizing it for not handling the crisis. He concluded sarcastically by remarking that after his visit he "left al-Hasa and did not come down with any sickness." He thanked God for that.

The exchanges in the letters section of *Akhbar al-Dhahran* highlight the importance that citizens had come to place on the state, its institutions, and what they expected of the government. In criticizing local councils, letter writers invoked notions of nation and community not found in official literature but appropriated from discussions about issues from around the region. Where government discourse blended with this new talk of community and state-society relations was on the issues of development and progress—interrelated notions that the state had championed but was failing to achieve, at least for some communities. The fallout over the failure of local state institutions to accommodate clear needs, as well as to meet high expectations, was clear.

Authorities from local and national government and officials from Aramco were well aware of the frustration of local citizens. Even so, they did little to address the sources of that frustration. In November 1960, five years after concerns about local environmental and public-health issues surfaced as matters of community contention, Saudi health officials convened two public-health conferences, one in Dammam and one in Hofuf. Aramco sent Phebe Marr, one of the company's researchers, to observe the conferences. Marr characterized the conference in Hofuf as "volatile" and reported that "delegates were almost entirely drawn from the local populace and viewed the conference as a forum for a thorough discussion of local government and education problems."[72] Local attendees blasted officials from the Hofuf municipal council with a familiar set of criticisms.

They accused the municipality of falling short on its duties to maintain public health standards, for not cleaning streets and public sewers, and for failing to drain swamps. Local officials passed the buck, arguing that the populace was not doing much to help maintain cleanliness. More important, though, officials also argued that they had not received sufficient financial support from the central government. A shortage of money meant they were unable to undertake projects like swamp drainage. The conference ended with the passage of several resolutions aimed at addressing some of the complaints, including resolutions for building public sewers, filling swamps, "contacting Aramco for aid in filling those swamps which are located near Aramco houses," and establishing a "Clean-up Day" in each municipality.

Citizens in al-Hasa interpreted the Hofuf conference as little more than a cosmetic effort to address their concerns, recognizing that the meeting itself was meant to be palliative and that neither the municipality nor the central government would do much to change the situation on the ground. Many in al-Hasa's population expressed their dismay a few weeks later. In December 1960 the oasis held elections for the municipal council. More than half of those eligible to vote boycotted the elections out of frustration about several issues, including "a desire for more efficient expenditure of funds allocated for municipal projects."[73] Most of the boycotters were Shiites, who in addition to ongoing discrimination, also suffered disproportionately from environmental neglect. As a result of their boycott, Shiites, who made up at least half of the oasis's population, were not represented in the municipal council that was elected.

Sustained complaining and simmering frustration about the government's poor handling of environmental policy generated few results. Neither the municipality nor Saudi Arabia's central authorities exerted much effort to address the sources of anger. The government allocated two million riyals for local projects in 1960, the vast majority of which went to the expansion of local streets. The focus on roads only intensified frustration about spending and environmental problems. Aramco's Phebe Marr observed that "the dissatisfaction with compensation and the scramble by influential residents and shopkeepers for better private streets resulted in increased pressures on the Municipal Council and in a succession of local committees complaining to the central government in Riyadh." She went on to note that "the result has been a shift of authority from the Municipal Council to the amirate [local governor] and to central government representatives in an effort to speed up development."[74] The shift of responsibility did little to alleviate the problems that beset al-Hasa and other communities in the Eastern Province. The expansion of the central government's responsibilities, and the locals' turning to authorities in Riyadh for support, reflected the fact that power in Saudi Arabia's periphery was increasingly connected to the center, and that the environment was at the heart of this connection. But it did not result in the central government's being attentive to the interests and concerns of its citizens.

In spite of their anger in the 1950s and early 1960s, citizens in the Eastern Province had not yet given up on the idea that they too belonged to the nation and the national community. They articulated this by criticizing members of local institutions while remaining careful not to malign the purpose and potential power of the institutions themselves. It was also clear that they had specific expectations about what their presence in the national community and the political system meant. They demanded the same services and the same commitment showed to communities elsewhere in the Arabian Peninsula. They also invoked the language and symbolism of development and modernization in an effort to offer an alternative vision not only for the relations between state institutions and citizens, but also for a framework in which all citizens could be part of the nation.

While some letter writers, and even editors, continued to insist on both the expectations and the values that should have linked citizens across communities, others clearly did not. Those who disagreed with the critics did not emphasize the notions of unity or shared responsibility, as Ibn Rashid's critique of Qatifi culture and the collective failure of its citizens demonstrates. It is painfully clear in hindsight that the marginalization of the towns and villages on the perimeter of the Eastern Province was not viewed by observers from the center as tragic, or even shocking. There is little in the historical record that explicitly suggests such apathy was deliberate or based on sectarian prejudice, but certainly those possibilities remain very real—even likely.

Contrary to the claims in Qatif and al-Hasa, not everything was great in Dammam, Dhahran, and al-Khobar either. There were real problems and real tensions even there, although the degree of deprivation and suffering was mitigated considerably as a result of the attention—and resources—received from both the state and Aramco. Even so, the perception among residents on the periphery that things were very much better elsewhere generated an intense debate in the Saudi press. The grim situation on the edge, the desire of residents to voice their anger, and the opportunity to do so in emerging newspapers shaped the way people spoke of the nation, state institutions, and the powerfully consuming notion of progress. But in spite of efforts to shed light on the poor conditions that dominated in the eastern periphery, the state did little to ameliorate them. The state's disinterest in the region's plight was made clear when it shut down the only public means through which residents could express their frustration and their only way of criticizing the government.

Critics made it clear not only that they believed development, technology, and technical management were at the center of the state's relationship to its citizens, as well as its responsibility toward them, but also that they had yet to benefit from them. Observers and contributors to the local press, while hopeful that the tough conditions that dominated in the outlying communities of Qatif, al-Hasa, and Jubail would be alleviated, believed that their being left behind was a deliberate result of the emerging oil order in the kingdom. While letter writers at midcentury were clearly angry with the failure of the state to meet their expectations, they were not rejecting the state altogether. But they perceived that the choices made by central and local government institutions were intrinsically economic and unfair. It is likely that the perception that the state had been neglectful in the 1950s when it came to addressing community concerns, especially environmental ones, helped mute enthusiasm for large technological undertakings such as the al-Hasa Irrigation and Drainage Project in the next decade.

It would be two decades before residents in the Eastern Province's predominantly Shia communities expressed their outrage in public again. Frustration boiled over in the late 1970s, culminating in a massive uprising in 1979 that revealed how community resentment over the politics of development, marginalization, and the failure of the state had continued to simmer after the mid-1950s. Why the gap between the frustration of the 1950s and the violence of the 1970s? It is unlikely that local anxiety about the dislocations and failures of modernization faded in this period. That residents, when they eventually rebelled against the Al Saud, articulated many of the same grievances that first appeared in the pages of the local press in the 1950s suggests that there was a clear continuity despite the twenty years separating the two eras.

The temporal distance between events can be attributed to several factors. The Saudi state became increasingly proficient at rooting out and oppressing dissenters. In addition to closing down provocative media, the government took various other measures to shut down any opposition, including arresting some prominent political activists and driving others into exile.[75] The effect on local politics in the Eastern Province was pronounced. As a result of the state's more authoritarian handling of local critics, most residents remained silent, preferring to keep grievances to themselves or to air their frustrations through private correspondence with regional and local representatives of the Saudi state.[76] In the predominantly Shia communities, the value of silent suffering was likely reinforced to some degree by the passive political tendencies of the local clerics and notables. Since the Al Saud had established its hegemony over the region in 1913, most Shia religious figures had embraced the belief that their role lay exclusively in the spiritual and not the political domain, preferring not simply to avoid criticizing the political system but to avoid participating in politics at all.

However, the political compliance of the clergy is not enough to explain why there were few public demonstrations of outrage against the failures of modernization in the 1960s and early 1970s. The most radical activists did not define themselves in religio-political terms, or as Shia Islamist, in this period. Most important, as a result of the Saudi crackdown in the mid- to late 1950s, many prominent would-be agitators were forced into exile, to Cairo, Beirut, and Baghdad. It is impossible to know with any precision the numbers of those who fled the kingdom and continued on with their political activism. The most dedicated Saudi Arabians in exile continued to propagandize against the Al Saud. This tendency was not unique to those from Saudi Arabia's Eastern Province, but some eastern exiles became particularly influential. A large number of those from the east, including Shiites, fled to Baghdad in the late 1960s and early 1970s, where they supported Iraq's Baath Party. From Baghdad, the Saudi Arabian Baathists published a political journal, *Sawt al-Tali'a* (Voice of the Vanguard), and smuggled it into the Eastern Province. Unlike the newspapers of the 1950s, which dealt with specific community issues, *Sawt al-Tali'a* focused more broadly on the failures of the Al Saud and particularly the family's unwillingness to support the cause of Arab unity.

Even into the mid-1970s there was little public political activism in Saudi Arabia's Eastern Province. By the end of the decade, the Arab-nationalist tendencies that had dominated the political outlook of many residents, including those who expressed their frustration in the 1950s and those who were radicalized in the 1960s and early 1970s, gave way to Islamist politics. A new generation of Saudi political activists emerged in the mid-1970s that turned to religion as a framework within which to express political dissent. Much like the Arab nationalists who wrote critically of the Saudi royal family from exile

in the 1960s and early 1970s, the radicalization of a younger generation of Saudi Shia youth took place abroad, in Iraq, Iran, and Kuwait.
Like their leftist counterparts, the Shia Islamists, who were also infu-
riated by the inequities in oil's domain, returned to the kingdom in
the mid-1970s, where they focused attentively on local frustration.
And as with the earlier generations of critics, oil and the environment fueled their anger. But unlike their predecessors, the Islamists
were better organized and more driven. And as a result of their efforts, the relative quiet that had characterized Saudi Arabia's Eastern
Province for two decades was shattered in 1979.

6

Frustration in the Eastern Province's Shia communities came to a head in late 1979. While community leaders in the 1950s and 1960s had remained mostly passive and sought various means to engage with Saudi authorities, the late 1970s were characterized by a turn to revolutionary politics. The sources of the transformation were twofold. From the early part of the 1970s a new generation of community leaders, motivated and politically ambitious, came of age. They increasingly used the emerging notion of political Islam to whip up revolutionary fervor, borrowing from Shia tradition as well as from the works of Sayyid Qutb and other twentieth-century political Islamist theoreticians who called for greater Islamic activism. For many Shiites, the call to Islamic radicalism was appealing. In spite of efforts by Shiite figures in the 1950s and 1960s to press for greater tolerance, inclusion in society and the nation, and the more equitable distribution of oil wealth, the reality was that Shiites faced severe forms of discrimination. The Saudi government did not just fail to heed calls for greater equity, it erected barriers to Shia advancement. These included limits on the kinds of work Shiites could take up. Jobs in the public sector, particularly in the police and military forces, were almost entirely closed off to Shiites. So, for the most part, were management positions in important industries, including at Aramco. The Saudi government also banned Shiite religious rituals and observances. The most important were bans on the construction of Shia mosques and the ban on the observance of Ashura, when Shiites publicly commemorated the martyrdom of their first imam, Hussein, the grandson of the prophet Muhammad.

Religious and social discrimination overlapped with other forms of inequality, particularly the unequal distribution of oil wealth. Since the 1950s, Shia communities had been mostly left behind in the kingdom's push toward modernization. By the late 1970s, when the country's oil and financial power was at its height, the disparities helped precipitate rebellion. Forced to endure tough environmental and social conditions and faced with deeply rooted forms of religious discrimination, Saudi Shiites took aim at the government and its surrogates, including Aramco. By calling for revolution, Shiites also were pushing back against and pointing out the contradictions in the way the Saudi government had linked its authority and legitimacy to its ability to manage and engineer the country's natural resources. Where the conquest of nature had served to expand the power of the central state, it had also created the very conditions for violent opposition.

For seven dramatic days in late November 1979, bloody violence between state security forces and thousands of frustrated Shiites rocked the Eastern Province of Saudi Arabia. Sparked by the regime's brutal repression of those Shiites staging a provocative observance of the officially banned commemoration of Ashura, the fury resulted in widespread death and ruin.[1] In the normally sleepy village of Qatif, perched on the Persian Gulf shore, Shia demonstrators burned the British bank as well as the offices of Saudi Arabian Airlines. They destroyed state-owned vehicles, attacked police, raided the national coast guard office in the village of al-Awamiyya, seized weapons from soldiers, and even occupied the old city in downtown Qatif, from which they held off the Saudi military for days. So deep did Shia enmity toward the Saudi state run that one group of rebels even burned a toy store owned by a government official.[2] Women and men marched in anger. Saudi security forces, which included 20,000 members of the Saudi National Guard, cordoned off the major roadways in order to localize the protest, control the flow of information, and, most important, prevent nearby oil facilities from being destroyed. Reports swirled that soldiers fired on virtually any public gathering of people—including at least one funeral procession, where they forced the mourners to flee and abandon the corpse in the street. State and hospital officials refused to release bodies from the morgue for burial until the uproar quieted, leveraging the dead as blackmail. The National Guard relied on the heavy firepower of helicopter gunships for crowd control, turning the region into a killing field.[3]

Before the rebellion, an event that Saudi Arabia's Shia refer to as the intifada, the community had long suffered from pervasive discrimination. The official religious orthodoxy of the Saudi government, Wahhabism, was based in part on the need to purify Islam and eliminate what its proponents deemed to be Islamic heresy throughout the Muslim world. The zealots behind the Saudi throne singled out Shiism as an especially condemnable deviation from what they considered the true faith. After the Saudi conquest of the Eastern Province in 1913, Shiites faced restrictions on their religious observance, limits on employment, harassment from police and religious officials, and the periodic threat of violence. And even when the government protected the community from aggression, Saudi leaders consistently condoned anti-Shia enmity expressed by religious scholars and permitted anti-Shia teaching in Saudi schools. Charges of apostasy have frequently been leveled as a means to justify the pursuit of violence against them. Forced to endure such opprobrium, it was hardly surprising that the persecuted minority eventually revolted against the acrimonious political and religious forces surrounding them. Decades of discrimination and oppression go a long way in explaining the intensity of the rebellion that unfolded in 1979.

While the uprising was partly born from the frustrations wrought by decades of official intolerance, the roots of discrimination against Saudi Arabia's Shiites and the forces that led to their turn to violence ran much deeper. At the heart of the uprising was a wrenching sense of rancor over the deplorable social and economic conditions that predominated in their communities.[4] Signs of opulence and abundance, of the wealth generated as a result of the kingdom's fabulous oil reserves, were all around by the late 1970s. But while they lived in a country that had come to enjoy extraordinary economic growth, Saudi Arabia's Shiites knew mostly poverty and hardship. As the kingdom grew rich in 1970s, with revenues from oil sales accumulating at a spectacular rate, they enjoyed little of the windfall. The government pursued ambitious plans to redistribute billions of dollars in oil money, spending lavishly on services and programs across the country. Its efforts yielded sparkling results. Cities glimmered as real estate and infrastructure development proceeded at a frantic pace. The conspicuous signs of material comfort took other forms as well. Well-cared-for Saudi citizens embraced the oil bonanza by spending money enthusiastically, turning the country into a marketplace for high-end imports, such as luxury cars and electronics. Profligacy became a lifestyle, with the best-off citizens spending copiously on palatial estates, global travel, and an army of foreign workers, perhaps most notably, legions of young Asian women who were virtually enslaved as domestic servants. Surrounded by those awash in new luxury, few Shiites enjoyed anything remotely resembling prosperity.

Their grinding poverty in the midst of rising affluence and unyielding prejudice stirred Shiites to action. Pent-up frustration gave way to outrage and then to revolt. A shared cultural identity and, perhaps most important, a sense of communal grievance—forged in the crucible of Saudi oppression—lent the uprising a religious ardor. A rising generation of religiously trained activists led the call to action and to arms, making clear that political power was deeply connected to religious identity and authority. But while religious identity and the shared experience of oppression determined who would take part in the uprising, at the heart of the communal anger were the contradictions and anxieties wrought by oil, oil wealth, and the various ways that the government chose or chose not to put oil to use. It is telling that it took more than six decades of direct Saudi rule before the kingdom's Shiites finally rebelled against tyranny, suggesting that religious discrimination alone was not enough to spur action.

And it is equally telling that the community unleashed its anger at the height of Saudi Arabia's prosperity and power as an oil-producing nation. The 1979 uprising, then, was as much about oil as religious difference.

The dehumanizing effects of poverty and discrimination were exacerbated not only by the great prosperity enjoyed elsewhere in the kingdom but also by the expectation, encouraged by the Saudi government, that largesse stemming from oil production would ameliorate social inequity all around. Oil's plenty, Saudi Arabia's leaders assured its citizens, would catapult the kingdom into an era of shared and sustained affluence. Shiites were under no illusion that discrimination would wane with greater wealth, but they came to believe that the impact of intolerance would diminish as social and economic opportunities expanded. After the oil boom the government accelerated the pace at which it constructed what would become an elaborate welfare state, providing services and investment in infrastructure and communities across the country. Shia communities had already seen some of this, although on a limited scale and with uncertain outcomes. Even before the oil boom, the regime raised expectations by engaging in a public discussion about developing the nation. The Eastern Province had been the site of several expensive development projects, including the Irrigation and Drainage Project in al-Hasa, which went into operation in 1971, as well as a smaller drainage project in Qatif. Following the oil boom, progress talk and development planning quickened and the state committed itself publicly and fully to developing the nation.

Whatever the government's assurances, the collective Shia hope of receiving social and economic benefits was quickly disappointed. Exclusion from the windfall, the realization that plenty did not in fact mean more for everyone, stirred discontent. The environment emerged as a central issue. Poor environmental conditions and the government's clear disinterest in addressing the public's long-standing concerns about limited access to water, degraded water infrastructure, and the health risks posed by antiquated and broken public facilities like sewage systems excited outrage. Equally upsetting were the unexpected and deleterious consequences of the work that the government did undertake. By the late 1970s residents of al-Hasa firmly believed that the Irrigation and Drainage Project had accelerated an environmental crisis there. Water resources were drying up and agriculture was dying. Exasperation about the environment and their own poverty was further compounded by the proximity of Shia communities to the source of the country's fortune. Saudi Arabia's oil lay in massive underground reserves almost directly beneath Shia communities and villages. Billions of barrels and trillions of dollars' worth of black gold lay tantalizingly close and yet out of reach. Proximity proved cruel in other ways as well. Favored communities in the region did prosper from oil. The cities of Dammam and al-Khobar, along with Dhahran, home to the local seat of government as well as the operations of Aramco, saw an influx of Saudis from around the country as well as an influx of oil money. Located a few kilometers from the main Shia communities of Qatif and al-Hasa, the oil "triopolis" stood as a gleaming example of what oil wealth could achieve—cities with modern conveniences and services, flush with revenue and abundant opportunity, the kingdom's Klondike on the Persian Gulf shore. Saudi citizens from central Arabia and farther west made their way to the east, where many earned considerable fortunes working for Aramco and affiliated industries. Aramco hired Shiites from the local oasis communities as well, but for the most part they enjoyed few opportunities to work in management or other more influential positions. For Shiites, jobs at Aramco and the rise of the oil cities served only as stark reminders of what was being withheld and of their second-class status.

The uneven distribution of oil wealth did more than establish the material conditions for revolt. Oil helped shape an entirely new political movement, turning a historically quiescent Shia community into an ideological force, one that equated Saudi authority and oil as forms of imperial power. The uprising, then, while driven by the material inequities of oil, also became ideologically about oil. Shia activists railed against oil and the contradictions of living in an oil state as a means to rally support and galvanize revolutionary fervor. Both before and after the uprising, oil and the Shiites' exclusion from oil wealth dominated political discourse. The focus on oil also turned the uprising into an anti-imperial movement, one that targeted the House of Saud as well as its American backers.

MYTHS OF REVOLUTION

The intifada erupted in parallel with tumultuous events elsewhere in the region, most notably in Iran. In February 1979 Ayatollah Khomeini returned to Tehran after a long period of exile, marking the culmination of Iran's revolution. Khomeini's popularity also signaled the important role that Islam and revolutionary Shiism had played in the fall of the shah of Iran. That the shah had been toppled heightened anxiety across the Middle East. That he had been ousted in part by the forces of radical Islam worked to further intensify regional uncertainties about the influence Iran would come to have in neighboring states. Iraqi president Saddam Hussein, driven partly by fear and partly by a sense of opportunity, launched an ill-conceived war against Iran in 1980, a conflict that lasted eight years, cost millions of lives, and paved the way for what has been a permanent state of war in the Persian Gulf ever since.

Saudi Arabia's leaders were particularly nervous about the power of the new Iran and its charismatic leader, Khomeini. Almost immediately after his return to Tehran in early 1979, Khomeini sought to export the revolution, calling on disillusioned Muslims across the Middle East to overthrow the brutal dictators who oppressed them. He reserved his most venomous vitriol for the Al Saud, attacking Saudi Arabia's leaders for their excessive corruption, their unholy alliance with the United States, and their claim to be the devoted guardians of Islam's sacred shrines in Mecca and Medina.[5] Khomeini considered the Shia communities in Iran's neighboring states, such as Kuwait, Bahrain, and Saudi Arabia, as naturally sympathetic audiences, among whom he believed the ideology of the revolution would find support and whip up fervor. He actively sought to distribute his message by beaming a powerful radio signal directly into the Eastern Province.[6] There is little doubt that the Iranian Revolution helped galvanize politics and energize dissent among Shiites in neighboring countries.[7] The revolution helped explain both the timing and some of the forces that encouraged Saudis to take to the streets.[8]

The Iranian Revolution did have tremendous implications for political life in Shia communities throughout the Gulf and in Saudi Arabia, although making sense of Iranian-Saudi connections has remained a challenge. There is little question that the Iranian Revolution emboldened Saudi Shiites and inflamed anger, even generating confrontational tendencies. Throughout 1979, Saudi Shia community leaders grew increasingly daring, undertaking measures that they had avoided in the past. But although the example of Iran was indeed influential, the uprising in Saudi Arabia was not a derivative event.[9] While the symbolic power of Iran was central—images from Iran's revolution, such as pictures of Ayatollah Khomeini, were common in Saudi Arabia—the 1979 uprising reflected the convergence of external factors with specifically local grievances and objectives. Although it is tempting to say otherwise, the Saudi uprising constituted something more than a response to Khomeini's call for the region's Shiites to embrace and carry out their own revolutions.

While Saudi Shiites regarded Khomeini as a source of political inspiration, most did not consider him as their religious or political authority *(marja'iyya)*, particularly in the areas affected by the uprising. Rather, since the early 1970s Saudi Shiites followed the *marja'* Ayatollah Muhammad al-Husayni al-Shirazi, who had fled Iran for Kuwait in the late 1960s and returned to Qom in 1979, after the fall of the shah.[10] In the 1970s his influence spread throughout the Gulf's Shia communities.[11] While al-Shirazi supported the overthrow of the Iranian regime, he was not a close supporter of Khomeini's principle of the rule of the jurisprudent *(wilayat al-faqih)*. Al-Shirazi advocated the creation of a clerical political class to help run the affairs of the state, although he sought the formation of a committee of senior *mujtahid*s rather than the rule of single powerful *faqih*. The difference between his vision and that of Khomeini did not generate personal tension between the two men, although they were clear rivals in Iran; there were more bitter relations between al-Shirazi and Khomeini's junior supporters, such as Ayatollah Ali Khamenei.[12]

It is difficult to assess the specific impact of al-Shirazi's influence on Saudi Arabia's radicalized Shia organizations and their activities in the 1979 uprising. The effect of al-Shirazi's direct leadership on local Shiite communities was clearly manifested elsewhere in the Gulf. In Bahrain, for example, where the Shiites constituted a majority of the population, Hadi al-Mudarrisi, an Iraqi who represented al-Shirazi on the island, founded the revolutionary Islamic Front for the Liberation of Bahrain (Al-jabha al-islamiyya li tahrir al-Bahrain) in 1980 and maintained direct relations with al-Shirazi in Qom.[13] While Saudi Arabian followers of the *marja'* al-Shirazi, led by Sheikh Hassan al-Saffar, founded the Shia Reform Movement in Saudi Arabia and then later the Organization for the Islamic Revolution in the Saudi Arabian Peninsula (Munathamat al-Thawra al-Islamiyya fii al-Jazira al-Arabiyya Al-Sa'udiyya, or OIR) in the late 1970s, they did not maintain close relations with the senior cleric, particularly after he left Kuwait for Iran in 1979. Sources indicate that Saudi Shiites communicated with al-Shirazi about events in the region later that year but did not seek his assistance or guidance in organizing them. Rather, the group maintained its local character and control, reflecting community interests and objectives. Members of the OIR certainly took inspiration from revolutionaries in Iran, even appropriating their symbols, but it seems likely that relations did not surpass the level of the symbolic.

For some Saudi Shiites the uprising did indeed constitute the local playing-out of a transnational Shia event. Yet on close inspection it becomes clear that the ideological character of the Saudi uprising was not framed exclusively in terms particular to the political Shiism emanating from Iran. Pamphlets circulated before and during the events of the fall of 1979, as well as what followed, identified various political groupings. Leftists who avoided specifically sectarian politics, as well as Islamists, mobilized and demonstrated in response to what they perceived to be years of neglect, and in reaction to the events of November 1979 themselves. Interestingly, the uprising's political complexity mimicked events in Iran, where the actions of Islamists and leftists helped drive out the shah. Khomeini and his supporters came to dominate the political system only later and only by violently driving out their leftist corevolutionaries. Unlike in Iran, Saudi agitators did not coordinate. Divided among themselves ideologically, Saudi Shia rebels lacked clear objectives and failed to formulate a sustainable vision.

THE GEOGRAPHY OF VIOLENCE

The violence of 1979 was concentrated in the villages and towns throughout the Eastern Province, from Qatif in the north to the al-Hasa oasis in the south. The disturbances were most intense and sustained in Qatif and surrounding communities in the north. More sporadic violence also broke out in towns with major oil facilities, such as Abqaiq in the south. Toward the end of the period of unrest, demonstrators targeted the three oil cities directly, taking their anger to al-Khobar, Dammam, and Dhahran, where they marched through the streets. The marches in the cities that administered the country's oil industry were intended to ensure that the rebels' message spread beyond the Shia heartland. While these cities had some Shia residents, the vast majority of those who lived in the oil triopolis came either from abroad (American and other foreign workers) or from central and western Saudi Arabia (members of the Sunni merchant elite and privileged clients of the Saudi regime). The demonstrations in the nerve center of oil were also a signal that the uprising was targeting the lifeblood of oppression and Saudi power. Although the activity and the heart of the hostility were centered in the coastal towns and villages nearest the oil operations, those who took part in the violence claimed to speak on behalf of all Shiites in the kingdom.

The Eastern Province officially got its name when the Saudi rulers moved the administrative capital of the region from Hofuf to Dammam in 1950.[14] Previously, at least according to the nomenclature used by the rulers in Riyadh, the region shared its name with the al-Hasa oasis, located in the southern part of the province. Historically, however, the region was home to two distinctly separate population centers, one in al-Hasa and another in Qatif, separated by more than 120 kilometers. Date agriculture dominated both communities, although rice and various other fruits and vegetables were also grown in each. Between them, they produced enough dates for export, supplying markets across the peninsula, throughout the Persian Gulf region, and as far abroad as South Asia and western Africa.[15] Qatif, situated on the Gulf coast, was also home to a vibrant fishing and pearl-diving industry.[16] The rich resources and relative wealth of al-Hasa and Qatif had long attracted regular and intense interest from imperialist powers, leading to invasions and conquests by the Portuguese, the Safavids, the Al Saud, and the Ottomans. In addition to having similar settled agricultural and trade patterns, the populations in both communities were, and are, predominantly Twelver Shia.[17] Population figures for the religious group are unknown and estimates vary widely, as their status remains controversial and sensitive inside the kingdom. In the early 1980s, Jacob Goldberg and others determined that the total number of Shiites in Qatif and al-Hasa was around 350,000.[18] The Shiites in both Qatif and al-Hasa shared various religious institutions in common, such as the *husseiniyya,* the prayer house that served as the center for religious and community services. Because the Al Saud forbade the building of Shia mosques, the *husseiniyya*s were particularly important in defining and shaping spiritual life.

Although the two communities had a faith in common, there were some differences between them, including demography and religious practice.[19] These differences did have an impact on the location and the intensity of the uprising. Even though violence was not sustained at the same level in every Shia community, most Shiites shared in the anger and frustration that fueled the rebellion. Those who did take to the streets and challenge the government claimed to speak on behalf of all Shiites in the kingdom. In Qatif the Shia constituted the vast majority of the population, perhaps around 95 percent. The demography of al-Hasa proved more balanced, as the Shia constituted roughly 50 percent of the oasis's population, although they dominated in the poorer and more remote areas. Social conditions in Qatif played an important role in generating and sustaining public defiance there. Qatif was home to several concentrated urban centers, including Safwa and Sayhat, as well as dozens of surrounding villages. More integrated than the Shia communities in the south, Qatifis occupied positions across the social spectrum. That Qatif was both urban and rural seems to have been a critical factor in animating the community. In al-Hasa, although the two main cities, Hofuf and al-Mubarraz, were major urban centers and home to large numbers of both Shiites and Sunnis, the vast majority of Shiites were poor landless peasants who lived in isolated villages on the outskirts of the oasis.[20] Marginalized, they were likely unable to sustain popular protest. Their different social universes did not mean that the two did not suffer through similar material hardships, however. While the Hasawi Shiites may not have participated broadly in the uprising, they were no better off than their neighbors to the north. Both communities found themselves on the outside when it came to state services and the financial benefits generated by great oil wealth.

In December 1979, the Organization of the Islamic Revolution in the Saudi Arabian Peninsula released a pamphlet on the seven statements the group had circulated during the unrest a few weeks earlier, exhorting people to take to the streets.[21] The OIR emerged from underground in the midst of the intifada itself and assumed a leading role in the community. In a brief introduction, the pamphlet's author (or authors) asked rhetorically, "[Was] what happened . . . merely an emotional uprising, one having no social or political foundation, as Minister of the Interior Prince Nayif bin Abd al-Aziz and Minister of Information Muhammad Abdu Yamani depicted it? Or did the Intifada possess an essentially social and political foundation?"[22] In answering, the authors outlined three reasons for the intifada and its character. First, they cited the "deprivation and misery" of Saudi Arabians throughout the kingdom, but particularly in the east. In making the case that regular citizens suffered unnecessarily, the authors argued that the state had conspired to mask the extent of its wealth while many Saudi Arabians knew only poverty and desperation. Challenging the government's announced total for daily oil production of 9.5 million barrels, the OIR argued that the true production figure was closer to 14 million barrels. According to their calculations, this generated $350 million in revenue *daily*. Given this, the authors asked, "What do you [foreign reader] imagine the condition of the people to be whose government possesses such wealth? If only the world knew the condition of our people and understood the extent of the deprivation and misery that our masses of oppressed [*jamahirna al-mustada'afa*] live in under the shadow of the Saudi regime."[23]

The pamphlet displayed pictures of dilapidated tin shacks with thatched palm roofs, with a caption stating, "In the land that houses one-quarter of the world's oil reserves, you find these homes."[24] Such housing was common all over the kingdom, they argued, "whether in the south in Najran, in Jizan, in Asir, or in Qatif or al-Hasa, all of the homes fail to meet the most meager conditions of health."[25] Thousands of people, the authors argued, possessed no running water or electricity as late as 1979. Even in Ras Tanura, site of the kingdom's massive oil refining facilities, power stations, a huge desalinization plant, and vast modern technological systems, thousands lived and toiled without utilities or basic services. Humiliation was heaped on top of misery. When Queen Elizabeth visited Dammam in 1978, the authors wrote, the local municipality erected barriers and fences so she would not be able to view "the mud hovels" or the extent of the people's despair.

The authors argued that Saudi oil money was being funneled into wasteful and excessive channels that did not serve the interests of Saudi citizens. Among the most egregious examples of profligacy, the OIR cited the $5.1 billion spent on American weapons in 1978 alone, including the controversial purchase of sixty American F16 fighter jets. Citing unnamed sources, the group declared its exasperation at the suggestion that the Saudi regime might be responsible for 23 percent of global arms purchases. The authors wondered, "Against whom will these weapons be used?" pointing out that the Saudi regime was not involved in any regional or global conflict and did not appear to be under threat of any direct attack.[26] American banks, they charged, were benefiting from petrocapital, as the dollars generated by oil sales routinely made their way back into Western markets and coffers rather than into Saudi communities. The worst abusers of the national wealth were members of the Saudi royal family, the OIR claimed. Alluding to various instances of state leaders' excess and opulent living, the authors expressed disgust and anger over the fact that, in contrast, many Saudi Arabians "suffered a crisis with [a shortage of] water as well as health and social services." The authors remarked: "When the people look at the exploitation and squandering of the [national] wealth—and every area in which they live is deprived, miserable, and suffering—is it not natural for them to behave in a revolutionary way, and for them to practice violence, and to persist in fighting for their rights and the protection of their wealth from the betrayal of the criminal Al Saud?"[27]

The authors also cited the absence of a constitution guaranteeing basic freedoms, such as free speech and freedom of the press, as the second factor that mobilized the public expression of frustration. Third was the hostile position of the Saudi regime toward the Iranian Revolution, which the authors heralded for its pan-Islamic message and its appeal for unity against Western and American imperialism. The three reasons outlined by the OIR for the outbreak of the intifada provide a glimpse of the complexity of grievances shared by those who took to the streets. While the latter two reasons speak to the OIR's specific ideological agenda, the group acknowledged that the long-term crises and anxiety born from social despair and the contradictions of oil and development planning fueled the intensity of the revolt. While some benefited and profited from the massive oil wealth, many—particularly minorities and those on the margins of power—seemed to have been intentionally left behind.

In its writings, the Organization of the Islamic Revolution used passion, anger, and the power of emotional rhetoric to rally support and sustain direct pressure on the regime. Importantly, it also framed hardship in very specific terms that tell us a great deal about the issues that galvanized unrest. The OIR not only juxtaposed popular "misery and suffering" with state opulence and wastefulness, but it also pointed out how the difference was predicated on the unfulfilled promise of development, which the regime had widely and very publicly marketed as the most important commitment it had toward Saudi citizens. The second five-year Saudi development plan released and widely celebrated in 1975, for example, claimed that the "fundamental values and principles which guide Saudi Arabia's balanced development" included the goal to "develop human resources by education, training, and raising standards of health." The plan emphasized the regime's desire to "increase the well-being of all groups within the society and foster social stability under circumstances of rapid change" by "develop[ing] the physical infrastructure to support [the] achievement of the above goals."[28] In the spring of 1979, the regime introduced its annual budget with much fanfare. King Khalid marked the announcement of the year's SR160 billion–budget by stating that the funds would "enable the government—God willing—to present increases in services to citizens all over the kingdom."[29] Minister of Information Muhammad Abdu Yamani remarked that "the most important goals include developing social and health services" in villages and settlements.[30] Local officials in the east echoed the state line. Prince Abd al-Muhsin ibn Jiluwi, the powerful governor of the Eastern Province, opined that the budget clearly identified the "happiness of the citizens" as the priority of the kingdom's regents. He declared that the huge budget was evidence of the royal family's commitment to the "development of the nation." In particular, he emphasized that in the east the focus would be on health and social services as well as developing human resources.[31] In the past, such declarations had served to heighten expectations. By the end of the 1970s they generated animosity.

According to local observers and activists, the regime—through both its national and local institutions—failed to deliver. While members of the royal family built luxurious villas, traveled around the world, and purchased expensive weapons—meanwhile fattening the wallets of American business—they did not act to provide the very services and basic welfare promised to Saudi citizens. Poverty remained widespread in those areas on the margins of power, and many tired of the state's failure to live up to its assurances. It appeared to the authors of the OIR pamphlet and others that the broken promise was premeditated—that the "criminal Al Saud regime" had engaged in a conscious act of "betrayal" that intentionally left thousands behind.[32] That people believed the Al Saud and its agents had willfully betrayed its citizens is ultimately more important than the truth of the claim.

As a result of intentional negligence or not, it was clear that hundreds of thousands of people were suffering, living in meager conditions, lacking basic services, and angry about it. Less than a year and a half before the outbreak of violence, and under pressure from community leaders to do something about deteriorating social conditions in Qatif, Deputy Minister of the Interior Ahmad bin Abd al-Aziz dispatched a royal decree to the governor of the Eastern Province ordering the formation of a committee to study the "backwardness and underdevelopment" that the region of Qatif "suffers . . . in all fields."[33] Little was accomplished, however, and as the situation worsened community anger became increasingly public. In the year before the uprising, social decay and the shortcomings of state services dominated local newspaper reporting in the Eastern Province, with the pages of *Al-Yawm*—the region's local paper, based in

Dammam—full of stories of suffering, investigative reports about administrative ineptitude, and angry letters from local citizens. While the press never targeted the royal family directly, the animosity toward local branches of government and the politics of development, and thus the central state, was clear.

Several environmental issues dominated discussion, the most important being the crisis in water management and diminishing resources, as well as the local municipalities' inability to manage the worsening situation. Contracting water resources, as well as failing water systems, reached a crisis stage in both the oasis of al-Hasa and Qatif and the surrounding villages. In 1979 alone more than fifty articles, letters, or pictures were published about the water problem in the province.[34] In the al-Hasa oasis, the problem was acute. Water resources—vital to the oasis's agricultural production—appeared to be in sharp decline, in spite of efforts over the previous two decades to manage them. As a result, local farmers and landowners had scrambled to dig their own deep wells and secure private access to the oasis's precious resource. This scramble, however, contributed to the further depletion of the already low water table. The water shortage was complicated by other factors as well, such as chemicals in the drinking water and water-borne disease from the mixing of freshwater with sewage. In one investigative report, Hussein al-Tantawi, an agitated reporter for *Al-Yawm*, drew attention to the deepening crisis. In response to a local initiative by the al-Hasa municipal council to find new sources of water, al-Tantawi questioned the wisdom of the council's handling of the problem, arguing that the water problems would probably repeat themselves because the board's planning had failed to take into account the growing population, increased demand, and the need to cover a wider geographic area. He further argued that the salt and chloride content of water throughout the oasis was outrageously high, over twice the international standard, which he declared "unacceptable," and said that disease-carrying microbes threatened the health of the oasis's citizens.[35] Al-Tantawi's account was not exceptional, although his report provoked a terse response from the Ministry of Agriculture and Water.[36] Similar problems plagued villages throughout the oasis, including in Hofuf and in more remote areas, like the old village of al-Jafar and especially in a cluster of Shiite villages in the area of al-Umran. In al-Umran, a community in the remote eastern periphery of the oasis, long marginalized from regional power, frustrated citizens spoke out about government negligence. Locals claimed that in spite of repeated claims about coming services, including the installation of water storage tanks, the rebuilding of crumbling homes, the provision of public lighting, and the building of a network for drinking water, the promises had gone unfulfilled for three years.[37]

In Shia Qatif and the surrounding area, the problem was even more dramatic. In a series of articles, editorials, and pictorial essays, *Al-Yawm* systematically documented the water problems in Qatif. Most important, as was the case in much of al-Hasa, the city of Qatif and its villages possessed no centrally planned or functioning system to deliver freshwater. Where there were old local systems, the pipes often lay exposed and disintegrating, pumping both freshwater and sewage into public areas. Safwa, a town just south of Qatif, had massive ponds of standing water and sewage that had seeped from the antiquated system. Tarut Island, which lay several kilometers to the east of Qatif, was of particular interest to the journalists at the newspaper. Remarkable for its natural beauty, its past fertility, its historic landmarks, and its potential for investment, the small collection of villages stood in virtual ruin. In a June article, the paper wondered if the citizens of Tarut would eventually be forced to drink seawater. Citing the island's two main problems as the absence of drinking water and year-round bogs, local citizens and authorities blasted the Ministry of Municipal and Village Affairs and its Committee for Environmental Health in the Eastern Province for neglect. They even suggested that the problems were the product of willful disregard. Citing a telegram from the Qatif municipal council, the paper quoted the following: "The drinking-water wells in Tarut are producing negative results and the reason for that is the absence of a functional drinking-water network . . . We previously raised the issue for your consideration . . . But it has not been completed this year. Now, the problems have grown worse and thus the citizens complain." The paper stated that "bogs remain throughout the year and in every area. The health of the citizens is gravely affected. [The citizens] request the establishment of offices there to follow the condition of [people's] health and not just author reports that have no effect or provide no speedy resolution."[38]

Raising the possibility of willful negligence, the director of Qatif's municipal council—passing the buck—went on record saying that in spite of the efforts of some local authorities to care for the health of the community, the Ministry of Agriculture and Water did not appear to be overly concerned with the problems of the general public. He remarked that "the Municipality undertook work to drain the bogs and budgeted for the [sewage] network. It raised the issue to the Committee of Environmental Health. The Committee agreed [to resolve problems] with the part of the project that is located on government land and hoped to secure agreement on the remaining part!!!" Ultimately, however, he claimed that the ministry's committee "left the part allotted to citizens in addition to the nongovernment land" to be sorted out among themselves.[39]

Other problems abounded. Ibrahim al-Ghudair, in a lengthy article, recorded the remarks of a Tarut resident who commented that "every day I see these hovels. If the sorrow of Darin [village] overcomes me, then I flee and enter al-Rabiyya [village] and I tour the homes made of palm fronds and old ramshackle tin shacks falling on the heads of their inhabitants."[40] Horrified, the author described the details of his trip to the island, relating various encounters with the poor residents there, including one child who, he guessed, "had not bathed in a month."[41] In another incident, exasperated by the potential for disaster, he determined that the municipal council used diesel gasoline as a spray against flies and mosquitoes. During an encounter with a regional official, he questioned how long the communities would have to endure their abject conditions, particularly the hovels and wretched living circumstances; the official told him, flippantly, "Until the residents destroy them and build more modern ones."[42]

Ali Yusuf al-Jarudi, a resident of Qatif, stated that "it is not a stretch [to say] that Qatif continues to have been deprived of projects since the 1975 budget and the second five-year plan, which is about to end without helping [the city] at all."[43] Al-Jarudi made it clear that, in his opinion, local officials "had not fulfilled their duties to the community . . . It is noticeable," he pointed out, "that Qatif suffers from a poverty of modern planning and that it is poor in industrial, commercial, luxury, and community areas." Even in areas where Qatif was historically rich, in agriculture, the communities were suffering from the lack of services and assistance. Over time, thanks to heavy seasonal winds from the west, Qatif's fertile fields were threatened by encroaching desert sand. In al-Hasa, the state had undertaken various projects to protect farms and farmers, including building barriers and planting patches of trees and shrubs to stave off the invading desert. Al-Jarudi argued that "although Qatif is among the most fertile agricultural areas in the kingdom, the Municipality is lost" in dealing with it.[44]

Abdullah al-Dubaisi, another writer, commented on Qatif and its "sick streets."[45] Al-Dubaisi condemned local administrators as well as those it had contracted with to undertake community projects. While he could not name the president of the municipality— implying that the local chief had not bothered to actually involve himself in community affairs—everyone in Qatif knew that local firms, awarded fat contracts for technical work, had "been responsible for the ills of the city and [had] delayed its convalescence." The dirty streets were particularly troubling. A possible solution, al-Dubaisi suggested, was to pave all the roads in the city and surrounding villages, thus eliminating the source of the filth. He seemed to understand that his plea was in vain, however, as he remarked that the government intended to "leave the dirt sitting in the streets and the neighborhoods of the city. It is satisfied to only treat the main streets and leave the rest." He underscored the depth of community ire, and foreshadowed future conflict, when he angrily stated, "We denounce this and the villages have not forgotten, for they are in greatest need of services."[46]

It is not as though the Eastern Province's local councils did nothing in their communities, though they had little real impact other than frustrating and insulting their poor residents. Community offices spent millions of riyals on various projects and campaigns. In the small, predominantly Sunni village of al-Jafar in al-Hasa, for example, the village council spent 200,000 riyals on cleaning and other services. It also staged a contest in which it awarded 6,000 riyals to the citizens with the cleanest homes.[47] Hundreds of thousands of riyals were allotted for planning meetings, addressing various water issues, and for beautification projects such as the building of public parks. Even in Qatif, local government reportedly budgeted over 400,000 riyals on health and social services, including researching the health status of ninety-four communities in 1979.[48] In Ras Tanura, the local governor commissioned the construction of a new 100-bed hospital and an international phone system.[49] Given the anger of letter writers and journalists, however, the impact of these initiatives proved minimal. In contrast, cities of Dammam, alKhobar, and Dhahran—the centers of administrative and business life in the region—enjoyed greater prosperity and attention. In the spring, the new 120-million-riyal Abdullah Fuad Hospital in Dammam opened its doors, complete with 300 beds, an intensive care department, a twenty-four-hour emergency room, an electronic lab, and even computers.[50] In September, 2 billion riyals were allotted for improving the water and sewage networks in Dammam and al-Khobar, a huge sum that underscored the central importance of services in the capital district and suggested, by comparison, indifference to other areas.[51] Dammam officials lavished literally hundreds of millions of riyals on community projects in the capital, overwhelming the support provided elsewhere. The difference revealed in the emphasis on the main cities of the region, seemingly at the expense of the outlying regions of Qatif and al-Hasa, was not lost on observers. *Al-Yawm* wondered "why municipal services focused only on the cities while the villages live in worse conditions?"[52] The participating officials proved unable to provide a reasonable answer, and after the May follow-up meeting, the paper concluded that "the seminar on utilities and services [was] transform[ed] into a seminar on limiting responsibility."[53]

The remarkable differences between community life in the urban outposts of Saudi power and that on the margins—both geographically and socially—generated intense frustration among those left out. As various accounts by citizens and journalists in *Al-Yawm* suggest, patience with the status quo had grown increasingly tenuous by the end of the decade. Worse was the seemingly dismissive and unsympathetic position of many of those in a position to ameliorate the struggles of so many thousands. Broken promises of development, environmental neglect, and the withholding of oil wealth roused specific grievances and provided a ready vocabulary for those angry with the regime. Without question, the politics of (un)development exacerbated the frustration produced by the hardships of daily life and gave rise to increasingly intense demands for attention, for a real commitment to deploying solutions in remote communities, and for the rejection of the state's seemingly prejudiced development strategy. It is impossible to know if widespread misery and social neglect, by themselves, would have generated the violence that gripped the Eastern Province in late November 1979. As the writing of the Organization for the Islamic Revolution made clear, however, repeated instances of apparent neglect by the regime and its failure to fulfill stated objectives certainly made the violence more likely. Ultimately, what provoked the uprisings in the fall and winter were local grievances born of social despair and political oppression, combined with the emergence of a willfulness on the part of Shia community leaders about expressing and practicing their ideological convictions—a willfulness that the regime in Riyadh sought to crush.

THE TURN TO VIOLENCE

Violence erupted in Qatif, and to a lesser extent in al-Hasa, in late November 1979. As we have seen, the political tension leading up to the uprising had deep historical roots. State oppression against the region's Shiites dated back to 1913, when the Al Saud and its warrior army conquered al-Hasa and Qatif. After the conquest, the Saudi regime relied on various forms of suppression to subdue the Shia minority but did not often engage in sustained or direct acts of violence.[54] That changed in the year before the uprising, when the state grew increasingly nervous about subversive activities in the remote towns and villages in the east. The first indication of the state's growing discomfort came about in the village of al-Awamiyya, located a few kilometers north of Qatif, in 1978. Reportedly, villagers there accosted a Saudi police officer. In response, according to an account of the events recorded by the Communist Party in Saudi Arabia, state security forces apprehended upwards of seventy people and detained them without a trial, a situation that persisted for many months. The Communists claimed that the people of the village "lived under the weight of oppression, ignorance, poverty and disease" and that "police negligence" served to only further provoke the "feelings of the people."[55] Perhaps not surprisingly, in the early stages of the uprising in November 1979, the people of al-Awamiyya assaulted various centers of the security forces and "disarmed them of not only their weapons, but also their military clothes, police miscellany, and their clocks."[56]

Although the state's nervousness, along with its willingness to react harshly to even a hint of subversion, was manifested much earlier, the showdown of 1979 was directly precipitated by the boldness of religious leaders in Qatif that summer. In August, the community's leaders proclaimed that they would publicly celebrate the banned ceremony of Ashura.[57] Similar provocations had been made by Shiites in Bahrain, a predominantly Shia island under Sunni rule, located twenty-five kilometers off the coast of Saudi Arabia, which was historically integrated with the Shia communities in the eastern Arabian Peninsula. In fact, public discord was evident much earlier in Bahrain than in Saudi Arabia. In mid-August, several waves of unrest rose up in Shia communities there.[58] On September 11 the disaffected staged demonstrations against the Bahraini government, provoking a heavy-handed response. Saudi security officials interpreted the rising boldness of the Shiites elsewhere in the Gulf as menacing to their own interests and the result of the dangerous influence of Iran. On September 13, *Al-Yawm* reprinted an article from the Bahrain-based newspaper *Akhbar al-Khalīj* that quoted the Bahraini minister of the interior as saying the government would "not permit the continuance of any demonstrations of nonsense in the country and that it [would] face them with all the violence and strength and severe measures" necessary. The paper reported that the police had dispersed the protestors, whom they belittled as "extremist" and an "insignificant group" committed to stirring up "chaos and tension" and destabilizing Bahrain. The message to potentially sympathetic and like-minded Saudis was clear. Also on September 13, to underscore the seriousness of the Saudi state's concern and frame of mind, the paper ran an article acknowledging for the first time that the Saudi regime was concerned with the regional impact of the Iranian Revolution. That day the Saudi foreign minister, Saud al-Faisal, attended a meeting in Bahrain in which regional leaders "deliberated on the prevailing political situation in the region since the success of the Iranian Revolution," a clear reference to the unrest there.[59] On October 2 and 3 Crown Prince Fahd hosted the Bahraini prime minister, Sheikh Khalifa bin Salman al-Khalifa, in Jidda to discuss the "security and protection" of Arab affairs in the Gulf.[60] Undeterred, the Saudi Shiites took to the streets in Safwa on November 26, when 4,000 marchers staged the first public mourning procession of Ashura.

On November 28 the Eastern Province turned into a killing field. That night, thousands came together and paraded through Sayhat, a small Shia community situated a few kilometers north of Dammam, angrily shouting antiregime slogans such as, "Oh [King] Khalid release your hands [from power], the people do not want you!"[61] Tension mounted as the marchers advanced on a group of agitated Saudi National Guardsmen. In the front ranks of the procession, nineteen-year-old Hussein Mansur al-Qalaf, a recent graduate of Aramco's Industrial Training Center, led the marchers in a violent and frenzied confrontation with the security forces.[62] Initially, the National Guard relied on using clubs and electric prods to control the crowd. In response, the attacking mob surged, hurling stones and wielding wooden canes and iron bars in defiance. According to one account, "At that point the security forces opened fire on the demonstrators."[63] Into the maelstrom al-Qalaf rushed, to aid one of his wounded friends, and Saudi forces gunned the nineteen-year-old down, making him the first martyr of the uprising. Al-Qalaf's comrades whisked him to the emergency room of the Dhahran hospital, but the facility's administration refused him treatment without prior permission from the government. They then raced him north to the hospital in Qatif, more than half an hour away, to no avail. Security forces there seized his body, refusing to return it to his family unless his father agreed "that the cause of his death were the stones of the demonstrators." His family refused and the body remained in the custody of the government for a week. Eventually the state returned al-Qalaf's corpse, on the condition that the family "not hold a funeral procession on his behalf and that they bury him secretly, which they did." According to legend, al-Qalaf's martyrdom fulfilled his self-prophecy, as he had allegedly told his frightened mother two days before his death, "You have six sons, it is for you that one of them should be martyred on behalf of Allah."[64] Over the next few days at least two dozen people perished and hundreds fell wounded in a crescendo of mayhem and violence that the regime effectively sealed off from the world. Scores were killed or wounded in various incidents, mostly in the Shia heartland in and around Qatif. Ten died under fire from security forces while crossing the bridge from Tarut. Various sources reported random killings as a result of heavy machine-gun fire from helicopters that strafed protesters and the surrounding neighborhoods.[65]

By December 3, after large marches of Shia in Dammam and al-Khobar, public protest ebbed as local dissidents withdrew. Public action flared again on January 12, as thousands took to the streets forty days after the fall of the first martyr in November, to mark the end of the period of mourning. An act of tribute, the public display was also a sign of defiance toward the regime. State security forces, including the National Guard, followed behind the January 12 processions, although there was no violence. The same was not true, however, on February 1, the first anniversary of Khomeini's return to Iran, when thousands again clashed with the regime's security troops in Qatif. According to a statement issued by the Committee for the Defense of Human Rights in Saudi Arabia (CDHR), crowds began milling in an area in downtown Qatif known as Martyr's Square—named for those who had been killed in the clashes there in November—early on the morning of the first.[66] For two hours in the late morning and early afternoon, they listened to orations calling for heroism and the absence of fear as well as stories from the Iranian Revolution. Around one o'clock they marched to the Qatif market and reassembled, carrying signs recalling martyrs and those arrested. They also railed provocatively against state brutality. Meanwhile, state security forces had also gathered, and they trailed the procession very closely.

The CDHR reported that wide-scale violence erupted after a military officer opened fire on the crowd, killing one and wounding many others. In response, the crowd surged on the officer and assaulted him. He was spared death only by the arrival of an ambulance and the rescue efforts of his colleagues. In the bedlam, the crowds torched buildings and vehicles throughout the city. The state declared a national emergency and the National Guard augmented its forces in subsequent days, protecting administrative offices such as the local municipality, the police station, and the local governor's office.[67] Throughout the rest of that month, the CDHR reported continuing acts of resistance as well as mass arrests and police brutality.

Expectations, among both locals and security officials, that the violence would endure persisted well into 1980. Aside from some minor skirmishes, however, it did not last, as local rebels turned to clandestine activity (and self-preservation) rather than open confrontation.

The observance of the religious ceremony of Ashura, and the state's swift resort to police violence to suppress it, have led observers to interpret the events that followed as religiously centered and even Iranian controlled. The initial turnout of marchers should certainly be attributed to the call by community clerics to honor the religious holiday, an explicitly political act. What transpired in subsequent days, however, assumed a more complex character. In the days after the protest turned violent, the numbers of marchers swelled by the thousands, something not expected by anyone in the province. On November 29, a day after the first deadly clash, the Communists estimated that 18,000 people marched in protest, a figure echoed by other observers.[68] The swelling ranks of angry protesters reflected a popular disaffection that, in many ways, transcended religious conviction. To be sure, identity mattered in the course of the uprising, in the sense that it was the Shia communities that suffered disproportionately in Saudi Arabia. However, religious identity did not predict the response or render it uniformly coherent. Indeed, the initial religious reasons for public gathering passed, and as the regime's forces brutalized the crowds, the protests became more populist and impassioned—driven by shared communal outrage at the regime's cruelty, combined with the already simmering anger over appalling social and environmental conditions and the broken promises of modernity. Although populist and unpredictable, there was a mixed ideological character to the intifada. Amid the violence, forces emerged and organized, competing for the favor of the masses, struggling to define the event and to sustain public pressure on the regime. The struggle to direct and generate public action persisted well into 1980, with various networks in the Eastern Province pressuring the regime for the amelioration of political and social grievances. In the end, the state extended limited concessions and superficially addressed core community issues—all the while rooting out political groups, crushing them, and driving political refugees underground or into exile.

During the uprising, two political networks clearly emerged as operating in the east, one Islamist and the other nationalist-leftist. On the Islamist front, the Organization of the Islamic Revolution assumed the mantle of religio-political leadership, drawing on Iran for inspiration—although not for leadership. The origin and operations of this group date back to 1975, when Hassan al-Saffar established the Shia Reform Movement in Saudi Arabia.[69] Mamoun Fandy writes that, under al-Saffar's direction, "leaders adopted a militant stance" between 1975 and 1980, and that "events in 1979 helped to further radicalize the movement, namely the coming of an Islamic government in Iran, the uprising in the Eastern Province, and the takeover of Mecca's Grand Mosque. Leaders of the Shia movement, including Sheikh al-Saffar, followed the Iranian line."[70] Madawi al-Rasheed writes that, in contrast, the Organization of the Islamic Revolution "began to take shape as the political outlet for the group [the Shiites] following the spontaneous events of 1979. Members of the organization were drawn from students in the University of Minerals and Petroleum (Dammam) and workers at the oil fields. The organization began broadcasting from Iranian radio stations in an attempt to reach the community in Saudi Arabia, and an information office was opened in Tehran to coordinate political activities."[71] Elements of both accounts are correct, as Hussein Musa shows. In his account, loosely organized Shia dissidents rallied around Hasan al-Saffar in the late 1970s, congealing formally only after the success of the Iranian Revolution.[72]

In the year before the uprising in 1979, Saudi Shiites took inspiration from the Iranian Revolution, a powerful example that stirred excitement and generated political enthusiasm throughout the region. Iran's example foreshadowed what transpired elsewhere, but it did not set the political terms. Musa writes that "the issue of authority [marja'iyya] played an important role in [the] polarization" of Shia politics throughout the Gulf.[73] Although various Shia groups agreed that political change was necessary, there were important "divergences" on the issue of who should lead. Throughout the Gulf, including in Saudi Arabia, many Shiites regarded Muhammad al-Husayni al-Shirazi as their communities' authority on political and juridical matters, not Khomeini, although Khomeini was a powerful and respected figure. And while Shiites in Saudi Arabia did revere the popular al-Shirazi, they went a step further and "sought to establish independence from the Iranian authorities and to establish local ones . . . in order to distinguish themselves from the Iranians."[74] They exhibited a specifically local sensibility, one in tune with their own community interests and needs and focused on social justice and oil. Musa argues that while they respected the Iranians, whom they encountered during the hajj and while abroad, the Shia Islamic movement in eastern Arabia "did not embrace the Iranians."[75]

Although the followers of al-Shirazi had been active within the Shia Reform Movement since 1975, the group's members were radicalized in 1979. They subsequently renamed the movement the Organization for the Islamic Revolution and announced that they would strive for change through confrontation.[76] Preparing for what was sure to be a charged public celebration of Ashura, the OIR adopted a threatening pose by dispatching ominous warnings to resident Americans in the Eastern Province and by calling for young Shiites to rebel. On November 24, the group sent an English-language letter to American employees at Aramco, whom the OIR viewed partly as surrogates for the Saudi royal family doing the bidding of the central authorities, and partly as imperialists exploiting the Shiites' natural and human resources. They threatened direct retribution against American citizens working in Saudi Arabia if the U.S. government involved itself in community affairs. In a menacing opening paragraph, the group wrote, "We realize the dubious role that you play in our country and toward our national resources. God willing, we will settle our accounts with you in the near future." Citing popular belief that American commandos and military personnel had arrived in Saudi Arabia in preparation for operations in Iran, they threatened, "We will not permit you to use our land and our resources against our Muslim brothers. Therefore, if your oppressive government takes any aggressive and military action against Iran, then you will be its victims here."[77] After the uprising, the OIR was quick to claim that its letter had forced 140 Americans and their families to flee the kingdom.

The group also circulated a flyer exhorting young Shiites to take to the streets. The impassioned call for action pleaded, "Oh, noble faithful: you are called forth these days to revive the case of Imam Hussein, to commemorate his memory, and to augment the climate of revolution in this great season of revolution. The best means to revive the issue of Imam Hussein, the great revolutionary, are the mourning processions that fill the streets and energize the people." The OIR cited several reasons for the need to undertake public processions, foremost being to honor Imam Hussein, Shiism's first martyr. In addition, it declared, "It is a practice of our religious freedom, which others try to take from us." Sensing community nervousness and fear about the possibility of Saudi retribution, the OIR sought to overcome such uncertainty by appealing directly to the impressionable and, hopefully, more passionate youth. The pamphlet encouraged the faithful "not to fear the police or security forces, for they will inevitably be put to flight by your endurance and persistence for mourning. Whoever suffers an injury such as a beating or imprisonment, God will be with him and give him great rewards. He will be a servant among the mujahideen along the path of Imam Hussein. As for your fathers who fearfully warn you from rebelling . . . rebel and do no heed their ban." And as for those unwilling to participate, the OIR declared that they "are cowards" and interested only in their own affairs.[78]

On November 27, the day after the first mourning processions took place in Safwa, the OIR, enthused by the initial turnout, circulated a second flyer in the community, this time targeting women. The flyer read:

Oh Faithful sisters: you live in these days celebrating the memory of Hussein and his revolution, whose events were not made only for heroic men. Rather, heroic women also participated. For next to the victims of Imam Hussein was his faithful widow Zaynab. And standing behind the exalted Ali [the Prophet's cousin and first Shia Imam] was his courageous mother, Layla. Behind his bravery, love enabled his heroism, his security, and his martyrdom. Faithful women participated in the revolution of Karbala' among the ranks of revolutionary men. Oh faithful sisters, as women participated in [that] revolution, it is incumbent upon you to participate now in memoriam.[79]

By appealing to women, the OIR hoped to accomplish two objectives, which it articulated by placing "two demands" on them. First, it called on women to "encourage your husbands, your brothers and your sons to participate." Second, the group called for them "to take to the streets yourselves," for women's participation would "energize the men and confuse the police. What would they do with women?" the OIR scoffed. "Would they imprison them?"[80] It turned out that they would. In its memorial to the intifada and its victims, published five years later, the OIR acknowledged one woman martyr, Fatima al-Gharib.[81]

After the killing of Hussein al-Qalaf, Saudi leaders finally grasped the seriousness of what was transpiring in the east and understood that force alone would not resolve the conflict. Earlier, it had attempted to pressure local merchants and various well-known persons, believing they could control the masses and rein in the protest. That gambit failed. On November 28, the regime dispatched Deputy Minister of the Interior Ahmad bin Abd al-Aziz to Dammam, who called various local leaders to the principality. According to the OIR, he assumed "a threatening tone," promising more violence if the demonstrations did not cease.[82] In response, those in the "vanguard" of the uprising mailed a letter to the deputy minister with a list of demands to be met before the violence would subside.

They remarked that the embittered crowds persisted in demonstrating as a result of police recklessness. Moreover, they claimed, the masses erupted spontaneously, under neither external nor internal control or planning. In fact, they commented, "The events were greater in severity and violence" than central planning could have produced, and said that without justice, the bloodshed would continue.[83] Justice would entail four concessions, including, first, the freeing of political prisoners apprehended in the course of the uprising and trials for police and wayward National Guardsmen. Second, they demanded religious freedom, an independent judiciary, the right to read and print Shia religious books, and the abolition of sectarian discrimination. Third, they sought an end to the U.S.-Saudi special relationship, reiterating their anti-imperialist position and their deep skepticism of American interests and ambitions in their country. Fourth, they demanded "that the authorities limit the negligence and manipulation of the interests of the citizens in the region, as the people live in terrible conditions and . . . continuous problems [result] from the crisis of the community and services . . . If the government is serious in treating the problem, then the street will be cleared."[84] The state's response to the list of demands is unknown, although the security forces did partially withdraw and as a result limited the opportunity for further violence.

In the closing days of the violence and in the weeks that followed, the OIR also used its power to communicate with outside groups, sharing the brutal details of what had transpired and trying to call global attention to the events. In addition to communicating with the outside world, including the United Nations and various press agencies, the group printed and circulated documents and materials it received from abroad. Along with encouraging support from Saudi Shia students in Iran, the OIR circulated the text of two telegrams from Ayatollah al-Shirazi, who lionized the protestors and condemned the brutality and "criminality" of the Saudi security forces.[85] Al-Shirazi's communication with the OIR leadership certainly reflected Iran's interest in events inside Saudi Arabia, and vice versa, but it did not indicate that the ayatollah played a role in coordinating or organizing the uprising in the kingdom. Most important, it seems, the OIR leadership believed that the telegrams from al-Shirazi extended legitimacy to their own efforts and thus validated their independence and abilities. It is clear that the Iranian example—its success as well as elements of Khomeini's message—resonated in Saudi Arabia. The terms of revolt in the kingdom, however, reflected local experience and concerns. The passion and power of the OIR's message aside, it is difficult to precisely determine the extent to which the community responded specifically to its call. The early turnout of 4,000 mourners on November 26 demonstrates considerable support. Tens of thousands responded to the violent turn of events on November 28, however, signifying that the masses took to the streets in reaction to state brutality.

While the OIR demonstrated leadership and vision, it was not alone in the Eastern Province. Alongside the Islamists, leftist nationalists expressed their views during the uprising as well. Importantly, however, non-Islamist elements also responded to the initial call to action. They had not been consulted by the Islamists and were unaware of what was to come. At least in the first few days, leftists did not exhibit leadership on the same scale as the OIR. The organizational contribution of the leftists seems to have been limited, with the biggest push coming after the most dramatic waves of violence in November—although, without question, they did participate in the uprising. The best sources available for the leftists' involvement comes from the efforts of the Communist Party of Saudi Arabia to collect and distribute details of the uprising. These include several eyewitness accounts as well as documents produced by other leftist organizations, such as the Committee for the Defense of Human Rights in Saudi Arabia, the Union of Democratic Youth, the Workers' Committee, the League of Democratic Women, the League of Students in Saudi Arabia, and a more loosely organized group that emerged during the uprising, calling itself the Assembly of Saudi Citizens. Several of these groups had a long history of leftist activity in the kingdom, and particularly in the Eastern Province. The Workers' Committee was formed in 1953, after the first strike by Arab employees of Aramco, although the Saudi regime's crackdown on its leadership in the late 1950s had curtailed its activities.[86] Some of the others had roots in organizations such as the Popular Democratic Party, which formed in the late 1960s and early 1970s. The Communist Party in Saudi Arabia took shape in 1975, born from earlier unions of laborers at Aramco.

These various organizations did not claim responsibility for generating mass dissent nor for leading events on the ground in November. The Communist Party's narrative argues that "the democratic forces tried to encourage the religious groups to not raise signs and slogans possessing a sectarian character . . . as it believed the regime would use it as a pretext for justifying oppression." The clerics refused to cooperate with the leftists according to the Communists who reported that "attempts were made to coordinate the two sets of forces [religious and leftist]. However, the religious leaders forbade this from the beginning, [believing] that their cooperation with politically progressive parties and organizations would bring them harm and that they alone were able to lead the events and what was facing them."[87] As a result, the leftist groups proceeded to participate independently, taking to the streets without local guidance or any specific objective. They carried their own banners, calling for the "fall of the Carter-Begin-Sadat alliance" and the repeal of Camp David. Others included nationalist slogans, such as "Through a free nation will the people find true happiness" and "Down with Khalid, Fahd, and Abdullah, the agents of imperialism."[88] Throughout the period of unrest, according to subsequent reporting, the leftists sought to emphasize the popular character of the uprising, all the while sympathizing with its anti-imperial and anti-American tone. During the first phase of events, in November and early December, it is clear that religious forces dominated the call to action and shaped the course of action. In the weeks and months that followed, however, the "progressive democratic" forces left their mark as well.

Throughout December the leftists coordinated and spearheaded various efforts to petition the government to address the social and political ills in the east and complaints about the violence of November. They pursued two sets of objectives. First, they implored the king to "lift the restrictions, pressures, and sectarian practices against the Shia and to grant them their religious rights." They beseeched the regent to end "the fraud and injustice against the people of Qatif" and to grant them equal rights alongside "the Sunna in every field of employment." In particular, they called for opportunities for educated Shiites, who held university degrees, to take positions in their respective fields of training, for "it is well known that not one of them [occupies] a position of responsibility in local government administration such as the Municipality, traffic police, and others." Second, the petitioners called for "scientific planning in developing Qatif and its villages, which are the worst of cities and regions. This includes the complete development of agriculture, which in the past played a vital role in providing the country with vegetables and fruit, as well as of the services and health sectors."[89] The petitions pointed out that many of the region's residents lived in squalid conditions and collapsing homes, which the petitioners blamed on greedy real estate speculation by the authorities. According to the CDHR, the government declared in response that it intended to form a committee to investigate the claims, to which a citizen reportedly remarked, "We the people of Qatif do not want paper projects, for we are sick and tired of promises and planning. All we want is the preservation of our spirit, our customs, and our honor."[90] As for the violence, the state pinned the blame for the deaths during the uprising on the protesters themselves, claiming that their action had "forced" the security forces to fire on them in self-defense.

The implications of the uprising resonated widely, both inside and outside the kingdom. The protests and violence of 1979–80 forced the regime to reflect on its domestic policies toward the minority Shiites, although little changed. Saudi Shiites did not rise up again in mass protest, reflecting their fear of another crackdown, improved state oversight of the community, and the absence of local political leaders (they fled the kingdom in the early 1980s). The OIR moved its operations to Damascus and London, where it published a monthly newsletter until the late 1980s. Much of the organization's critical gaze continued to focus on the uneven distribution of oil wealth and the toll of what it continued to call Saudi imperialism. And in spite of the government's claims that it would address the social, political, and environmental concerns of Shiites, activists abroad and at home continued to point out that little had changed, well into the twenty-first century.

The uprising captured the attention of foreign observers, who, after long neglecting the fate of the Shiites in the oil kingdom, "discovered" in the events of 1979 something exceptional and powerful, a compelling story that seemed to speak to various domestic, regional, and global forces. Yet interpretations of the event have proved wide-ranging. While Shiites in Saudi Arabia were responding to and were inspired by regional events, they were not instruments of Iranian influence or a fifth column for Khomeini's revolutionary regime. Claims of irredentism are well wide of the mark and do little to explain the local factors that mobilized rebellion. Various observers have argued that ideology drove the violence, or that social and economic conditions accounted for the despair and the eventual course of events. The truth is that both factors figured greatly in the calculus of events and that important complexities and contingencies accounted for the route of the uprising and the violence that it generated. Although the violence was sparked by the regime and its handling of the Ashura ceremonies, the intifada proved to be of mixed character. Sectarian tensions aside, the uprising was not only about social despair or the "generic" suffering of the poor masses. It emerged from a specific kind of dislocation born of Saudi Arabia's experience with oil, and the government's mismanagement of oil wealth. More specifically, and what many observers have missed, is that the uprising was also a rebellion against a government that claimed that its power and credibility flowed from its ability to manage nature.

For its part, sensing the potential long-term threat of a radicalized minority in its midst, particularly one in the oil-rich Eastern Province, the royal family was driven to plot a political course that would protect its interests above all else. Saudi rulers' sense of anxiety about the tenuous nature of their power was challenged not only by the Shia uprising but also by a second incident that occurred on the other side of the country, in the holy city of Mecca. In November 1979 a group of Sunni Islamists, led by the rebel Juhayman al-Utaybi, stormed and occupied the Mecca mosque, Islam's holiest site, for more than two weeks. They justified their siege by charging the royal family with apostasy and failing to uphold strict Islamic values. Like the Shiites, Juhayman and his followers claimed that their anger was the result of frustration about the process of modernization that had taken place in the kingdom in the heyday of oil. In part, their disillusion followed from the failure of development to achieve its objective of providing material comfort for all. But the Mecca rebels were motivated more by a profound sense of spiritual alienation. Where rioting Shiites expressed anger that they had been left behind, those who stormed the Mecca mosque believed that development and the rapid accumulation of wealth had led the Saudi leaders to forsake the conservative Islamic principles that were supposed to be embodied in and protected by the state.[91] Their political protest was in many ways a protest against development and the creation of the Saudi technostate that had taken shape over the course of the twentieth century. They claimed, contrary to the government's narrative, that science and technology were not compatible with Islam.

Fearful that the uprising might spark even more widespread outrage, the Saudis responded by co-opting the message of the radicals and laboring to renew their Islamic credentials by spending large amounts of revenue in the 1980s on religious institutions, universities, and programs. Saudi leaders also exerted considerable effort in encouraging and promoting an elite coterie of highly visible religious scholars and clergy who rose to prominence and popularity. And most notably, Saudi Arabia supported the jihad in Afghanistan as a means to restore its credibility. Although the country's leaders had always used Islam to justify the political order and especially their own political power, in the 1980s Islam became increasingly politicized.[92]

The Islamic turn marked a partial departure from the politics of development. Saudi leaders continued to celebrate their own role in leading the kingdom on the path to progress, but they articulated the terms more carefully, particularly regarding the moral values that development was supposed to embody. The century-long obsession with controlling nature and using science and technology as instruments of political control also continued to be a priority. But increasingly in the 1980s the Saudi government diverted considerable sums of its oil revenue to building up austere Islamic institutions at home and abroad. In adopting the message of Sunni radicals, the royal family deflated the power of its rivals and redirected its ideological program so that it was more in line with the potentially powerful conservative forces at home. The impact on environmental policy and politics would be profound.

7

The year 1979 and the events that shook the kingdom marked a turning point in Saudi Arabia's domestic affairs. In the aftermath of the twin uprisings in Mecca and the Eastern Province, Saudi leaders pursued new paths in securing their political authority at home. Oil continued to play a vital role, but revenues were directed in new ways to meet what leaders perceived to be growing threats. Controlling nature and the country's natural resources, and using the abundance of oil to create new sources of water, retained a heavy emphasis. But while managing and remaking the environment remained a source of political power, the political role that water, agriculture, and land played was transformed. Scientists and engineers continued to enjoy considerable influence after 1979. And state leaders continued to view technology and technology-driven development as part of their overall program for managing the kingdom and projecting its power. However, the part that technology, scientists, and engineers played in the political administration of the kingdom shifted considerably during the 1980s. Most notably, Saudi leaders set aside the suggestion, partially cultivated in the 1960s and 1970s, that the country's identity—what it meant to be Saudi—was connected to being modern, to science, and to the effective use of technology in promoting the social and economic welfare of Saudi subjects. Instead, under pressure and confronted with criticism that the royal family had been swept up in the materialism and excess generated by its vast oil wealth, Saudi Arabia's rulers turned their attention in the 1980s to cultivating anew the image of themselves as Islamic leaders and the image of Saudi Arabia as an Islamic state. The technostate remained, as did the centrality of the environment to political authority, but the political logic of both would be reconfigured in the 1980s.

THE RETURN TO FAITH

The violent uprisings in 1979 generated deep anxiety among the ruling elite as well as doubt about the continued security of the existing political order. Along with the protests in the Eastern Province in 1979 and the lingering enmity they fostered between the Al Saud and the kingdom's Shiites, the occupation of the Grand Mosque in Mecca by Sunni rebels that November, led by Juhayman al-Utaybi, constituted an existential crisis for the ruling family.[1] To some extent both events represented responses to the influx of oil money and the programs it financed. For the Shiites, the uprising was an expression of anger at having been left out. Oil, the wealth it generated, and the development programs it made possible either exacerbated social tensions in Shia communities or were withheld from them altogether. Violence followed. For the followers of Juhayman, the decision to take hostage one of Islam's holiest sites reflected deep unease about the social and cultural toll of oil wealth. The oil-fueled frenzy that marked the 1970s, from the massive spending on development programs to the gluttony of garish consumerism, stoked fears among the most zealous Muslims that the kingdom was poised to forsake its faith in favor of Western-style materialism.[2] The rapid transformations wrought by oil alienated as many as it enriched, partly through exclusion but also partly through disillusion. Not everyone proved enamored of wealth or able to access the oil riches in the ways they wished. Anxiety and violence in Mecca and Qatif set in motion a profound political transformation.

Saudi Arabia's rulers responded to both uprisings harshly, using overwhelming force to crush the Shiites as well as Juhayman and his rebels.[3] The military mobilization lasted well beyond the events themselves while the government bolstered its domestic police forces as well as its intelligence capabilities in order to ward off future threats. In addition to ramping up surveillance and police powers, the country's rulers moved to counter the different ideological forces it believed were behind the criticisms against it. Although the country's Shiites were primarily motivated by domestic grievances, the rise of Shia Iran as a regional power in 1979, and especially the rise of the anti-Saudi Ayatollah Khomeini, who advocated the overthrow of the Al Saud and sought to export his revolutionary philosophy to Iran's neighbors, provided the primary lens through which leaders interpreted the uprisings in Saudi Arabia.[4] Countering the perceived Khomeini threat internally became a key part of Saudi domestic policy.[5] Saudi Arabia became a hotbed of anti-Shiism and anti-Khomeiniism in the 1980s, with the government encouraging and subsidizing clerical sermons against Shiism as well as the production of an array of anti-Shia tracts.[6]

Juhayman al-Utaybi posed a different kind of ideological threat than Khomeini, although he and his followers were just as hostile to the ruling family and the contemporary political state of affairs. He mounted a frontal assault on the very credibility of the Saudi royal family by challenging their commitment to Islam and Al Saud's legitimacy as head of an Islamic state.[7] At the heart of Juhayman's message was the complaint that the Saudis had too openly embraced Western-style modernity and had moved too far away from the religious principles that were supposed to make up the foundation of a true Islamic state. Oil and money demolished the family's and the government's resolve to resist the temptation of materialism, breeding moral corruption and devastating religious sensibilities. Juhayman argued not only that oil-fueled modernization had led to the displacement of Islamic values, but also, and worse, that oil allowed for the subordination of religious scholars as minor players in the political system. By the late 1970s the scholars, who had played an important role in mustering support for the Saudis in the first two decades of the century, had been enfolded in what one Middle East historian calls "an amoeba-like embrace" by the Al Saud, and rendered mostly powerless. As early as the 1950s, he writes, "the *'ulama* were firmly in their place as paid civil servants, hired and fired by the king."[8] After the bureaucratization of the religious scholars, "religion remained a central element in state discourse and ideology, although the authority of religious leaders was highly restricted. Saudi rulers recognized, or at least maintained, that their authority derived from Wahhabi principles, even if few of its monarchs were openly pious or faithful."[9] For Juhayman this represented a monumental departure from—indeed a corruption of—the historic partnership that had enabled the Al Saud to conquer the Arabian Peninsula and establish their suzerainty earlier in the century. He also blasted the religious scholars for their part in creating a morally corrupted political system. He criticized the ulama for their uncritical submissiveness to the Saudi regime and for not advocating more openly and willfully for the creation of an Islamic state administered by religious scholars and based on Islamic law.

The events of 1979 sent a powerful signal to the Saudis that they were dangerously vulnerable. They had been caught completely off guard by the nature of the threats and, worse, were unsure how deep the anti-Saudi sentiment ran. The kingdom's leaders agonized over the possibility that there were more than a few potential Juhaymans lurking in hidden corners, plotting revolution. So fearful were they about the possible appeal of Juhayman that they used especially brutal means to send the message that any dissent would be dealt with harshly. After the security forces had ousted the rebels from the mosque, those who were captured were sent to cities around the country where they were beheaded in public executions.

Particularly unnerving for the Saudis, given the historic religio-political alliance that made their rule possible, was the fact that the insurgents who occupied the Grand Mosque brandished an austere Islamic message as an instrument to challenge Saudi power. While the Saudis mobilized ideologically against Khomeini, and provided massive amounts of material aid to Saddam Hussein and the Iraqis in their war against Iran, they responded to Juhayman's challenge by reinventing their approach to managing the domestic political arena. The shift in domestic political strategy came about under the leadership of King Fahd, and it was profound.[10] Fahd sought to reinforce his family's legitimacy and security "by appropriating the power of Islam" and reinventing the Al Saud's religious credentials.[11] In doing so, he sought to undermine the potential appeal of Juhayman's and other critics' anti-Saudi messages by co-opting them. The scale of the effort to revitalize Saudi Arabia as an Islamic state was massive. Still flush with billions of dollars in oil revenue in the early 1980s, the government undertook extensive measures to cast itself as Islamic and to remake the public sphere along the same lines.

Although the effort to reinvent itself was partly an effort to strengthen the royal family's political bona fides, it was also part of a process in which the government reinvented the nature of its relationship to its subjects as well as the principles according to which Saudi citizenship would be determined. Whereas King Faisal had earlier called for Saudi citizens to serve themselves and the nation by pursuing development, embracing science, and carrying out the work of progress to build a foundation for material prosperity, the post-1979 framework for belonging in Saudi Arabia would once again be based on adhering closely to the principles of Wahhabi Islam and recognizing the absolute moral and political authority of the royal family. Government authorities enforced the new framework by expanding the power of the religious police, who imposed a strict moral code on the Saudi public by drawing attention to and punishing those who abrogated the principles of Wahhabism. The government also expanded the network of Islamic institutions that came to dominate the civic sphere in the 1980s and afterward. In particular, Saudi leaders oversaw the construction of new madrasas (religious schools) and universities, which "fostered a new generation of sheikhs, professors and students," leading to a widespread Islamic resurgence.[12] Gwenn Okruhlik, a scholar of Islamist political trends in Saudi Arabia, has noted that "by 1986, over 16,000 of the kingdom's 100,000 students were pursuing Islamic Studies. By the early 1990s, one-fourth of all university students were enrolled in religious institutions. They had ideas and resources: intellectuals, computers, fax machines, libraries and everything necessary for mobilization. This generation of students serves as bureaucrats, policemen, *mutawwaʿ*, *shariʾah* judges, or preachers in some twenty thousand mosques in the country."[13]

The implications for Saudi Arabia's political order were far-reaching as religious leaders assumed greater power. But while the role of scientists, engineers, and technology faded from public view, their importance did not. The government continued to pursue modernization schemes and limited infrastructural and technological development, although its ability to do so would be limited by the mid-1980s, when the price of oil collapsed and restricted its ability to finance the kind of projects it had bankrolled only a few years before. In the last two decades of the century "development planning," complete with the uninterrupted composition, publication, and implementation of the five-year development plans that first appeared in 1970, remained a central part of domestic policymaking. The government continued to pursue technological and scientific matters, but it did so more discreetly. The symbolic power that the state had previously placed on modernization was modified. Government leaders backed away from emphasizing the values that they had previously argued were bound up with being modern, as they had become a political liability. State officials saw peril in attaching themselves and the identity of the regime to anything that smacked of Westernization and Western values, especially since the rejection of Westernization was at the heart of Juhayman's rebellion. More intensively than in any other period in its history, and at the expense of all other considerations, Saudi Arabia played up and embellished its Islamic credentials. Oil, which had always been described as one of God's blessings on the kingdom, would now be used to do God's work.

Saudi leaders continued to celebrate their own role in leading the kingdom on the path to progress, but they articulated the terms more carefully, particularly regarding the moral values that development was supposed to embody. Development became less about technological progress and more about moral and religious progress. In 1983, King Fahd delivered a policy speech in which he declared,

> The State is composed of a population and a Government that represents and works for the well-being of the people. A nation may attain its aspirations and achieve the goals of advancement it has set for itself through the efforts and struggle of its people. Yours is a responsibility of great significance in the eyes of Allah, and your prospects for constructive work are bright. Therefore, hold fast to your ideals and values, and never slacken your pace . . . An enormous responsibility falls on the shoulders of our young men, in particular since they are the pillars of construction at present and the masterminds of further development in the future. They owe it to themselves and their heritage not to imitate the lost youth in the West and not resign themselves to lascivious pleasures, lest they fall into the abyss of nothingness.[14]

The state continued to finance development projects and pursued, at least rhetorically, the diversification of the economy. And the state continued to provide assistance to farmers and to encourage agricultural production and expansion, although its priorities shifted from encouraging small farming to supporting large industrial farms, which were often owned by members of the royal family. The century-long obsession with controlling nature and using science and technology as instruments in political control also continued to be a priority. The provision of water to citizens in major cities as well as in smaller village outposts persisted as a key concern. Most important, geology and especially geological efforts to locate unknown and untapped sources of oil continued to be viewed by Saudi officials as being of paramount concern.

The reorientation of the domestic political strategy in the early 1980s had important effects on how oil wealth was used, what kinds of programs were funded, and whose interests were served. Some key elements of the old political order went unchanged. The institutions that had been created during the period from the 1950s to the 1970s remained the important parts of the bureaucratic machinery that bound citizens to the state and projected state power into communities across the country, particularly the ministries that oversaw agriculture, water, and electricity. Even though it traded the ideology of Islamic modernity for that of Islamic austerity, the state continued to spend money on large technological projects when it could, especially when it came to maintaining and extending its centralized control over nature. By the 1980s the Ministry of Agriculture and Water had overseen the construction of more than two hundred dams—in a country with no rivers or lakes. And the country spent billions of dollars in oil revenue—effectively turning oil into water—in building massive desalination plants. More than twenty of them were constructed along the Red Sea and Persian Gulf coasts. But tapping water from the desert or from the sea, and the provision of agricultural loans, tools, seeds, and encouragement were not only instruments of political dominance; they were also packaged as part of the relationship that the state was *supposed* to exhibit toward those over whom it ruled. Service, formerly defined as a mutually beneficial relationship between ruler and ruled, was redefined in mostly functional terms: the state provided services as part of its contract with its citizens. Although the state no longer focused on the modern symbolism of its technopolitical practices, administrative and political officials understood that Saudi Arabian citizens still demanded the provision of services such as cheap electricity and water.

Some of the uglier aspects of Saudi policy also remained, particularly in the Eastern Province, home to so much angst and frustration about past patterns of neglect and abuse. After the uprising in 1979, the government indicated that it wished to address the social and environmental roots of Shiite violence, and implied that its failure to share the oil wealth was to blame for the violence. In response to the demands of the rebels, Saudi leaders undertook efforts to ameliorate the social despair of residents in Qatif and surrounding areas. In early December, for example, local administrators in Qatif came up with 700 million Saudi riyals for a new sewage network.[15] Ten days later, the Ministry of Agriculture and Water committed 3.25 million riyals to an experimental farm in Qatif.[16] On December 11, a 39-million-riyal project was announced to improve Qatif's streets.[17] And Al-Hasa was not ignored. That same week, the oasis's governor announced 1 billion riyals for various projects.[18] While these efforts underscored that the government understood the problem, they were nevertheless underwhelming. One observer, Jacob Goldberg, noted that "a comprehensive plan was launched, aimed at improving the living standards of the Shiite population. It included an electricity project, the re-asphalting of streets, new schools for boys and girls, a new hospital, the draining of large areas of swamps, and projects for additional street lighting, sewage, and communications. Perhaps most important," he wrote, "the government decided to provide loans, through the Real Estate Development Fund, to town residents to build new homes for themselves."[19] It is tempting to conclude that Shiites' passivity reflected their satisfaction with the government's efforts. Citing a trip by King Khalid to Qatif and al-Hasa the next year around Ashura, and the friendliness with which Qatif community leaders and the regent interacted, Goldberg concluded that "it seemed that the desire to mend fences was mutual. While the government realized that it had to reassess its policies toward the Shiite population, the Shiites on their side felt that they had to reevaluate the situation, given the new Saudi attitude."[20] Citing their subsequent attitudes and willingness to cooperate with the regime, Goldberg remarked that "once these issues started to be dealt with, the Shiites became satisfied and abandoned any idea of challenging or confronting the Saudi regime."[21]

Shared resolve to overcome the social imbalances that helped generate violence did not mark an end to discriminatory political practices. The Saudi will to develop the Shia areas, while certainly beneficial, was a stopgap measure aimed at deflating the immediate causes of protest, rather than a long-term commitment to the social welfare of the communities. Although the initial efforts to uplift the depressed areas were promising, the regime did not persist in its commitment. Very little of the state's oil fortune made its way into Shia communities, even after the uprising. Then, in 1986, the price of oil collapsed dramatically, marking an end to the kingdom's record profits. While oil continued to bring in considerable wealth, the government was forced to rein in much of its spending, meaning that the overlooked areas continued to be neglected. By the end of the 1980s, grievances about social problems and environmental crises, such as the lack of water in the al-Hasa oasis, endured. Many of the revolutionaries, almost all of whom had gone into hiding in exile, continued to brand the government as an imperial power and to charge it with the theft of "Shia" natural resources, including oil and water. Their anger was understandable. Discrimination persisted, in Shiites' limited access to jobs, education, travel, and resources. Security forces continued to harass and terrorize local residents throughout 1980, and the heavy security presence no doubt accounted for the passing of the 1980 Ashura season in relative quiet.[22] While the regime did release more than one hundred Shia political prisoners on the eve of the holiday in 1980, many hundreds more had fled the country, preferring exile to the prevailing conditions in the kingdom.[23]

Perhaps the most misleading claim related to the newfound Saudi benevolence is that it worked to assist Shiites in accumulating new real estate and constructing new homes. The Committee for the Defense of Human Rights recounted that in an "attempt to soak up the vengeance" of local Shiites, the Saudi authorities announced on January 22, through the municipality, that it was "distributing applications for ownership of land to those citizens who owned neither land nor home. On January 23 hundreds of people gathered near the Municipality of Qatif to obtain their applications." Given that useful land was scarce in the municipality, there were limited numbers of applications and therefore little land to be distributed. In an alleged act of duplicity on the part of the state, police and intelligence officers reportedly stood in line and, upon the opening of the office, rushed in with local citizens and absconded with hundreds of applications, depriving many of the opportunity to become landowners.[24]

True or not, the story reflects a basic distrust on the part of locals for state representatives, indicating that the allegedly mutual desire to settle hostility was fantasy. In interviews with local citizens twenty-five years after the intifada, many residents said they refused to apply for land, as they suspected the program was an attempt to break up the contiguity and integrity of the community and thus make it easier for the central state to monitor and control affairs there.[25]

The community's suspicion of the government's good intentions was not unfounded. In the aftermath of the uprising, the government razed Qatif's historic downtown [*qal'a*], in whose maze local rebels had holed up and held off security forces for days during the uprising. The destruction of the old city was viewed with deep anger and as a violation of the community's identity and spirit. For those who owned property there, what followed was even more frustrating. In 1980 a committee was put in place to iron out the financial settlements for those who had lost their homes, shops, and property. According to Hamza al-Hassan, the committee did not include any former landowners. In the end, the committee determined former owners would be recompensed for half the actual value of the land, much to their outrage. In 1981, in response to what they understandably perceived as unfair treatment, owners organized and presented nine different petitions demanding redress of the situation. As a result, Minister of the Interior Prince Nayif responded by outlawing community petitions.[26] Five years later the issue was still not resolved and the former landowners had yet to receive their compensation. On November 15, 1985, the group of owners sent a note to the governor of the Eastern Province complaining that the local court still "would not accept the registration of our property [*awqafna*] and will not return our heritage [*irthna*]."[27]

HARVESTING SECURITY

While it appeared that Saudi policy had gone mostly unchanged, Saudi Arabia's pursuit of mastery over nature, especially with respect to agricultural policy, did undergo a significant restructuring in the

1980s. The approach changed most notably in 1979, as the government intensified the pursuit of agricultural self-sufficiency in order to achieve "food security" and sought to end, once and for all, Saudi dependency on foreign food imports. The shift in focus was partially the result of the failure of earlier policies. Urbanization had proceeded rapidly, and after the early 1970s agriculture's percentage of the kingdom's GDP lagged behind most other sectors. In part this was the result of the oil boom and a reflection of the massive influx of oil revenues into Saudi Arabia's coffers, which overwhelmed the contribution of every other sector in the Saudi economy, including agriculture. But there was also a real decline in the number of Saudis willing to remain on their farms and a corresponding drop in production.[28] In addition to attempting to control the movement of people and the kingdom's urban demography, Saudi leaders and agricultural experts had mostly struggled to expand and intensify existing farming patterns and output in order to wean the country off foreign food imports. From the 1960s, the state had built dams, extended loans, and imported new technologies to perfect and expand cultivation that already existed, such as the growing of dates in the oases of the Eastern Province. Alongside the massive efforts to make "traditional" farms and farmers more efficient and productive, agricultural planners engaged in agricultural experimentation, including attempts to diversify the crops being grown and programs to stimulate the raising of livestock for domestic consumption. Most failed. Saudi Arabia remained almost totally dependent on food imports well into the 1970s.

In the late 1970s and 1980s, oil-rich Saudi planners determined to guide the kingdom to agricultural self-sufficiency. One observer noted that there was a strategic rationale behind the drive to self-sufficiency, noting that Saudi planners feared "that food exports to Saudi Arabia might some day be cut off by Western countries in order to pressure Saudi Arabia to change its oil policies."[29] While geopolitical considerations likely played a role in the restructuring of Saudi agricultural policy, the stated desire for food security and self-sufficiency was not altogether new, although the fact that the Saudis appeared financially capable of making it happen was. Perhaps not surprisingly, the Saudi government failed to meet its objective. In fact, by the mid-1980s it appeared that agricultural policy was still primarily oriented toward political rather than economic goals. What changed was that while agriculture remained an area in which the government sought to demonstrate its ability to master nature and project power, agricultural and hydrological policies became primarily oriented toward enriching members of the royal family and their allies. The political logic that had dominated efforts to know and harness nature in previous decades, as another means by which to redistribute oil wealth, gave way during the oil boom. But unlike other facets of the welfare state that were built after 1973, such as public health facilities and infrastructure, spending on agriculture went to the political and financial elite. Promoting investment in food, while rhetorically tied to concerns with national security, was really about lining the pockets of those close to the government, securing the support of the country's financial elites, and, just as important, reinforcing the total dependence of those elites on oil revenue and the goodwill of the country's leaders.

The most spectacular aspect of post–oil boom agricultural policy was the effort to promote wide-scale wheat cultivation. Given Saudi Arabia's intemperate climate, and particularly its dearth of water resources, wheat was a curious choice. Already straining under the pressure of limited water resources, and with billions of dollars being handed over to build massive desalination plants, the state's commitment to wheat cultivation only added to demands on the available sources of water, requiring as much as 1,300 to 1,500 cubic meters of water for every ton of wheat.[30] A recent observer of Saudi agricultural policies has commented that growing wheat in the desert requires two to three times more water than is used in more temperate environs.[31] Although in reality Saudi Arabia had little hydrological cushion to spare, studies of the country's water resources carried out in the early 1980s apparently convinced the kingdom's leaders that more water was available from underground aquifers than they had previously believed, emboldening the government to press ahead with the ambitious wheat-cultivation program.[32] For a time, the program performed impressively well. In 1971 wheat production totaled only 74,000 tons.[33] That number grew dramatically. From 1980 to 1992 production skyrocketed from 142,000 tons of wheat to 4.1 million, an amount that overwhelmed domestic demand and the country's storage capacity.[34] The kingdom proved so productive that Saudi Arabia became a net exporter, selling or donating wheat to neighboring states as well as to places as far afield as republics of the former Soviet Union in the 1990s.[35] For a time, Saudi Arabia ranked as the world's sixth-largest wheat exporter. The effect on the domestic agricultural sector was dramatic, leading to 12 percent growth in agricultural production in the 1980s.[36]

Saudi Arabia's success owed little to market forces. Growing wheat in such amounts was made possible only with considerable subsidies for wheat farmers and through the building of massive systems to pump, store, and irrigate with water from the country's ancient—and nonrenewable—underground aquifers. The government announced in 1979 that it would purchase wheat from Saudi farmers at three to six times the price of imported wheat, and it created the Grain Silos and Four Mills Organization (GSFMO) to manage domestic procurement. At the start of the program the government guaranteed every wheat farmer the price of 3,500 Saudi riyals (more than US$900) for every ton of wheat grown. In the period from 1980 to 2005 the country spent an estimated $85 billion, 18 percent of the revenue it generated from the sale of oil, on growing wheat. In 2005 the government continued to guarantee a price of $500 per ton of wheat, while the same amount in international markets fetched $120. In addition to the money, the environmental cost of wheat cultivation was very high. In the first twenty years of the program, authorities devoted more than 300 billion cubic meters of water to irrigating wheat farms, which the economist Elie Elhadj likens to the equivalent of six years' flow of the Nile River. The scale of Saudi water consumption was staggering considering its lack of resources. In 1980, as the wheat program was getting off the ground, the country consumed a little more than 3 million cubic meters of water for various purposes, including agriculture. Over the next fourteen years, it consumed 140 billion cubic meters. More than two-thirds of all the water used since 1980 has been nonrenewable.[37]

Saudi Arabia did suffer through a few significant hiccups. Budgetary constraints brought on by the drop in the kingdom's oil revenue in the middle of the 1980s forced it to scale back the scope of the program. Production of wheat dropped precipitously following the first Gulf War, from a high of 4 million tons to 1.2 million tons in 1996, when thousands of investors fled from wheat. There were additional financial pressures as well. The Saudi government bankrolled much of the cost of the first Gulf War to drive Saddam Hussein from Kuwait—and plunged the kingdom into debt. Even in the face of being overdrawn, in 1991 the government paid $2.1 billion to Saudi wheat farmers for a crop that was reportedly worth less than $500 million. Financial pressures soon grew too burdensome to sustain past levels of subsidy and support, and Saudi Arabia's fiscal struggles were not helped by the country's extravagant spending on defense and security. Since 1980 the country had spent hundreds of billions of dollars procuring expensive weapons systems, recycling many of its petrodollars back to American military contractors. While wheat production lagged in the late 1990s, the boom in oil prices in 2002 helped turn the wheat program around. By 2005 production numbers had risen again to 2.5 million tons a year, again more than domestic demand.

Although production and growth levels were staggeringly high for more than a decade, in the end wheat farming made little economic sense. Some foresaw the long-term risks in the Saudi program. In 1983 John Rusling Block, the U.S. secretary of agriculture, visited Saudi Arabia and described its agricultural policies as "crazy." Other American officials remarked that the "growing of cereals at an exorbitant cost in the desert makes about as much sense as planting bananas under glass in Alaska."[38] In 2008, the Saudi leaders finally agreed and announced their intent to abandon the project altogether. In January of that year, officials disclosed that they would reduce the subsidies provided to wheat farmers by 12.5 percent per year. By 2016, the government declared, it would become wholly dependent on imports for its wheat and cereal needs. An anonymous government official told one journalist that the "reason is the water resources."[39] The strain on the country's water resources had finally proved too much to bear. Even in the middle of the third oil boom, when prices rose as high as $147 for a barrel of oil, the government announced the end of wheat subsidies because Saudi leaders no longer felt they could justify the environmental costs of growing wheat in the desert.

Even though it was wildly successful in its ability to produce sheer quantities of wheat, Saudi Arabia's project was not designed to reward the average farmer for hard work. And unlike earlier iterations of Saudi agricultural planning, the goals of this government policy had little to do with using state control over nature and natural resources to secure the government's political, institutional, and administrative power. But the wheat program remained a political project, designed to shore up support, and stave off dissent, among merchants and other elites. It is likely that the stated pursuit of agricultural self-sufficiency did factor in the decision to commit vast resources to agriculture. In 1989 the total area under cultivation stood at 1.5 million hectares, more than double the area in 1980. But while more land was being farmed, ownership was consolidated in fewer and fewer hands. According to the U.S. Library of Congress, in 1989 more than 56 percent of the area under cultivation in Saudi Arabia was taken up by more than 7,000 "special projects"—projects owned and operated by members of the royal family, or their political or business allies. More than 67,000 landowners received plots of land that averaged less than 6 hectares each, while seventeen "companies" received over 15,000 hectares each, considerably more than the 400-hectare limit originally imposed on corporate farmers. Clearly, the state's bias was toward larger operations.

It is likely that the vast majority of these companies were owned by extended members of the royal family as well as citizens who maintained close financial and personal relations with them. This is certainly what most Saudis believe. Saudi citizens have interpreted the wheat program as evidence of government excess and see it as a powerful symbol of corruption.[40] Access to subsidies and government support was a key perk for family members and close supporters of the royal family. The Saudi government has long handed out allowances to members of the royal family—as rewards for being part of the ruling crowd. More important, though, the subsidization of agriculture in general, and wheat farming specifically, was just one part, albeit an expensive and particularly visible part, of the post–oil boom political shift in which the government increasingly used its oil wealth to buy and reward continued political support. The government took a large part of the massive amount of money generated in the 1970s and 1980s and created a techno-agricultural network that distributed much of it to its retinue. For decades, oil wealth had been used as a form of patronage, with revenue being redistributed as a means to secure the political authority of the Saudis. The oil boom accelerated this trend, bringing in vast amounts of new revenue with which the government was able to further incentivize cooperation and co-option within Saudi society. Finding ways of redistributing oil revenue further tied commercial, social, and potential political elites to the government, wedding their politico-economic fortunes with that of the state itself. In addition to fattening the wallets of loyal allies, it is likely that the wheat program was designed to buy off potential rivals after the disconcerting events of 1979. Not all critics and would-be dissidents of the regime were Islamist, a fact the Saudis understood well. As a result, many Saudis now believe that the government handed out land and subsidized wheat agriculture partly to buy political support and security for the royal family from those who might have become political rivals.[41]

The government's announcement in 2008 that it was ending the wheat-subsidy program sent a new message, that fears about the fate of the country's fragile water resources were more pressing than handing out patronage to social and commercial elites. Perhaps, after thirty years, Saudi leaders believed that threats of the immediate post-1979 era had passed and that the investors who profited from the program were now as dependent on the government as the government was on them. In some sense, this would mean that efforts to use oil wealth to create overlapping dependencies succeeded. The Saudi government and private investors quickly hinted they were ready to move on.

While the Saudis have set a course at home that depoliticizes land, agriculture, and farming, they have shifted their environmental gaze elsewhere. Amid rising inflation and food costs, Saudi leaders publicly disclosed in 2008 that they were looking to fulfill their agricultural needs abroad, not just by importing food but by using oil wealth to buy land and invest in farming in other countries, such as Mali, Ethiopia, Thailand, Ukraine, Pakistan, Sudan, Turkey, and Egypt.[42] Almost a century after setting out to control and remake their own natural resources, the Saudis are moving on to the next frontier, using oil as a means to create natural fiefdoms abroad. The outsourcing of agriculture is no less political than the patronage-based land politics of the 1970s and 1980s, although some of the dynamics have changed. The quest for "food security" continues to serve as a justification for Saudi agricultural policy. Even as the kingdom decided to end its expensive wheat-subsidy program, the country's leaders were confronted with rising wheat and rice prices in 2008. Fears that prices would escalate further provided the impetus not just to search for food markets in Africa and Asia, but to take possession of vast tracts of foreign land to ensure that Saudi Arabia would own the means of food production. The Saudi government has developed a program, the King Abdullah Initiative for Saudi Agricultural Investment Abroad, that will provide hundreds of millions of dollars in subsidies for private companies to undertake agricultural programs for Saudi Arabia in Africa and elsewhere.[43]

The pursuit of African and Asian farmland has raised considerable concerns. While African governments, in particular, have been eager to sell land at giveaway prices, it is far from certain that Saudi

Arabia will in the end be able to serve its food-security concerns. Many of the new sites of agricultural investment are in countries that have historically struggled to feed themselves, including Sudan and Ethiopia, where famine has ravaged local populations. It remains to be seen how those governments will handle pressures to fill local need if famine threatens indigenous communities while food being grown on sprawling plantations owned by Saudi Arabia is exported abroad. Saudi land purchases have also frustrated local farmers in Ethiopia, who have lost access to traditional grazing and farming land. Already bitter toward local governments for confiscating lands and assuming ownership in the 1970s, new rounds of displacement as the result of land sales to investors from Saudi Arabia have intensified the people's frustration, generating intense political opposition. Further, the new patterns of agricultural investment have invigorated conversations about neo-imperialism. The legacy of colonialism in Africa continues to shape politics in fundamental ways, including fueling distrust of investment by former colonizers in the West. The memory of colonialism, and fears of future expropriation by investors and governments from places like Saudi Arabia, have made the new agricultural land grab potentially dangerous, as locals and their supporters elsewhere fear the emergence of new imperial relations in Africa and wonder about the specter of "land wars" in the future.[44] The political consequences of Saudi Arabia's pursuit of foreign agricultural land and its efforts to conquer nature in Africa and elsewhere are yet to be determined. Saudi political authority is not at stake in the rice paddies of Asia and wheat fields of Africa. It is entirely possible, however, that awakening the ghosts of empire abroad will generate considerable political costs for those regimes doing business with the kingdom, as the Saudis dump their concerns about environmental development and the politics of nature into the laps of foreign leaders. The globalization of Saudi agriculture has not necessarily ended the politics of nature in the kingdom. But, and perhaps more important, it has allowed Saudi Arabia's leaders to distribute the political risks and consequences abroad.

The political authority of the House of Saud has historically been tied to the ruling family's command over Arabia's natural resources. Oil has been the lifeblood of Saudi power since the 1930s, fueling the consolidation of the modern kingdom and providing the wealth that helped finance the political primacy of the Saudi royal family. Other less abundant resources, most notably water, also proved to be vital to the political fortunes of the Saudis. Over the course of the twentieth century, capturing, controlling, engineering, and even making freshwater have been just as important to Saudi political authority as controlling oil. After all, while oil brought in much needed revenue, which served as the financial backbone of the state, water—in short supply in arid Arabia—was the key to life for the millions of people who lived under Saudi rule. Water was also the key to controlling land and agriculture. Although oil wealth helped spur the building of large, sprawling cities in Saudi Arabia and helped transform the kingdom into a place dominated by its urban environments, well into the 1970s most Saudi subjects still remained connected to some form of settled or pastoral farming, dependent on both land and water for their livelihood. Having control over water and land, then, was equivalent to having control over the productive capacities of society, the movement of its people, and the territory of the nation. The conquest of nature, a conquest accomplished through science and technology and through the work of a global network of experts, scientists, and engineers, was linked to the creation of Saudi Arabia's national space, its territoriality, and the relationship that the kingdom's subjects would have to their rulers. Moreover, during the course of the twentieth century the conquest of Arabia's natural resources helped shape the very nature of the state and political authority itself. It was in large part the result of Saudi Arabia's environmental politics that the kingdom was transformed from an empire into a modern authoritarian state.

By the end of the twentieth century, political authority and nature remained closely connected, although the oil boom of the 1970s changed the relationship in important ways. Whereas the Saudis derived political authority from their ability to control and exploit resources like water and land in the first six decades of the twentieth century, after the oil boom water and land were most important as forms of political patronage. The Saudi government built expensive desalination plants, subsidized expensive agricultural projects, and handed out land as patrimony, gifts to the country's citizens, gifts that the Saudis hoped would placate their desire for greater political rights or more direct access to power.

While control over the environment was important to political authority, and while the Saudis succeeded in using their primacy over nature to secure their political fortunes, the environment was also a source of vulnerability. Uneven environmental policies, particularly the inconsistent ways the kingdom distributed oil wealth, alongside the impact of environmental projects opened the central authorities to criticism. Frustration with local and national government was pronounced in the oil- and water-rich Eastern Province, home to the country's large Shia minority. Shiites in the Eastern Province eventually revolted against their Saudi masters in 1979, a rebellion fueled by a combination of revolutionary fervor, environmental activism, and anger at having been left behind in the age of great oil wealth. Radical politics were the exception to the rule, however. Rather, while Saudi Arabia's Shiites drew attention for their violent rejection of Saudi political authority in the late 1970s and throughout the 1980s, community leaders had previously used frustration over environmental degradation in Shia towns and villages to urge Saudi leaders to not only give them increased political rights and ease discrimination, but also to allow them to enjoy equal status as citizens in the Saudi nation. Shiites tapped into ideological currents that emerged in the 1950s and crystallized in the 1960s, in which Saudi leaders increasingly came to link science, the productive use of the environment, technology, and oil to what it meant to be Saudi. At midcentury, authorities at the height of power argued that while Islam and tradition shaped the character and special qualities of nationalism and belonging in Saudi Arabia, so too did development, modernization, and the pursuit of modernity. The uneven implementation of this vision in Shia communities eventually sparked challenges to Saudi political authority.

Rebellion in the Shia community, along with the seizure of Mecca's Grand Mosque in 1979 by Sunni rebels, ultimately compelled the Saudis to pursue an alternate ideological program, and for a while the environment and the importance of science and technology took a backseat. The rise of radical Islamism, in both its Sunni and Shia forms, led Riyadh to renew its own religious credentials and to set aside the public embrace of modernization as a marker of the nation. Instead, Saudi leaders cast their lot with the radicals and co-opted religious austerity as the essence of the nation. The Islamicization of Saudi Arabia over the past thirty years has come at considerable cost for Saudi Arabia's rulers, however. The events of 1979 led to the empowerment of religious scholars in Saudi Arabia, to an extent that was unanticipated and undesired by the kingdom's rulers. There is an axiom among observers of the kingdom that the Al Saud derived its legitimacy from a social and political contract the family forged with religious scholars back in the eighteenth century. And it is true that successive Saudi leaders have been dependent on Wahhabi clergy for credibility. But this relationship has been more fraught and contentious than harmonious.

Over the twentieth century the Al Saud, while acknowledging the importance of Islam and while bestowing upon Wahhabi religious scholars power over spiritual and cultural matters, sought to ensure that the clergy would enjoy limited political power. As they built the modern state, Saudi Arabia's leaders worked to demote the scholars from their position as partners in power to subordinates, institutionalizing them and diminishing their political potential by relegating them to the bureaucracy. By the late 1970s, at the height of the oil boom and the modernization craze, the clergy were at the nadir of their political influence. But the events of 1979 marked the return of Islam as a key part of the kingdom's political identity and political order, and they also marked the triumphant return of the clergy and other religious figures to political influence. As the Saudis attempted to co-opt Islam for their political ends, they became dependent on the clergy for their legitimacy. Over the past three decades, the kingdom's rulers have been at least partially captive to the power of the religious scholars, an undesirable position from the perspective of the royal family.

This relationship has come under pressure in recent years, however. Saudi Arabia's leaders appear to be attempting once again to limit the political influence of the clergy. King Abdullah has led this political gambit, taking on the religious establishment. There are many reasons why Abdullah has taken up the struggle. The terrorist attacks of September 11, 2001, in the United States, in which fifteen of the nineteen airplane hijackers were Saudi citizens, along with a violent al Qaeda campaign in 2003 inside Saudi Arabia itself, motivated the kingdom's leaders to confront religious extremism and to reassert the ultimate political authority of the royal family. This confrontation took multiple forms. Saudi security forces used overwhelming force to crush al Qaeda militants and terrorist networks in the kingdom. During 2003 and 2004 in Saudi Arabia, street clashes and gun battles between terrorists and police erupted frequently. The result was the dismantling of al Qaeda's network and infrastructure in Saudi Arabia, where the kingdom successfully crushed the terrorist group's ability to operate. Overlapping with the intense military crackdown, Saudi leaders launched an intense public relations campaign that aimed to convince citizens that terrorism and al Qaeda threatened the kingdom's security, and more important, that Islamic radicalism represented a form of spiritual deviance and a betrayal of the nation. The state began to promote new ways of thinking about what it meant to be a Saudi, to expand the substance of Saudi nationalism. Where the emphasis after 1979 had been placed on an austere interpretation of Islamic orthodoxy, an interpretation that was exclusivist, sectarian, and destabilizing, Abdullah, both as crown prince and then later as king, began calling for a greater emphasis on dialogue, tolerance, and coexistence.

Saudi leaders also began to challenge the official clergy's primacy over various social and religious matters, further eroding the influence they had gained after 1979. Perhaps most visibly, in February 2009 Abdullah removed Saleh al-Luhaydan, formerly head of the country's judiciary, and Ibrahim al-Ghaith, formerly head of the country's feared religious police, from their posts. The sacking of two of the country's most important and contentious religious figures— al-Luhaydan had embarrassed the kingdom in the fall of 2008 when he issued a religious edict justifying the murder of owners of satellite television stations that broadcast morally questionable content— sent a clear message that Saudi Arabia's leaders had limited tolerance for clerics who challenged Abdullah's new push for dialogue and coexistence.

Political expedience and the possibility that al Qaeda could plunge the kingdom into chaos, a frightening although remote possibility at the height of violence in 2003, explain only part of the motivation for limiting the influence of the clergy. When Abdullah became king in 2005 he was championed by his subjects, as well as by outside observers, as the great hope for political reform in Saudi Arabia. Although his political reformist credentials have been overstated, Abdullah has worked to control some of the excesses and extremist tendencies that characterized politics in the kingdom in the 1990s and the early twenty-first century, by calling for religious tolerance and the loosening of some restrictions on women and even Shiites.[1] It is most likely, however, that Abdullah's political calculus had a much more basic aim than promoting reform, namely to restore the absolute political authority of the royal family and shore up Saudi centralized power.[2] The effect has been the beginning of a process to dismantle the post-1979 political order that brought the clergy its greatest influence since the first part of the twentieth century.

The environment and the kingdom's natural resources have not played a particularly visible role in this transformation. Oil wealth, particularly the massive amounts of revenue generated during the third oil boom that started in 2002, remains critical to maintaining the political order and the Saudis' grip on power. And water also remains important to Saudi political authority, although its importance is mostly as a form of patronage, as water is subsidized and provided to Saudi citizens as a basic component of the welfare state. Agriculture's connection to domestic political authority diminished significantly with the decision to end state subsidies. However, while the politics of nature and Saudi Arabia's environmental policies have undergone a considerable transformation, science, technology, and development have once again emerged as politically important. Specifically, King Abdullah has pointed to science and technology as areas in which the kingdom should aim to become relevant globally and at home. The most visible symbol of the renewed emphasis on science and technology is a sprawling new research university dedicated to the pursuit of scientific knowledge and achievement.

On September 23, 2009, Saudi Arabia celebrated with great pomp and circumstance the grand opening of the King Abdullah University of Science Technology (KAUST). King Abdullah heralded the new university, which overlooks the Red Sea near Jidda, as a new House of Wisdom, a reference to the great library and research center founded in ninth-century Baghdad. It was in Baghdad at the original House of Wisdom that Arab scholars made seminal contributions to the advancement of science, agriculture, medicine, and mathematics. The great center of learning was destroyed in the thirteenth century by Mongol invaders. At the launch of Saudi Arabia's newest scientific endeavor, Abdullah personally invoked the original. His statement, published on KAUST's Web page, reads, "Wishing to rekindle and spread the great and noble virtue of learning that has marked the Arab and Muslim worlds in earlier times, I am establishing King Abdullah University of Science and Technology on the Red Sea in the Kingdom of Saudi Arabia." By linking the long history of Arab scientific achievement to the kingdom and attempting to make Saudi Arabia the future site of an Arab scientific renaissance, the king sent a powerful message about what he views as Saudi Arabia's path forward. He also used the opening of the new university as an opportunity to emphasize his claims for tolerance and coexistence, stating that "the University shall be a beacon for peace, hope, and reconciliation and shall serve the people of the Kingdom and benefit all the peoples of the world in keeping with the teachings of the Holy Quran, which explains that God created mankind in order for us to come to know each other."[3]

The opening of KAUST also figures into the ongoing conversation in Saudi Arabia about what constitutes the substantive and symbolic nature of the nation. The king has deliberately facilitated a dialogue about the Saudi nation. His focus on science and technology, and his use of oil wealth to build up local expertise, which the king hopes will ultimately help the kingdom diversify its economy, establish a foundation for a future after oil, and make Saudi Arabia internationally competitive in science, are signals that these areas should figure prominently in how both Saudis and outsiders think about the kingdom.

While the new university has figured and will figure prominently as a symbol for the new and more open Saudi nation, its basic political role fits squarely within Abdullah's push to marginalize the clergy, undermine religious extremism, and reconsolidate the authority of the ruling family. The king made it clear that the university represents a kind of neutral physical space inside Saudi Arabia. As a major research institution, KAUST was created to bring in foreign scientists and experts and to support their work. But it was also founded to encourage Saudi citizens to pursue scientific and technical study and to allow them to do so without interference from religious scholars or authorities. This was made most clear by Abdullah's demand that men and women at the university, students, faculty, and staff, not be subject to the same rules that govern gender elsewhere in the country. Most important, this meant that men and women would be able to mix freely, that they would not be bound by the restriction of gender segregation that predominates outside campus walls. The issue proved immediately controversial. In October 2009, just a few days after KAUST's opening ceremony, Abd al-Aziz al-Shethri, a prominent cleric and a member of the Council of Senior Ulama, the highest religious authority in the kingdom, criticized coeducation and the mixing of men and women at the new university, remarking that to allow this was forbidden in the land that was home to Islam's two holiest sites. Al-Shethri also called for the creation of a committee to make sure that instruction at KAUST complied with Islamic law. King Abdullah immediately sacked al-Shethri, publicly rebuking him for criticizing KAUST, its mission, and, by implication, the king himself.

The university's political role also has some historical resonance. King Faisal made similar statements in the 1960s and 1970s about the important role that science and technology needed to play in shaping the character and direction of the kingdom. At the height of Saudi Arabia's first modernization push, the country's leaders outlined a similar vision for how the kingdom could and would become modern. Rhetorically, at least, Faisal and others emphasized the need to balance the pursuit of modernity with traditional values, to hold fast to the Islamic foundations of society while pursuing scientific and technological achievement. Abdullah has decided on a similar trajectory, even establishing a permanent religious endowment *(waqf)* for KAUST, making it both a scientific and a religious institution. Abdullah's call for scientific and technical achievement balanced with fidelity to "tradition" marks a return to an earlier era in which the management of science and technology was not only an important instrument of domestic statecraft but also a public symbol of the state's authority and its ability to govern, to rule. Science, technology, and development projects were manifestations of centralized power. And by suggesting that untended, scientific and technical development could somehow threaten Islamic values, Faisal in the 1960s and Abdullah in the early twenty-first century made the claim that the royal family was necessary as both the agent of progress and the custodian of tradition. What is old is new again in Saudi Arabia. What remains to be seen is whether the country's rulers can or will continue to pursue the same trajectory. Abdullah's initiatives are highly personalized, and it is unclear whether others in the Saudi family share his enthusiasm for a future Saudi Arabia in which science and technology will continue to play the same role. And the ultimate success of Abdullah's gambit, both his challenge to the clergy and the return to scientific and technological politics, depends on oil: how long the kingdom's reserves of petroleum will last, and whether it can continue to command high prices. Both are unknown—as are the roles that science, technology, oil, and water will play in the future.

On Transliteration and Translation

The endnotes follow the standard transliteration system used by the *International Journal of Middle East Studies*. In the body of the text, most Arabic words appear without the *ayn* and *hamza*, for ease of reading by nonspecialists. Unless otherwise indicated, English translations of Arabic titles and texts are my own.

1. The Nature of the State

1. Douglas E. Kneeland, "An Alaskan Iceberg Upstages a Saudi Prince at Conference in Iowa," *New York Times*, October 7, 1977, 23.
2. Youssef M. Ibrahim, "Saudi Will Deliver Icebergs—at a Price," *New York Times*, April 15, 1975, 29.
3. Kneeland, "Alaskan Iceberg Upstages a Saudi Prince."
4. "Towing Icebergs," *Time*, October 17, 1977. Antarctic icebergs were preferred for transoceanic voyages. Their flatter, more regular topography and features made them more desirable. Prince al-Faisal arranged for an Alaskan iceberg to be brought to Ames because of Alaska's relative proximity and convenience.
5. Ibid.
6. The Saudi and Kuwaiti governments had previously inquired about the feasibility of using icebergs as a means to address their respective water problems. Earlier in the 1970s both countries approached Gulf Oil, the American oil company operating in Kuwait, about using the company's tankers to tow icebergs. The company reportedly explored the possibility of doing so but ultimately rejected the proposals.
7. Steven Rattner, "20 Desalination Plants to Cost Saudis 15 Billion," *New York Times*, May 24, 1977.

8. "Saudi Arabia Leads World in Water Desalination," *Arab News*, June 16, 2008. In April 2009 Saudi Arabia opened the largest desalination plant in the world, a $6 billion project in Jubail, in the kingdom's Eastern Province. The Jubail plant is designed to provide 800,000 cubic meters of water daily to cities throughout the province; Siraj Wahab, "World's Largest Desalt Plant Opened," *Arab News*, April 29, 2009.

9. The concession agreement between Aramco and the Saudi Arabian government was a constant source of friction. Although Aramco agreed in principle that the oil belonged to Saudi Arabia, the company did not always observe the commitment in practice. The major oil companies that made up Aramco (Chevron, Texaco, Exxon, and Mobil) determined the amount of oil that would be pumped from the ground, and how and where it would be refined, transported, priced, and marketed. Some Saudi officials and leaders believed that they had given away too much to the American oil giant. The two parties revised the concession agreement on several occasions. In 1950 they pledged to split the revenues evenly between them in a fifty-fifty sharing deal. Ultimately the Saudis nationalized the company, assuming full ownership of Aramco in 1980. They renamed the company Saudi Aramco in 1988.

10. Saudi Arabia's ambition was extraordinary in scale. Its vast oil reserves, and the massive quantities of energy and wealth it was able to create, made the impossible seem possible. But while the scale and the spectacular level of energy consumption that oil enabled seem to suggest that the kingdom's experience was exceptional, it was not. Saudi Arabia's twentieth-century environmental saga is part of a longer history of the rise and fall of energy regimes. The human pursuit of energy, and the complicated environmental consequences of that pursuit, have long been experienced around the world. The role of fossil fuels, and the role of oil in particular, is relatively new. For more, see Edmund Burke III, "The Big Story: Human History, Energy Regimes, and the Environment," in Edmund Burke III and Kenneth Pomeranz, eds., *The Environment and World History* (Berkeley: University of California Press, 2009), 33–53, and J. R. McNeill, *An Environmental History of the Twentieth-Century World* (New York: W. W. Norton, 2000).

11. For detailed discussions about challenges to Saudi power, particularly those from within the royal family in the 1950s and 1960s, see Madawi

al-Rasheed, *A History of Saudi Arabia* (New York: Cambridge University Press, 2001); Sarah Yizraeli, *The Remaking of Saudi Arabia: The Struggle between King Saʿud and Crown Prince Faysal, 1953–1962* (Tel Aviv: Moshe Dayan Center for Middle East and African Studies, 1997); Robert Vitalis, *America's Kingdom: Mythmaking on the Saudi Oil Frontier* (Stanford, Calif.: Stanford University Press, 2006); Nadav Safran, *Saudi Arabia: The Ceaseless Quest for Security* (Ithaca, N.Y.: Cornell University Press, 1988).

12. For a brilliant analysis of similar trends in Venezuela, see Fernando Coronil, *The Magical State: Nature, Money, and Modernity in Venezuela* (Chicago: University of Chicago Press, 1997).

13. For more on oil and the resource curse, the deleterious effects of boom-time prosperity on oil-producing countries, and the impact of oil wealth on the political systems of oil producers, see Terry Karl, *The Paradox of Plenty: Oil Booms and Petro-States* (Berkeley: University of California Press, 1997); Michael Ross, "Does Oil Hinder Democracy?" *World Politics* 53, 3 (April 2001): 325–361; and, for a critique of the argument that oil wealth predicts authoritarian political outcomes, see Thad Dunning, *Crude Democracy: Natural Resource Wealth and Political Regimes* (New York: Cambridge University Press, 2008).

14. Violence was not the only important instrument in the Saudi political arsenal. Throughout the century, the kingdom's leaders worked to build relationships with disparate social groups as a means to shore up their central authority. These included merchants and guilds in the Hejaz region, tribal elites, and other notables across the peninsula. Intermarriage, appointments to prominent regional political positions, tax concessions, and favorable terms of trade were all employed by the royal family to consolidate support. See al-Rasheed, *A History of Saudi Arabia;* Kiren Aziz Chaudhry, *The Price of Wealth: Economics and Institutions in the Middle East* (Ithaca, N.Y.: Cornell University Press, 1997); and Guido Steinberg, "The Shiites in the Eastern Province of Saudi Arabia (al-Ahsaʾ), 1913–1953," in R. Brunner and W. Ende, eds., *The Twelver Shia in Modern Times: Religious Culture and Political History* (Leiden: Brill, 2001).

15. The approach to the study of the Saudi state in which I am primarily interested is mostly concerned with the internal dynamics of Saudi

rule, the ruling strategies deployed by the state to secure its authority and security domestically, and the challenges to power it faced in the twentieth century. See Timothy Niblock, ed., *Social and Economic Development in the Arab Gulf* (New York: St. Martin's Press, 1980); Safran, *Saudi Arabia: The Ceaseless Quest for Security;* Mordechai Abir, *Saudi Arabia in the Oil Era: Regime and Elites: Conflict and Collaboration* (London: Croom Helm, 1988); Yizraeli, *The Remaking of Saudi Arabia;* Alexei Vassiliev, *The History of Saudi Arabia* (London: Saqi Press, 1998); al-Rasheed, *A History of Saudi Arabia;* and Daryl Champion, *The Paradoxical Kingdom: Saudi Arabia and the Momentum of Reform* (New York: Columbia University Press, 2003).

16. The most enduring feature of most studies of Saudi society and culture is the dominance of a central argument that Saudi Arabia's rulers and its society are essentially "traditional" and that each has historically been and continues to be culturally and socially determined by a timeless Islam. Studies that purport to examine Saudi Arabia's social and cultural history tend to look uncritically at the importance of religion, and even adopt the official state narrative that the Saudis are the guardians of the faith and that Saudi society is essentially "conservative" as an article of faith. See in particular David E. Long, *The Kingdom of Saudi Arabia* (Gainesville: University Press of Florida, 1997); Thomas Lippman, *Inside the Mirage: America's Fragile Relationship with Saudi Arabia* (Boulder, Colo.: Westview Press, 2004); Vassiliev, *History of Saudi Arabia;* Rachel Bronson, *Thicker Than Oil: America's Uneasy Partnership with Saudi Arabia* (New York: Oxford University Press, 2006). For a superior take on the importance of religion in Saudi Arabia historically, see David Commins, *The Wahhabi Mission and Saudi Arabia* (New York: I. B. Tauris, 2006). F. Gregory Gause has noted critically that a "conventional wisdom" exists in the field of Saudi studies that assumes the existence of an unchanging traditional influence on Saudi Arabia, especially its political order, in which religion, tribe, and family exert the most profound influences. F. Gregory Gause, *Oil Monarchies: Domestic and Security Challenges in the Arab Gulf States* (New York: Council on Foreign Relations, 1994), 25.

17. Since the eighteenth century, when the Al Saud wedded the family's fortunes to the austere religious revivalist movement founded by Muhammad ibn Abd al-Wahhab known as Wahhabism, Islam has been a

powerful force in Saudi politics. In building a conquering army—an imperial army—the Saudis used Wahhabism as a means to marshal support. Religious scholars recruited a warrior class through a blend of enticement and compulsion. They promised both material and spiritual salvation for those who embraced the message and threw their support behind the Al Saud, while assuring that damnation would follow for those who chose otherwise. Their evangelism produced results, compelling thousands to join what would become the formidable Ikhwan fighting force. The Ikhwan led several wars of conquest, sacking and occupying al-Hasa in eastern Arabia in 1913 and the holy cities of Mecca and Medina a decade later. They used often brutal methods, massacring entire communities and calling at times for widespread ethnic cleansing of those who refused to embrace their religious proclivities.

18. The Ikhwan did revolt against its Saudi benefactors from 1926 to 1929, accusing the Al Saud of religious infidelity. The Al Saud vanquished the rebellion.

19. Chaudhry, *The Price of Wealth,* 59.

20. Arun Agrawal, *Environmentality: Technologies of Government and the Making of Subjects* (Durham, N.C.: Duke University Press, 2005); Michel Foucault, *Security, Territory, Population: Lectures at the Collège de France, 1977–1978,* ed. Michel Senellart (New York: Palgrave Macmillan, 2004).

21. Timothy Mitchell captures the intimate connection between the institutional authority of the state and land, property, and space. He writes that "frontiers are demarcated as fixed lines. The movement of population and goods across those lines is controlled in unprecedented ways, and marginal forms of political life, where allegiance to central authority was graduated or variable, increasingly gave way to more uniform and vigorous methods of control." Timothy Mitchell, *Rule of Experts: Egypt, Techno-politics, Modernity* (Berkeley: University of California Press, 2002), 12.

22. Kiren Aziz Chaudhry has written that "the initial impetus for rapid expansion of the territory controlled by the Al Saud was largely internal, driven not by religious zeal but by the more mundane motive of revenue." Chaudhry, *The Price of Wealth,* 53.

23. I rely on Gabrielle Hecht's notion of technopolitics to show that devel-

oping Saudi Arabia was a major component of a deliberate strategy in which state leaders sought to use technology and science to establish their political authority. Gabrielle Hecht, *The Radiance of France: Nuclear Power and National Identity after World War II* (Cambridge, Mass.: MIT Press, 1998), 15.

24. For more on Aramco's struggle against Arab nationalism, see Vitalis, *America's Kingdom.*

25. Michael Adas, *Dominance by Design: Technological Imperatives and America's Civilizing Mission* (Cambridge, Mass.: Belknap Press of Harvard University Press, 2006); James Ferguson, *The Anti-Politics Machine: "Development," Depoliticization, and Bureaucratic Power in Lesotho* (Minneapolis: University of Minnesota Press, 1994); Arturo Escobar, *Encountering Development: The Making and Unmaking of the Third World* (Princeton, N.J.: Princeton University Press, 1994).

26. See Frederick Cooper, *International Development and the Social Sciences: Essays on the History and Politics of Knowledge* (Berkeley: University of California Press, 1998).

27. See James Scott, *Seeing Like a State: How Certain Schemes to Improve the Human Condition Have Failed* (New Haven, Conn.: Yale University Press, 1998); Thomas P. Hughes, *Networks of Power: Electrification in Western Society, 1888–1930* (Baltimore: Johns Hopkins University Press, 1983).

28. For another view of the relationship between politics and the environment, see Myrna I. Santiago, *The Ecology of Oil: Environment, Labor, and the Mexican Revolution, 1900–1938* (New York: Cambridge University Press, 2006).

29. Timothy Mitchell, "The Limits of the State," *American Political Science Review* 85 (1991): 77–96. In practice, there were not always clear distinctions among the state, society, and the host of domestic and international actors that operated in the kingdom until near the end of the century.

30. Scott, *Seeing Like a State,* 4–5. While Saudi Arabia appears to embody the four conditions that James Scott argues are necessary for technical disaster (the administrative ordering of nature and society, an ideology that views science and technology as a cure for various natural and social ills, an authoritarian state, and a prostrate civil society that lacks

the capacity to resist modernization schemes), in reality the kingdom was not strong enough to be considered authoritarian in the middle decades of the twentieth century. Nor was it up against a "prostrate civil society." In fact, even though some technological projects failed, they actually strengthened the Saudi state and contributed to its becoming authoritarian by increasing its presence in local communities and enrolling local people in administrative and governmental networks in which they had not previously been involved. Priya Satia provides an additional critique of Scott that is applicable in the case of Saudi Arabia. She notes, contra Scott, that rather than being disinterested in local knowledge, British colonizers in Iraq "fetishized" it in order to justify violence. Similarly, Saudi leaders and the Western engineers and technologists who operated on their behalf often demonstrated a keen interest in understanding local systems in order to control them. See Priya Satia, "The Defense of Inhumanity: Air Control and the British Idea of Arabia," *American Historical Review* 3, 1 (February 2006): 16–17.

31. While it is certainly the case that science and technology were instruments of state power, as Scott argues, they also shaped the ways that state actors understood the meaning of legibility. Legibility, much like authoritarianism, was also an outcome of state technopolitical practice.

32. Fouad al-Farsy, *Saudi Arabia: A Case Study in Development,* 4th ed. (New York: Kegan Paul International, 1988), 82–94.

33. So thorough is the purging of the Shiites from the national narrative that Saudi historians, including Shia authors who publish inside the kingdom, avoid discussing the group at all, even refusing to mention the group by name. Some studies of the Eastern Province avoid mentioning that the vast majority of the residents there are Shia. See, for example, Abdullah Nasir al-Subaiʿi, *Al-Hayāt al-ʿilamiyyat wa al-thaqāfiyyat wa al-fikriyya fi al-mantiqa al-sharqiyya, 1930–1960: Darāsat fi tarʿkh al-mamlaka al-ʿarabiyya al-saʿudiyya,* 2nd ed. (Riyadh: Al-Warāq Bookstore, 1979), *Iktishāf al-naft wa atharhū ʿala al-haya al-ijtamāʿiyya fi al-mantiqa al-sharqiyya, 1933–1960* (Riyadh: Al-Waraq Bookstore, 1979), and *Iktishāf al-naft wa atharhū ʿala al-haya al-iqtisādiyya fi al-mantiqa al-sharqiyya, 1933–1960* (Riyadh: Al Waraq Bookstore, 1979); Abdullah Hassan Mansur Abd al-Muhassan, *Min*

turāth jazīrat tarūt (Jubail, Saudi Arabia: Industrial Support Printers Limited, 1986), and *Al-Amthāl al-shaʿbīya fī al-sāhil al-sharqī li al-mamlaka al-ʿarabiyya al-saʿudiyya* (Jubail, Saudi Arabia: Industrial Support Printers, 1986); Khalid bin Jabir al-Gharib, *Mantiqat al-ihsa ʿabr atwār al-tārikh,* 2nd ed. (Khobar, Saudi Arabia: New National House for Publishing and Distribution, 1988); Muhammad bin Abdullah abd al-Qadr Al-Ansari al-Ahsa'i, *Tuhfat al-mustafīd bi tārikh al-ihsa fī al-qadīm wa al-jadīd,* 2 vols. (1962; Riyadh: Secretary General for the Saudi Centennial Celebration, King Fahd National Library, 1999); Hamad al-Jasir, *Al-muʾajam al-jugrāfi lil bilād al-ʿarabiyya al-saʿudiyya al-mantiqa al-sharqiyya (al-bahrain al-qadīm),* 4 vols. (Riyadh: Manshurat for Research and Translation and Publishing, 1979); Talat Ibrahim al-Lutfa, *Athar mashrūʿ al-rai wa al-saraf ʿala mantiqat al-ihsa* (Riyadh: King Saud University, 1986); Muhammad bin Abdulatif bin Muhammad al-Malhum, *Kānat ʿashbuh bi al-jāmaʿat: qisāt al-taʿlīm fī muqātaʾāt al-ihsa fī ʿahd al-malak ʿAbd al-ʿAziz* (Riyadh: House of Doctor al-Malhum for Publishing and Distribution, 1999). The Shia author Muhammad Said al-Muslim was imprisoned briefly for discussing the details of Shiism and oppression in the 1960s in his book on the Eastern Province. To secure his release, al-Muslim edited out sensitive details in subsequent editions. Muhammad Said al-Muslim, *Sāhil al-dhahab al-aswad: Darāsa tārikhiyya insāniyyat li-mantiqat al-khalīj al-ʿarabi,* 2nd ed. (Beirut: Dar Maktabat al-Hayat, 1962).

34. Sheila Carapico, "*Arabia Incognita:* An Invitation to Arabian Peninsula Studies," in Madawi al-Rasheed and Robert Vitalis, eds., *Counter-Narratives: History, Contemporary Society, and Politics in Saudi Arabia and Yemen* (New York: Palgrave, 2004), 9–33.

35. I spent ten months in 2003 carrying out research in Riyadh and in various places in Saudi Arabia's Eastern Province. The process of finding a host institution and obtaining an entrance visa took one year. Extending the visa once I was in the country required regular visits to various branches and offices within the Ministry of the Interior. And the acquisition of a visa is no guarantee of successful research. With several poorly organized exceptions, Saudi Arabia has no major public research libraries or open archives. I carried out most of the research for this project in the small library at the King Abd al-Aziz City for Sci-

ence and Technology, the library at the King Faisal Foundation (whose closed stacks, antiquated catalog system, and censor-minded librarians render effective research a challenge), and the King Fahd National Library; I also made use of oral histories and the private libraries of sympathetic Saudi citizens.

2. Imperial Geology

1. Karl S. Twitchell, Letter to H. E. Shaikh Abdulla Sulaiman, December 30, 1948, Karl S. Twitchell Papers, Public Policy Papers, Department of Rare Books and Special Collections, Princeton University Library.

2. Ibid.

3. John Craven Wilkinson, *Arabia's Frontiers: The Story of Britain's Boundary Drawing in the Desert* (New York: I. B. Tauris, 1991).

4. The two largest deserts are the Rub al-Khali in the south and southeast (the Empty Quarter) and the Nafudh in the northwest.

5. Guido Steinberg, "Ecology, Knowledge, and Trade in Central Arabia (Najd) during the Nineteenth and Early Twentieth Centuries," in Madawi al-Rasheed and Robert Vitalis, eds., *Counter-Narratives: History, Contemporary Society, and Politics in Saudi Arabia and Yemen* (New York: Palgrave, 2004), 78.

6. In a report written in 1974, the Ministry of Agriculture remarked that "traditionally agriculture in Saudi Arabia has been centered around oases and wadi [valley] channels scattered throughout the kingdom where springs and shallow ground water are available or where rainfall alone is sufficient for the cultivation of crops . . . This situation arose from the severe climactic conditions and lack of irrigation water for agriculture over many centuries." Kingdom of Saudi Arabia Ministry of Agriculture and Water, *Seven Green Spikes, 1965–1972: Water and Agricultural Developments* (Riyadh: Ministry of Agriculture and Water, 1974).

7. H. St. John Philby, *Sa'udi Arabia* (London: Benn, 1955), 66.

8. Steinberg, "Ecology, Knowledge, and Trade in Central Arabia," 82.

9. Philby, *Sa'udi Arabia*, 266.

10. Hamza al-Hassan, *Al-Shi'a fil-mamlaka al-'arabiyya al-sa'udiyya*, vol. 2 (Mu'assasat al-Baqī li-Ihya'a al-Turāth, 1993), 293–294.

11. Muhammad Said al-Muslim, *Sāhil al-dhahab al-aswad: Darāsa*

tārikhiyya insāniyyat li-mantiqat al-khalīj al-ʿarabi, 2nd ed. (Beirut: Dar Maktabat al-Hayat, 1962), 205–206.

12. Alexei Vassiliev, *The History of Saudi Arabia* (London: Saqi Books, 1998), 225.

13. The hajj provided only an intermittent source of cash, particularly in the first half of the twentieth century when a depressed global economy and global wars dissuaded would-be pilgrims from traveling. To supplement the disappointing pilgrimage taxes, the Saudis instituted a national taxation system in 1925, one that depended mostly on, and was even articulated in terms of, agricultural production and agricultural property. Abd al-Aziz called it a religious tax, *zakat,* a reference to the annual tithe that is proscribed for Muslims. He demanded that *zakat* paid in kind be extracted "from among livestock of average quality, and that *zakat* paid in cash . . . [and] be based on the average price of livestock." In addition to livestock, farmers were compelled to pay taxes on dates, raisins, and assorted nuts. Because they were so rare in the peninsula, fruits other than dates were exempted. The rate of taxation depended on the agricultural techniques employed, with a rate of 5 percent for irrigated land and 10 percent for those who did not irrigate. The lower rate for irrigated farming would seem to suggest a tax break for those who produced in greater bulk, an indication that the young state sought to encourage others to adopt similar means and thereby expand the amount of revenue, and thus taxes, being generated. Aside from waging war, tax collecting was among the earliest practices engaged in by the state. Abd al-Aziz dispatched minor royal family members and provincial leaders appointed during the process of conquest and expansion to collect *zakat* from both settled and Bedouin communities. The *zakat* system would be halved in the 1950s as oil revenues expanded, making the taxes less necessary. The state did away with taxes altogether in the 1970s. See Vassiliev, *History of Saudi Arabia,* 304.

14. See Kiren Aziz Chaudhry, *The Price of Wealth: Economics and Institutions in the Middle East* (Ithaca, N.Y.: Cornell University Press, 1997); Daryl Champion, *The Paradoxical Kingdom: Saudi Arabia and the Momentum of Reform* (New York: Columbia University Press, 2003).

15. Abdulaziz H. al-Fahad, "The ʿImama vs. the ʿIqal: Hadari-Bedouin Conflict and the Formation of the Saudi State," in Madawi al-Rasheed and Robert Vitalis, eds., in Madawi al-Rasheed and Robert Vitalis, eds.,

Counter-Narratives: History, Contemporary Society, and Politics in Saudi Arabia and Yemen (New York: Palgrave, 2004), 35–36.

16. The Al Saud relied on its clerical partners, on whom it bestowed considerable power, to convince skeptics of the legitimacy of the message. To spread the faith, King Abd al-Aziz dispatched devotees known as *mutawwaʿa*, religious figures who lacked the higher religious training of the more senior sheikhs, but who made up for their lack of credentials with zealotry. While Muhammad Ibn Abd al-Wahhab may not in fact have been a proponent of offensive jihad, as Natana Delong Bas has argued, once hitched to the political ambition of the Al Saud, Wahhabism was imbued with more specifically political aims. In the twentieth century the Al Saud helped connect the strict interpretative framework of Wahhabism, which viewed anyone who deviated from a set of narrow beliefs and rituals as guilty of apostasy and thereby deserving of either death or conquest, with its political aim of controlling the Arabian Peninsula. See Natana Delong Bas, *Wahhabi Islam: From Revival and Reform to Global Jihad* (New York: Oxford University Press, 2004).

17. The Al Saud relied on several incentives to induce permanent settlement. The *mutawwaʿa* stressed that proper faith required sedentary living, a precept embodied in the name for the settlements: *hujjar* (sing. *hijra*). The choice of the word *hijra* for individual settlements was an intentional and symbolic choice, as it harked back to the early Islamic era, specifically to the Prophet Muhammad's migration from Mecca to Medina, a seminal event in the formation of Islamic belief and tradition. Saudi political leaders and their religious lieutenants demanded that the tribes abandon their nomadic lifestyle for the *hujjar*. While Islam lent ideological substance to sedentarization, the location of *hujjar* near water resources and the potential for agriculture gave the Al Saud hope that the sedentarization program would be sustainable. In little over a decade the number of settlements jumped from one to more than two hundred, with most located close to other water resources spread across Najd. In addition to providing weapons for the jihad and building mosques and schools, the Al Saud gave the Ikhwan money, seeds, and the equipment necessary to engage in various kinds of settled agriculture.

18. John S. Habib, *Ibn Saʾuds Warriors of Islam: The Ikhwan of Najd and*

Their Role in the Creation of the Sa'udi Kingdom, 1910–1930 (Leiden: Brill, 1978), 16. Another significant objective was to harness but not eliminate the mobile fighting power of the Ikhwan. Habib notes that the Saudi king's military goal was to keep the Ikhwan "mobile enough to cross the length and breadth of the peninsula, and sedentary enough to be in a specific locality when he needed them."

19. Ibn Khaldûn, *The Muqaddimah: An Introduction to History*, trans. Franz Rosenthal, abridged and ed. N. J. Dawood, Bollingen Series (Princeton, N.J.: Princeton University Press, 1969).

20. FAO cited in Karl S. Twitchell, *Saudi Arabia: With an Account of the Development of Its Natural Resources*, 3rd ed. (New York: Greenwood Press, 1969), 21.

21. See Vassiliev, *History of Saudi Arabia*, 412–419; J. S. Birks and C. A. Sinclair, "The Domestic Political Economy of Development in Saudi Arabia," in Timothy Niblock, ed., *State, Society and Economy in Saudi Arabia* (New York: St. Martin's Press, 1982), 199–200. Vassiliev estimated the population in the 1960s to be 3.5 to 4.5 million people. However, there were no census data and all figures must be viewed as loose estimates, as the wide range indicates.

22. Ministry of Agriculture and Water, *Seven Green Spikes.*

23. Thomas Lippman, *Inside the Mirage Mirage: America's Fragile Relationship with Saudi Arabia* (Boulder, Colo.: Westview Press, 2004); Anthony Cave Brown, *Oil, God and Gold: The Story of Aramco and the Saudi Kings* (Boston: Houghton Mifflin, 1999); Wallace Stegner, *Discovery! The Search For Arabian Oil* (Beirut: Middle East Export Press, 1971); Philip McConnell, *The Hundred Men* (Peterborough, N.H.: Currier, 1985).

24. In his study of Aramco and the United States in Saudi Arabia, Robert Vitalis tackles many of these myths. See Robert Vitalis, *America's Kingdom: Mythmaking on the Saudi Oil Frontier* (Stanford, Calif.: Stanford University Press, 2006). See also Robert Vitalis, "Black Gold, White Crude: An Essay on American Exceptionalism, Hierarchy, and Hegemony in the Gulf," *Diplomatic History* 26, 2 (2002): 159–185.

25. Twitchell, *Saudi Arabia*, 212.

26. Ibid.

27. Ibid., 213.

28. Ibid., 215.
29. Karl Twitchell, "Water Resources of Saudi Arabia," *American Geographical Review* 34, 3 (July 1944): 368.
30. Ibid., 368–369.
31. Twitchell, *Saudi Arabia,* 216.
32. Ibid.
33. Ibid., 219.
34. Shortly after obtaining the concession for operating in Saudi Arabia, the California Arabian Standard Oil Company was formed. It would be renamed the Arabian American Oil Company in 1944. In 1936 the Texas Oil Company purchased a 50 percent interest in the concession. In 1948 the concession was reorganized once again, with holdings redistributed as follows: 30 percent to Socal; 30 percent to Texas Oil Company; 30 percent to Standard Oil Company of New Jersey; and 10 percent to Socony-Vacuum Oil Company.
35. Twitchell, *Saudi Arabia,* 45.
36. Asir Trip Reports to King Ibn Saud—Riyadh, regarding Roads, Irrigation, Agriculture, Archaeology in Asir and Nejran, April 15–July 15, 1940, Karl S. Twitchell Papers, Public Policy Papers, Department of Rare Books and Special Collections, Princeton University Library.
37. Twitchell, "Water Resources," 366.
38. *Report of the United States Agricultural Mission to Saudi Arabia* (Cairo, 1943), 1.
39. Twitchell, *Saudi Arabia,* 49.
40. There is no indication in any of Twitchell's writings that he saw anything wrong with the expansion and consolidation of Saudi power. He certainly never wrote about local resistance to or animosity toward the Al Saud, but this does not mean that he was unaware of such sentiment. His various accountings of his and the agricultural mission's work are apolitical in tone, yet it is clear from them that Twitchell understood whose political interests were being served.
41. They claimed that thousands of acres of land could be brought under cultivation in al-Hasa (10,000 acres), Qatif (3,000), Asir, and Najd (1,000). In both Najd and Hejaz, however, they argued that the potential for expanding the area being farmed was limited and that more could be achieved by intensifying and perfecting agricultural methods.

42. *Report of the United States Agricultural Mission,* 46.

43. Ibid., 48.

44. Ibid., 58.

45. Ibid., 84–85.

46. Ibid., 68.

47. Ibid., 68–69.

48. See Michael Adas, *Dominance by Design: Technological Imperatives and America's Civilizing Mission* (Cambridge, Mass.: Belknap Press of Harvard University Press, 2006).

49. Daniel Yergin, *The Prize: The Epic Quest for Oil, Money, and Power* (New York: Touchstone, 1991); Nathan Citino, *From Arab Nationalism to OPEC: Eisenhower, King Saʿud, and the Making of U.S.-Saudi Relations* (Bloomington: Indiana University Press, 2002).

50. Letter to Sulayman al-Hamad, Assistant to the Minister of Finance, June 4, 1949, Karl S. Twitchell Papers, Public Policy Papers, Department of Rare Books and Special Collections, Princeton University Library.

51. Letter from John Crane to Karl Twitchell, February 4, 1938, Karl S. Twitchell Papers, Public Policy Papers, Department of Rare Books and Special Collections, Princeton University Library.

52. Letter to Charles Crane, February 27, 1938, Karl S. Twitchell Papers, Public Policy Papers, Department of Rare Books and Special Collections, Princeton University Library.

53. Letter to John Crane, February 16, 1938, Karl S. Twitchell Papers, Public Policy Papers, Department of Rare Books and Special Collections, Princeton University Library.

3. The Dogma of Development

1. Welles Hangen, "Saudi Arabia's New King Stresses Home Development and Arab Arms," *New York Times,* December 1, 1953, H1.

2. In 1938 revenue from oil amounted to US$500,000. In 1948 it jumped from US$17,500,000 to US$31,500,000. It nearly quadrupled in 1951 to US$110,000,000, and then doubled again in 1952 to US$212,200,000.

3. See Kiren Aziz Chaudhry, *The Price of Wealth: Economics and Institutions in the Middle East* (Ithaca, N.Y.: Cornell University Press, 1997), and Daryl Champion, *The Paradoxical Kingdom: Saudi Arabia and the Momentum of Reform* (New York: Columbia University Press, 2003).

4. Kingdom of Saudi Arabia, Ministry of Agriculture and Water, *Seven Green Spikes, 1965–1972: Water and Agricultural Developments* (Riyadh: Ministry of Agriculture and Water, 1974), 9.

5. Oral interview, Arthur N. Young, February 24, 1974, Truman Presidential Library, Independence, Mo., www.trumanlibrary.org/oralhist/young.htm#transcript. Point Four was a U.S. program to provide technical assistance and economic aid to developing countries. The program operated from 1949 to 1953.

6. Daniel Da Cruz, "Dry—But Why?" *Aramco World* 18, 4 (July/August 1967): 6.

7. Ministry of Agriculture and Water, *Seven Green Spikes*, 180.

8. Historians and other observers of Saudi Arabia often point to the demonstration farm at al-Kharj as the kingdom's first experiment with development. King Abd al-Aziz founded the farm in 1938 and relied initially on the efforts of two Egyptian and Iraqi managers. He later pressured Aramco to take over the farm. The heavy emphasis on al-Kharj has served a number of political and intellectual agendas. Americans, including Thomas Lippman and Anthony Cave Brown, like to claim that the project was the first example of the United States' benevolent intent in Saudi Arabia and that it demonstrates the goodwill of American political and commercial interests in facilitating the modernization of Saudi agriculture. Literature published by Aramco, which helped operate the farm from 1945 to 1959, points to the company's work at al-Kharj as a central part of its "friendship" with the kingdom. Lippman and Brown rely heavily, and mostly uncritically, on Aramco's narrative. Thomas Lippman, *Inside the Mirage Mirage: America's Fragile Relationship with Saudi Arabia* (Boulder, Colo.: Westview Press, 2004); Anthony Cave Brown, *Oil, God and Gold: The Story of Aramco and the Saudi Kings* (Boston: Houghton Mifflin, 1999). In *America's Kingdom*, Robert Vitalis has demonstrated that the American role at al-Kharj was actually minimal, was pursued only because it helped reduce pressure from the Al Saud and not as a result of goodwill, and hardly qualified as development, since the only people who benefited from the crops produced at al-Kharj were members of the royal family in Riyadh. Robert Vitalis, *America's Kingdom: Mythmaking on the Saudi Oil Frontier* (Stanford, Calif.: Stanford University Press, 2006).

9. Timothy Niblock, "Social Structure and the Development of the Saudi

Arabian Political System," in Niblock, ed., *Social and Economic Develop-ment in the Arab Gulf* (New York: St. Martin's Press, 1980), 77.

10. Vitalis, *America's Kingdom;* Helen Lackner, *A House Built on Sand: A Political Economy of Saudi Arabia* (London: Ithaca Press, 1978); Mordechai Abir, *Saudi Arabia in the Oil Era: Regime and Elites: Conflict and Collaboration* (London: Croom Helm, 1988).

11. Madawi al-Rasheed and others downplay the importance of these po-litical movements, noting correctly that they did not enjoy widespread support across the kingdom. Madawi al-Rasheed, *A History of Saudi Arabia* (New York: Cambridge University Press, 2002). Nevertheless, the Al Saud took them very seriously, as demonstrated by Vitalis and others. For an account of the politicization of Saudi Arabian society during the 1950s, see Abir, *Saudi Arabia in the Oil Era,* 64–107.

12. Niblock, "Social Structure and the Development of the Saudi Arabian Political System," 77–99.

13. King Faisal is often pointed to as the first "modernizer" among the Al Saud. This moniker is not particularly helpful, especially since most who use it imply a value judgment, usually inferring or stating outright that it was Faisal who finally placed Saudi Arabia on the path to prog-ress and modernity and all the benefits that that journey was supposed to entail. It is true that Faisal's tenure marked a tactical shift in gover-nance, in which modernization and development programs assumed greater importance in state policy and rhetoric, but the strategic goal of ensuring the survival of the royal family remained the same. It is more useful, then, to view Faisal as the first Saudi monarch to deploy the lan-guage of development in the service of protecting and expanding the central authority of the Al Saud. It is also important to note that devel-opment discourse was not entirely new in Saudi Arabia. There had been talk of development since at least the late 1930s, and it had intensi-fied in the late 1940s when Aramco resumed operations after World War II. But development as an institutionalized and centrally coordi-nated policy did not exist in any serious form until the 1960s.

14. Alexei Vassiliev, *The History of Saudi Arabia* (London: Saqi Books, 1998), 365.

15. According to Vassiliev, in a major speech delivered "in al-Taif on 6 Sep-tember 1963, Faisal listed the projects that were to be given priority: de-

velopment of a telephone network, roads and airports; settling of the Bedouin; a reduction in water charges; the construction of a metallurgical works, an oil processing plant in Jidda and a paper and pulp mill; prospecting for and exploitation of other mineral resources; opening a college of petroleum and minerals; and a reduction in electricity prices." Vassiliev, *History of Saudi Arabia,* 366.

16. *Al-Manhal* 6, 20 (December 1959): 341.

17. Vassiliev suggests that "the head of government tried to attract the growing middle class by the promise of new legislation and 'independent bodies' to supervise its implementation, as well as the lure of an economic upsurge. To enlist the support of the ordinary people, Faisal promised to raise their standard of living, provide them various social benefits and protect them from unemployment." Vassiliev, *History of Saudi Arabia,* 365.

18. Ministry of Agriculture and Water, *Seven Green Spikes,* 9.

19. *Al-bank al-zirā'ī al-sau'dī: Al-taqrīr al-sanawī, 1384–1385;* in English, *The Saudi Agricultural Bank: Annual Report, 1964–1965* (Jidda: Saudi Agricultural Bank), 7. (The bank's annual reports are henceforth cited as *SAB,* with the appropriate year.)

20. Norman C. Walpole, *Area Handbook for Saudi Arabia,* American University, Foreign Area Studies Division (Washington, D.C.: U.S. Government Printing Office, 1966), 221.

21. The Ministry of Agriculture and Water stated that the average holding was 2.2 hectares in 1975. Ministry of Agriculture and Water, *Seven Green Spikes,* 7. Ramon Knauerhase suggested that in the early 1970s, 67 percent of all peasant families owned parcels of less than 1 hectare. Ramon Knauerhase, *The Saudi Arabian Economy* (New York: Praeger, 1974), 120.

22. Vasili Ozoling, *The Economy of Saudi Arabia,* cited in Vassiliev, *History of Saudi Arabia,* 414.

23. Vassiliev, *History of Saudi Arabia,* 416.

24. Ibid.

25. Ibid.

26. *SAB, 1964–1965,* 21.

27. Ibid., 17.

28. *SAB, 1968–1969,* 6.

29. *SAB, 1974–1975,* 5.

30. *SAB, 1968–1969,* 22. The geographic distribution of loans raises questions—about the bank's activities and why certain areas had a higher rate of borrowing than others—that are difficult to answer. From the beginning, the central office in Riyadh awarded the highest number of loans, 83 percent. That number dropped to 27.5 percent five years later, although it still made the most loans. Jidda and Buraydah made 23.2 percent and 22.3 percent of the loans, respectively, in 1968–69, approximating the rates from the central office (and up from 4.7 percent and 1.8 percent, respectively, five years earlier). But the loan rates in the Hofuf branch in the Eastern Province remained mysteriously low in the first five years of the bank's operation. From 1964 to 1969 the Hofuf branch made 7.2 percent of the total number of loans. The number actually declined to 6.9 percent in 1967–68 before increasing to 8.5 percent in 1968–69. *SAB, 1968–1969,* 11–12.

31. Ibid., 14.

32. Ibid., Appendix 26.

33. Ibid., 6.

34. *SAB, 1974–1975,* 5.

35. Ministry of Agriculture and Water, *Seven Green Spikes,* 21.

36. Vassiliev, *History of Saudi Arabia,* 409. Vassiliev claims that "Gross Domestic Product expanded from SR8.6 billion in 1962 to SR21.3 billion in 1973 at a rate of around 1.6 percent per annum, but most of this was a result of rising oil revenues" (409). The Saudi Ministry of Information notes that "the total value added by agriculture in 1974/75 was estimated at $SR1.4 billion or 8.6 percent of private non-oil GDP, reflecting a growth rate of about 3.6 percent over the last five years. With a very large and growing gap between food consumption and local production, the planners have devoted special attention to easing restraints and increasing productivity." Kingdom of Saudi Arabia Ministry of Information, *Saudi Arabia and Its Place in the World* (Lausanne: Three Continents Publishers, 1979), 6. The Saudi Ministry of Planning gave slightly different figures in the second Saudi five-year development plan, saying that GDP rose from SR3.185 billion in 1969 to SR23.98 billion in 1974. Kingdom of Saudi Arabia Ministry of Planning, *Second Development Plan, 1975–1979* (Riyadh: Ministry of Planning, n.d.), 38.

37. Mohammed Hussein al-Fiar, "Faisal Settlement Project, Haradh, Saudi Arabia: A Study of Nomad Attitudes toward Sedentarization," Ph.D. diss., Michigan State University, 1977, 84.

38. Ministry of Agriculture and Water, *Seven Green Spikes*, 15.

39. Vassiliev, *History of Saudi Arabia*, 420.

40. *SAB, 1974–1975*, 10.

41. *SAB, 1964–1965*, 20; *SAB 1974–1975*, 8.

42. *SAB, 1964–1965*, 20.

43. *SAB, 1974–1975*, 8.

44. From 1969 to 1971 SRI, which was officially part of Stanford University until the mid-1970s, also undertook work on specific agricultural sectors. The Saudi-based SRI field teams authored several reports on how to improve livestock production among the Bedouin as well as how to improve the production and marketing of agricultural commodities. See Stanford Research Institute (SRI Project ECH 8680): Ibrahim Daprab, *Selected Commodity Situations in Saudi Arabia, with Views on Policy Alternatives;* Earl O. Heady, *A Synthesis of Policies to Attain the Goals of the Agriculture Sector Plan of the Ministry of Agriculture and Water;* Clarence J. Miller and Bruce Barber, *A Program for the Improved Marketing of Agricultural Commodities in Saudi Arabia;* Howard Sprague, *Improvement of Livestock Production by Bedouin Nomads on Semidesert Rangelands of Saudi Arabia* (Menlo Park, Calif.: SRI, 1971).

45. Stanford Research Institute, *A Plan for the Development of the Agriculture Sector in Saudi Arabia: Proposed Courses of Action for a Near-Term Plan of Growth* (Menlo Park, Calif.: SRI, 1971), 16.

46. Ministry of Agriculture and Water, *Seven Green Spikes*, 12.

47. See James Scott, *Seeing Like a State: How Certain Schemes to Improve the Human Condition Have Failed* (New Haven, Conn.: Yale University Press, 1998).

48. Ministry of Agriculture and Water, *Seven Green Spikes*, 12–14.

49. Ibid., 12.

50. Ibid., 16.

51. Ibid.

52. Ibid., 89.

53. Ibid., 167.

54. Ibid.

55. Mohammed Hussein Saleh Ebrahim, "Problems of Nomad Settlement in the Middle East with Special Reference to Saudi Arabia and the Haradh Project," Ph.D. diss., Cornell University, 1981, 164.

56. Vassiliev, *History of Saudi Arabia,* 421.

57. Al-Fiar, "Faisal Settlement Project," 9–27.

58. Ministry of Agriculture and Water, *Seven Green Spikes,* 149.

59. There are no reliable figures for the Saudi population in any period, although most put the population in the 1960s and early 1970s at 4 to 6 million.

60. Vassiliev, *History of Saudi Arabia,* 421. The Arab League, or League of Arab States, was established in 1945 to promote cooperation among member nations in matters of economic and social development and foreign policy.

61. Federico Vidal, report on Bedouin migration to Ghawar, untitled manuscript, 1973.

62. Ibid., 2.

63. Ibid., 27.

64. Ibid., 16.

65. Ibid.

66. Karl S. Twitchell, *Saudi Arabia: With an Account of the Development of Its Natural Resources,* 3rd ed. (New York: Greenwood Press, 1969), 75.

67. Ministry of Agriculture and Water, *Seven Green Spikes,* 149. Aramco, which maintained a gas-oil separation plant near Haradh, had carried out its own hydrological survey in the area in 1963 and reported to the Ministry of Agriculture that there was potential for agricultural work there.

68. Ministry of Agriculture and Water, *Seven Green Spikes,* 147.

69. I located the reports, surveys, and studies carried out by Wakuti, as well as those undertaken by the Italian engineering firm Italconsult, in the library of the King Abd al-Aziz City for Science and Technology in Riyadh, Saudi Arabia.

70. "Saudi Arabia Orders a Custom Built Oasis," *New York Times,* May 4, 1967, 53. See also Al-Fiar, "Faisal Settlement Project," 119.

71. Ministry of Agriculture and Water, *Seven Green Spikes,* 147.

72. Al-Fiar, "Faisal Settlement Project," 120.

73. Ibid., 198.

74. Ibid., 127.

75. Ibid., 154–155.
76. Ministry of Agriculture and Water, *Seven Green Spikes*, 154.
77. Timothy Mitchell, "The Limits of the State," *American Political Science Review* 85 (1991): 77–96.
78. Lisa Wedeen, *Ambiguities of Domination: Politics, Rhetoric and Symbols in Contemporary Syria* (Chicago: University of Chicago Press, 1999).
79. *SAB, 1964–1965*, 7.
80. Al-Rasheed, *A History of Saudi Arabia*, 121–126.
81. Ministry of Information, *Second Development Plan*, 4.
82. Fouad al-Farsy, *Saudi Arabia: A Case Study in Development* (New York: Kegan Paul International, 1978).
83. King Faisal Ibn Abd al-Aziz, "The Duties Incumbent upon Us," in *Da'wat al-haq: Al-majmu'a al-kāmila li-khābāt wa aqwāl wa ahadīth sāhib al-jalala malak Faisal bin 'Abd al-'Aziz*, al-Juz al-Thani (Riyadh: Dar al-Faisal al-Thaqāfiyya), 1; translation is mine.
84. Ibid., 3.
85. Ibid., 5.

4. Engineering the Garden

1. Robert Vitalis, *America's Kingdom: Mythmaking on the Saudi Oil Frontier* (Stanford, Calif.: Stanford University Press, 2006), esp. ch. 6.
2. F. S. Vidal, "Date Culture in the Oasis of Al-Hasa," *Middle East Journal* 8, 4 (Autumn 1954).
3. Anti-Shiism played a central role leading up to the revolt of the Ikhwan against King Abd al-Aziz ibn Saud in 1926, as leading Ikhwani figures claimed that the Saudi regent had refused to deal with them according to the strictures of Wahhabi sharia, which demanded either their forced conversion or their destruction.
4. "The al-Ihsa' Irrigation and Drainage Project: Reviving One of the Greatest Oases of the Arabian Peninsula," *Qafilat al-Zayt*, February/March 1972, 3.
5. Philipp Holzmann, "Technical Reports," December 1971, 3.
6. James Scott, *Seeing Like a State: How Certain Schemes to Improve the Human Condition Have Failed* (New Haven, Conn.: Yale University Press, 1998).
7. "Closing in on Malaria," *Aramco World* 12, 3 (March 1961).

8. Carole Hicke, oral interview with Richard Daggy, April 21, 1996, in *Health and Disease in Saudi Arabia: The Aramco Experience, 1940s–1990s*, ed. Armand P. Gelpi (Berkeley: University of California, 1998), content.cdlib.org/ark:/13030/kt8m3nb5g6/.

9. "Closing in on Malaria," *Aramco World*.

10. The Saudi Arabian government took over the malaria program in 1957 with help from the World Health Organization. In 1960 infection rates climbed again in Qatif, although the higher incidence was attributed to the appearance of a second species of malaria-bearing mosquito, named *fluviatilis;* while immune to dieldrin, it was brought under control with the renewed use of DDT.

11. Hicke, interview with Richard Daggy.

12. Ibid.

13. Yitzhak Nakash writes that, after his appointment as governor of the al-Hasa province in 1913, "Bin Jiluwi embarked [on] a campaign intended to force the conversion of Shiʿis to Wahhabism, ordering Shiʿi legal courts to follow Hanbali law, introducing new prayer guidelines, and prohibiting the Shiʿis from performing their rituals." Yitzhak Nakash, *Reaching for Power: The Shiʿa in the Modern Arab World* (Princeton, N.J.: Princeton University Press, 2006), 46.

14. In 1940, two years after oil was discovered in Saudi Arabia, what was then California Arabian Standard Oil Company (CASOC) employed 2,668 Saudi Arabian workers, compared with 382 non–Saudi Arabians, a figure that included Americans. The total number of workers dipped during the war, but the proportion remained heavily slanted toward Saudi Arabian employees. The number of workers swelled in the last year of the war and then immediately after. In 1945, the year of the first labor strikes, 92.5 percent of the company's workers hailed from Saudi Arabia (8,099 out of 10,683). See California Arabian Standard Oil Company and Arabian American Oil Company annual reports (1940–1945).

15. Turnover rates were high early on, approaching 91 percent in 1945, but they stabilized within a decade and a half, dropping to 3 percent by 1959. See Ibrahim S. al-Abdullah al-Elawy, "The Influence of Oil upon Settlement in al-Hasa Oasis, Saudi Arabia," Ph.D. diss., University of Durham, 1976, 375.

16. Hicke, interview with Richard Daggy.

17. Article 23 of the 1933 oil concession states: "The enterprise under this contract shall be directed and supervised by Americans who shall employ Saudi Arab nationals as far as practicable, and insofar as the Company [Aramco] can find suitable Saudi Arab employees, it will not employ other nationals."

18. F. S. Vidal, *The Oasis of al-Hasa*, Arabian American Oil Company, Local Government Relations, Arabian Research Division (1955). Vidal also published a condensed version of his report, entitled "Date Culture in the Oasis of al-Hasa," in the *Middle East Journal* 8, 4 (1954): 417–428.

19. See Abdullah Nasir al-Subaiʿi, *Iktishāf al-naft wa ātharihī ʿala al-haya al-iqtisādiyya fī al-mantiqa al-sharqiyya, 1933–1960*, 2nd ed. (Riyadh: Sharif Publishers, 1989), 71.

20. Vidal, *The Oasis of al-Hasa*, 13–15.

21. Vitalis, *America's Kingdom*, 68–70.

22. See F. S. Vidal and George Rentz, *The Aramco Reports on Al-Hasa and Oman 1950–1955* (Cambridge: Cambridge University Press, 1990); F. S. Vidal, "Bedouin Migration in the Ghawar Oil Field, Saudi Arabia," Field Research Project, Miami, 1975.

23. Vitalis, *America's Kingdom*, 204.

24. In 1951 the Saudi newspaper *Al-Bilad Al-Saʿudiyya* put the population total at 500,000, which is considerably higher than every other estimate. Most estimates vary between 150,000 and 250,000. See Vidal, *The Oasis of al-Hasa*, 17. In a 1957 article in Aramco's Arabic-language monthly magazine *Qafilat al-Zayt*, a local commentator put the oasis's population at 280,000. *Qafilat al-Zayt* (Ramadan, 1957), 13.

25. See Vidal, *The Oasis of al-Hasa*, 40–41, Table 6, for a breakdown of the size and population of some villages. Data on al-Mubarraz are from p. 109. Figures on Hofuf from Vidal, "Date Culture in the Oasis of al-Hasa."

26. Vidal, *The Oasis of al-Hasa*, 40–41.

27. Ibid., 96.

28. Ibid., 105–106.

29. Ibid., 179.

30. Ibid., 149.

31. Ibid., 154–155.

32. Ibid., 162–163.

33. Ibid., 166–167.
34. Vidal says that the probable ratio was 60 percent Shiite and 40 percent Sunni. He noted that "all four orthodox schools of religious law and ritual are found among the Sunnites of Al-Hasa. The overwhelming majority is now Hanbalite—which is the official Saudi interpretation—with varying degrees of allegiance to Wahhabi rules." Ibid., 34.
35. This strategy was hardly unique in the kingdom's history. Saudi Arabian narrative strategies became even sharper later in the century. But the peculiar absence of the Shiites from state sources and other media make it clear that discussing them at all was taboo. Similar patterns developed elsewhere in the kingdom as well, particularly in the Hejaz and in the southern and southwestern provinces, where other tribal and religious minorities made their home.
36. Aramco's Arabic magazine *Qafilat al-Zayt* normally adhered to the government standard of not discussing Shiites. In a reproduction of a local radio-broadcast transcript, a 1957 issue of the magazine did mention that Shiites and Sunnis lived side by side in al-Hasa, although it offered no additional insight.
37. Vidal, *The Oasis of al-Hasa,* 96.
38. Ibid., 112.
39. Ibid., 96.
40. Ibid., 32.
41. Ibid., 35.
42. Absentee landownership dates back at least to the sixteenth century, when the Ottoman Empire awarded fiefdoms in al-Hasa to its janissary military leaders. See Jon E. Mandaville, "The Ottoman Province of al-Hasa in the Sixteenth and Seventeenth Centuries," *Journal of the American Oriental Society* 90, 3 (July–September 1970): 504–506. The Ottomans also ruled over al-Hasa between 1871 and 1913. For two accounts of Ottoman administrative rule in the late nineteenth and early twentieth centuries, see Abdullah bin Nasir al-Subai'i, *Al-hakim wa al-idāra fi al-ahsa' wa al-qatif wa Qatar ithna' al-hakim al-'uthmānī al-thānī, 1871–1913* (Riyadh: King Fahd National Publishers, 1999), and Muhammad Hassan al-Idrus, *Al-haya al-idāriyya fi sanjaq al-ihsa* [sic] *al-'uthmānī* (Abu Dhabi: Dar al-Mutanabi Publishers, 1992). It is also worth noting that nineteenth-century Ottoman administrators, who

imposed taxes on al-Hasa's merchants and farmers, also sought to expand the oasis's agricultural area. The basic rules governing property rights were also established in this period, with the Ottomans setting up four kinds of ownership: private property, government-owned land, land overseen by endowments *(awqāf),* and common land. See Abdullah bin Nasir al-Subaiʻi, *Iqtisād al-ahsaʼ wa al-qatif wa qatar ithnaʼ al-hakim al-ʻuthmānī al-thānī, 1871–1913* (Riyadh: King Fahd National Publishers, 1999), 34–38.

43. Vidal, *The Oasis of al-Hasa,* 37. Vidal went on to note that "from the point of view of over-all social structure, the al-Hasa garden villages are fairly simple. The population of the hamlets and the smaller villages consists of only one class, that of the agricultural workers, since the land owners live in the big towns. In the larger villages, a rudimentary upper class is found, consisting of a few families of landowners who dominate the village economically and socially. The rest of the population is also made up of garden laborers. In recent years, some villagers who had left to do contracting work have returned to build permanent residences in the place of origin, though still working outside. It is possible that these people may start competing for social prominence with the older leading families, but a more likely prospect is that the new rich will marry into the village aristocracy" (37–39).

44. Sami Labban, "Al-nakhala fī mādīha wa hādiriha wa mustaqbalha," *Qafilat al-Zayt,* September/October 1964, 28. According to Labban, a Saudi who graduated from the American University in Beirut thanks to assistance from Aramco, in addition to their high sugar content, dates contain high levels of iron, potassium, calcium, vitamin A, and vitamin B.

45. Unlike al-Hasa, which is located well inland from the coast, Qatif sits on the shore of the Gulf.

46. Although there are no data on how well small farmers and day laborers fared in this system, there is no reason to believe that they were able to compete or to take advantage of the system as well as their larger competitors and employers could. The system did not provide a means of escape for those lower in the socioeconomic hierarchy.

47. Al-Hasa converted to a cash economy in the early twentieth century.

48. Vidal, *The Oasis of al-Hasa,* 193.

49. Vidal, "Date Culture in the Oasis of al-Hasa," 215.
50. Vidal, *The Oasis of al-Hasa*, 196. Debt grew, as well, among small farmers and landless workers in the twentieth century. With the decline of date prices, borrowing from larger merchants to buy foodstuffs increased, leading to a cycle of indebtedness from which it proved difficult to break free.
51. Vidal, "Date Culture in the Oasis of al-Hasa," 215.
52. Vidal, *The Oasis of al-Hasa*, 186.
53. William Tracy, "The Restless Sands," *Aramco World* 16, 2 (May/June 1965).
54. Vidal noted, in particular, "agricultural malpractice that produced a rise in the ground water table. The inefficient drainage system of al-Hasa does not carry the surplus water far enough. The land gets waterlogged through inadequate dams and too shallow ditches, and the root zone is kept insufficiently aerated." Vidal, *The Oasis of al-Hasa*, 187.
55. The irrigation system predated the arrival of the Saudis, but once the family's representatives took control of the oasis they recorded the distribution rights in the Finance Office. Subai'i, *Iktishāf al-naft*, 77.
56. Ibid.
57. Vidal, *The Oasis of al-Hasa*, 136.
58. Ibid.
59. Ibid., 137.
60. One of the largest springs in the oasis, al-Haql had a discharge rate of approximately 22,500 gallons per minute. Vidal, *The Oasis of al-Hasa*, 120; see also "'Ain," *Aramco World* 11, 10 (December 1960). There were several women's bathhouses along the length of the watercourse leading from al-Haql. Aside from al-Haql and al-Khudud, which also had a discharge of more than 20,000 gallons per minute, there were two other large springs in al-Hasa, Ayn Umm Sabaa and Ayn al-Harra. Together, the four largest springs produced more than 150,000 gallons of water per minute.
61. Vidal, *The Oasis of al-Hasa*, 141–142.
62. The sharing of technical and other data was stipulated in the 1933 oil concession. Article 26 of the concession states that "the Company shall supply the Government with copies of all topographical maps and geological reports (as finally made and approved by the Company) relating

to the exploration and exploitation of the area covered by this contract."

63. "Harvest without End," *Aramco World* 11, 9 (November 1960).

64. Tracy, "Restless Sands."

65. Atalla Ahmed Abohassan, "Sand Stabilization by Afforestation in al-Hasa Oasis, Saudi Arabia," Ph.D. diss., Michigan State University, 1976, 2.

66. Ibid., 2; Tracy, "Restless Sands."

67. See John Hidore and Yahya Albokhair, "Sand Encroachment in al-Hasa Oasis, Saudi Arabia," *Geographical Review* 72, 3 (July 1982): 350. See also Yahya Albokhair, "Sand Encroachment in al-Hasa Oasis, Saudi Arabia," Ph.D. diss., Indiana University, 1981.

68. Hidore and Albokhair, "Sand Encroachment," 350.

69. Ibid., 356.

70. Ibid., 354; Abohassan, "Sand Stabilization," 22–30.

71. The cost of the first decade of the Sand Control Project ran to about 25 million Saudi riyals. Al-Elawy, "The Influence of Oil," 382.

72. Tracy, "Restless Sands."

73. The government also experimented with nonirrigated trees, which did not survive as well as those that were irrigated. Tracy, "Restless Sands."

74. Hidore and Albokhair, "Sand Encroachment," 356. Another Saudi Arabian observer, the geographer Ibrahim al-Elawy, argues that migration and not sand encroachment was most responsible for the decline of the agricultural area. He claims that between 1950 and 1967 the oasis had contracted from 16,000 hectares to 8,000, a loss of 50 percent, but that only 1.7 percent of that loss was due to sand encroachment. He argues that the more compelling reason for the loss of area was the decision by former agricultural workers to take up jobs in the oil industry and related fields. See al-Elawy, "The Influence of Oil," 270. Al-Elawy seems to have gotten his figures wrong. In fact, the gross area of the oasis measured 16,000 hectares in 1951, not the cultivated area. There are no figures for the total area under cultivation in 1951, although by 1963 it measured around 8,000 hectares. By 1968, according to the consulting firm Italconsult, the gross area of the oasis had declined to 11,290 hectares. The area under cultivation was just under 8,000 hectares, representing only a marginal loss from five years earlier. While al-Elawy is

likely correct that migration played a major role in the loss of farming area, sand encroachment, although it took place more slowly, did constitute a legitimate source of concern.

75. Tracy, "Restless Sands."

76. List of ministry goals reproduced in Abohassan, "Sand Stabilization," 3, based on Kingdom of Saudi Arabia, Ministry of Agriculture, *Sand Dune Project in al-Hasa,* 1962, 1–5.

77. See al-Elawy, "The Influence of Oil upon Settlement in al-Hasa Oasis"; Abohassan, "Sand Stabilization by Afforestation in al-Hasa Oasis"; Albokhair, "Sand Encroachment in al-Hasa Oasis."

78. In the contract hiring Wakuti, the Saudi Arabian government outlined its technical ambition as well as its and the company's legal obligations. It is interesting to note that the Saudi government stipulated that Wakuti had to abide by the country's boycott of Israel if it wanted to operate in the kingdom. To prove that the Swiss firm was indeed honoring that commitment, Saudi Arabia demanded a manufacturer's certificate stating that no materials were manufactured or made in Israel, as well as a statement from the Swiss Chamber of Commerce attesting to the country of origin of all materials. Wakuti and Ministry of Agriculture, *Al-Hassa Irrigation and Drainage Project, Part I: Civil Work,* 1964, 25 (Wakuti tender contract).

79. Wakuti engineers remained on board in an advisory capacity, working closely with Philipp Holzmann engineers to ensure that the project was implemented according to specifications.

80. Wakuti and Ministry of Agriculture, *Al-Hassa Irrigation and Drainage Project, Part I: Civil Work,* 321. Wakuti wrote that the irrigated area measured 10,400 hectares but that 2,400 hectares out of that total were "in insufficient state with poor or minor yields." Of the 8,000 that enjoyed sufficient yields, 4,750 hectares were dedicated to dates, 880 to alfalfa, 1,150 to rice, and 1,120 to vegetables and fruits. When he carried out his studies in 1951, Vidal claimed that the total area of the oasis measured around 16,000 hectares, although he did not specify the area under cultivation.

81. Wakuti, *Studies for the Project of Improving Irrigation and Drainage in the Region of al-Hassa, Saudi Arabia,* vol. 4: *Study on Water Resources and Agricultural Engineering,* 1964, 1.

82. Ibid., 20.

83. Philipp Holzmann, *Technical Reports*, December 1971, 3.

84. Italconsult, *Final Agricultural and Water Report*, 1969, 127.

85. Ibid., 128. The oasis was 68 percent urban and 32 percent rural by the time Italconsult carried out its study.

86. Wakuti, *Al-Hassa: Irrigation and Drainage Project, Kingdom of Saudi Arabia*, December 1971, 5.

87. Wakuti, *Studies*, vol. 4: *Water Resources and Agricultural Engineering*, 26.

88. Wakuti, *Studies for the Project of Improving Irrigation and Drainage in the Region of al-Hassa, Saudi Arabia*, vol. 2: *Study on Present Conditions*, 1964, 229.

89. Italconsult, *Final Agricultural and Water Report*, 142.

90. Wakuti, *Studies*, vol. 2: *Present Conditions*, 232.

91. Ibid., vol. 4: *Water Resources and Agricultural Engineering*, 53.

92. Wakuti and Ministry of Agriculture, *Al-Hassa Irrigation and Drainage Project, Part I: Civil Work*, 3.

93. Ibid., 52.

94. Wakuti, *Studies*, vol. 4: *Water Resources and Agricultural Engineering*, 27.

95. Wakuti, *Al-Hassa: Irrigation and Drainage Project*, 11–20. The Philipp Holzmann company also put down more than 1,500 kilometers of roads in order to carry out its work. The irrigation and drainage canals were kept separate, effectively doubling materials and space required for the project. Reflecting on the total distance covered by the irrigation canals, Wakuti wrote in 1971 that "this length corresponds to the distance from London to Rome" (11).

96. Philipp Holzmann, *Technical Reports*, 16.

97. Ibid., 3–5.

98. Ibid., 27. Wakuti put the figure at 7 million cubic meters of earth. Wakuti, *Al-Hassa: Irrigation and Drainage Project*, 22.

99. Philipp Holzmann, *Technical Reports*, 6.

100. Ibid., 29.

101. The company used more than 270 trucks and cars, 25 bulldozers, 14 loaders, 26 excavators, 28 mobile cranes, and 9 tower cranes to complete its work.

102. Philipp Holzmann, *Technical Reports*, 8.

103. For example, congratulatory articles that emphasized the technological achievement of the IDP appeared in Aramco's Arabic magazine *Qafilat al-Zayt* in March 1972 and then again almost twenty years later, in July 1991. *Al-Manhal,* one of Saudi Arabia's longest-running cultural magazines, published a laudatory piece in its December/January 1972 issue. The good news spread beyond the kingdom. The Kuwaiti monthly *Al-ʿArabī* also celebrated the IDP in an August 1974 article.

104. Wakuti, *Studies,* vol. 2: *Present Conditions,* 28.

105. Clyde, Criddle, Woodward, Inc., *Comments on Review of al-Hassa Project Report by Wakuti for Minister of Agriculture and Water, Saudi Arabia,* n.d., 1.

106. Tor Eigeland, "The Twice Used Water," *Aramco World* 21, 6 (November/December 1970).

107. Italconsult, *Final Agricultural and Water Report,* 24–27.

108. Ibid., 38.

109. The firm argued that 71 percent of all farms had a maximum area of one hectare or less. Ibid., 37.

110. Ibid., 18.

111. Ibid., 33.

112. Ibid., 38.

113. Ibid., 34.

114. Ibid.

115. See Michael Adas, *Machines as the Measure of Men: Science, Technology, and Ideologies of Western Dominance* (Ithaca, N.Y.: Cornell University Press, 1989), and *Dominance by Design: Technological Imperatives and America's Civilizing Mission* (Cambridge, Mass.: Belknap Press of Harvard University Press, 2006).

116. Eigeland, "Twice Used Water."

117. Talat Ibrahim Lutfi, *Athar mashrūʿ al-rai wa al-sarraf ʿala mantiqat al-Ihsaʾ: Dirāsa fī al-tughayr al-ijtimāʿi al-qurawī bil-Mamlika al-ʿArabiyya Al-Saʿudiyya* (Riyadh: King Saud University Press, 1986), 126.

118. Zayn al-Abadin al-Rahman Rajab, "Dirāsat fī mawāradihā al-maʾiyya wa taʾthīrihī fī al-istikhdām al-rīfī al-ʿard", in *Ad-Darah* 3, year 16 (October–December 1980): 122–124.

119. Rajab, "Dirāsat," 124.

120. Lutfi, *Athar mashrūʿ,* 112.

121. Rajab, "Dirāsat," 125.

122. Lutfi, *Athar mashrū'*, 113.

123. This information is based on interviews I conducted during fieldwork in al-Hasa in September and October 2003.

5. The Black Gold Coast

1. Abd al-Qadūs al-Ansari founded and first published *Al-Manhal* in 1937 in the city of Medina. Although the magazine was not an official organ of the Saudi regime, al-Ansari was aware that his journal's survival depended on maintaining the goodwill of the ruling family. Permission to found *Al-Manhal* was granted directly by the Advisory Council to King Abd al-Aziz, only after the group reviewed al-Ansari's personal history, education, and writing samples. The actual printing of *Al-Manhal* was made possible only through the direct assistance of Muhammad Said Abd al-Maqsud, the editor of *Umm al-Qura,* the government's official weekly. According to *Aramco World,* al-Ansari served as an adviser to the Saudi government later in his life. See "Portrait of an Editor," *Aramco World* 15, 1 (January/February 1964).

2. Salah al-Zakir, "Dhahran in My New Life," in *Al-Manhal* 9 (September and February 1948–49): 11–12.

3. Abd al-Qadūs al-Ansari, "This Is the Eastern Province," *Al-Manhal,* April 1956, 514–523.

4. See Robert Vitalis, *America's Kingdom: Mythmaking on the Saudi Oil Frontier* (Stanford, Calif.: Stanford University Press, 2006), for a powerful deconstruction of the Aramco development myth.

5. The annual reports by Aramco, titled *Report of Operations to the Saudi Arab Government by the Arabian American Oil Company* for each year (first published in 1947), devoted considerable space to the efforts of the oil company to develop individuals' skills, assist communities, help employees, and provide technical and human support (like health care) in the villages and areas surrounding the oil facilities.

6. Vitalis, *America's Kingdom,* 35.

7. Although its first few issues were published in and circulated from Beirut, the home of *Akhbar al-Dhahran* was the city of Dammam. See Muhammad Abd al-Rizaq al-Qasha'mī, *Al-Bidayāt al-sahifa fī al-mamlaka*

al-ʿarabiyya al-saʿūdiyya, al-mantiqa al-sharqiyya (Riyadh: King Fahd National Library, 2002), 20. I am grateful to Mr. al-Qashaʿmī for making his study available to me in Riyadh.

8. See Hamza al-Hassan, *Al-Shiʿa fil-mamlaka al-ʿarabiyya al-saʿudiyya,* vol. 2 (Muʿassasat al-Baqī li-Ihyaʾa al-Turāth, 1993), for dramatic details and evidence of the state's role in the depression of the date market in the late 1940s and early 1950s.

9. Abdullah bin Khamis, "My Impressions of al-Hasa," *Akhbar al-Dhahran* 1 (December 26, 1954).

10. Muhammad Said al-Muslim, *Sāhil al-dhahab al-aswad* [The Black Gold Coast] (Beirut: Dar Maktabat al-Hayat, 1962). Details of al-Muslim's imprisonment are available in the newsletter of the Organization for the Islamic Revolution in the Arabian Peninsula, *Al-Thawra al-Islamiyya* 105 (December 1988): 22. Al-Muslim was also forbidden to travel outside Saudi Arabia.

11. Al-Zakir, "Dhahran in My New Life," and al-Ansari, "This Is the Eastern Province."

12. The cities and villages that came to form the edge of the Eastern Province by the middle of the twentieth century had for centuries been the only viable settled communities in the region. It was only after the discovery of oil that Dammam, al-Khobar, and Dhahran grew as residential areas, supplanting the ancient communities that surrounded them and assuming primacy in the commercial and political sectors.

13. Bin Khamis, "My Impressions of al-Hasa."

14. Aramco also enjoyed considerable power in the Eastern Province, but it does not appear that citizens in the region saw the company as possessing political power like that of ibn Jiluwi or the Al Saud.

15. See Nadav Safran, *Saudi Arabia: The Ceaseless Quest for Security* (Ithaca, N.Y.: Cornell University Press, 1988); Mordechai Abir, *Saudi Arabia in the Oil Era: Regime and Elites: Conflict and Collaboration* (London: Croom Helm, 1988); Sarah Yizraeli, *The Remaking of Saudi Arabia: The Struggle between King Saʿud and Crown Prince Faysal, 1953–1962* (Syracuse, N.Y.: Moshe Dayan Center for Middle Eastern and African Studies, 1997).

16. See Vitalis, *America's Kingdom,* and al-Hassan, *Al-Shiʿa fil-mamlaka al-ʿarabiyya al-saʿudiyya,* for the most thorough accounts of the strikes, the forces propelling the unrest, and the various responses.

17. See Robert Vitalis, "Black Gold, White Crude: An Essay on American Exceptionalism, Hierarchy and Hegemony in the Gulf," *Diplomatic History* 26, 2 (Spring 2002): 185–213.

18. See Madawi al-Rasheed, *A History of Saudi Arabia* (New York: Cambridge University Press, 2002), 114. Al-Rasheed captures the essence of why political activity has been hard to detect in Saudi Arabia. She notes that it typically has simmered below the surface, stating that "most of those who can be described as 'political activists' were not drawn from major tribal groups. In fact, their activism was motivated by a desire to overcome their marginality in a society that still defined people's status and achievements along old tribal lines." A common though less thoughtful and more misleading line of analysis argues that with the exception of "a prolonged period of political and economic uncertainty in the late 1950s and early 1960s the people of Saudi Arabia have largely remained united behind the Al Saʿud . . . Where dissent has manifested itself, as in the labour unrest of the 1950s in al-Hasa or in the shattering November 1979 attack on the Grand Mosque of Mecca, it has been isolated from the main body of Saudi opinion." James Buchan, "Opposition in Saudi Arabia," in Timothy Niblock, ed., *State, Society and Economy in Saudi Arabia* (London: Croom Helm, 1982), 106.

19. Helen Lackner, *House Built on Sand: A Political Economy of Saudi Arabia* (London: Ithaca Press, 1978), 89.

20. Ibid.

21. See al-Hassan, *Al-Shiʿa fil-mamlaka al-ʿarabiyya al-saʿudiyya.*

22. I was unable to review issues of *Al-Fajr al-Jadīd* due to the newspaper's rarity and the fragile condition of those holdings still in existence at the King Fahd National Library in Riyadh.

23. *Al-Ishaʿāʿ* was the least controversial of the three papers, and the only one not forcibly closed by Saudi authorities. Its editor, Saad al-Buwaradi, focused primarily on literature and cultural issues, although he often included materials of regional and national interest. Al-Buwaradi closed the paper of his own accord in 1957 and moved to Oman.

24. Abd al-Karim al-Juhayman, *Muzakarāt wa Zikriyyāt min Hayati*, vol. 1 (Riyadh: Dar al-Shabal, 1995); second edition published in al-Qashaʿmī, *Al-Bidayāt al-sahifa*, 175.

25. The Yaqub brothers published only four issues of *Al-Fajr al-Jadīd*. Reflecting on the paper's closure four decades later, Yusuf remained ignorant of the precise reasons for the paper's closure. In a letter written and published in al-Qashaʿmī, he remarked that it could have been an article critical of Aramco and the position of one of its employees on the situation in Palestine. Unlike al-Juhayman, al-Yaqub was exiled after his arrest and allowed to return to the kingdom only in the 1970s under an amnesty program offered by King Faisal. See al-Qashaʿmī, *Al-Bidayāt al-sahifa*.

26. Abd al-Karim al-Juhayman, letter to al-Qashaʿmī, 1421, in al-Qashaʿmī, *Al-Bidayāt al-sahifa*, 41.

27. Editorial, *Akhbar al-Dhahran*, September 13, 1955, quoted in al-Qashaʿmī, *Al-Bidayāt al-sahifa*, 24–25. This use of "free pulpit" *(minbar hurra)* is an excellent example of the power of religious symbolism in political discourse. A *minbar* is the pulpit found in mosques, from which prayer leaders and learned scholars direct services and present sermons.

28. Al-Rasheed, *A History of Saudi Arabia*, 120.

29. Ibid., 112–113.

30. Ibid., 110–112.

31. See Walid Khaduri, ed., *ʿAbdullah al-Tariqi: Al-Aʿmāl al-Kāmila* (Beirut: Center for Arab Unity Studies, 1999), for the most comprehensive collection of al-Tariqi's works.

32. Al-Rasheed, *A History of Saudi Arabia*, 115. Al-Tariqi died in Cairo at the age of eighty, in 1997.

33. Ibid., 116–117. See also Nathan Citino, *From Arab Nationalism to OPEC: Eisenhower, Kind Saʿud, and the Making of U.S.-Saudi Relations* (Bloomington: Indiana University Press, 2002). Saudi Arabia viewed the deteriorating situation in Yemen as a security threat. In September 1962 an Egyptian-supported military officer, Abdullah al-Sallal, deposed Imam Muhammad al-Badr, the Yemeni king. Subsequently, violence between royalists and republican rebels aroused Saudi concerns. Particularly troubling to the Saudis was the presence in Yemen of 20,000 Egyptian troops, who were supporting the rebels.

34. Mamoun Fandy, *Saudi Arabia and the Politics of Dissent* (New York: Palgrave, 1999), 44–45. Fandy notes that issues such as the fate of the

Dhahran Air Base, which the United States leased from the kingdom for military purposes, were controversial in the kingdom and generated intense unease among Saudi citizens. Frustration over the role of the West and the appearance of colonialism angered many and certainly facilitated support for Arab nationalism, particularly since it was leaders such as Nasser who spoke out most forcefully against imperial machinations.

35. *Al-Isha'ā'*, year 1, issue 9 (April 1956): 32.

36. See interview with Muhammad al-Subai'i, the Syrian publisher of the journal *al-Muslimūn*, ibid., 35–36.

37. *Al-Isha'ā'*, year 1, issues 10 and 11 (May and June 1956).

38. The use of *umma*, which literally refers to the "Muslim" rather than the Arab community, is another example of the power of religious symbolism. The author also used the term *watan*, which embodies more of a sense of nation or homeland connected to a state or polity, to describe what he was talking about. Letter from "one among you" in Dhahran, *Al-Isha'ā'*, year 1, issue 11 (June 1956), 20.

39. *Al-Fajr al-Jadīd* 1 (March 6, 1955). Quoted in al-Qasha'mī, *Al-Bidayāt al-sahifa*, 51.

40. The word *dijāl* is another example of religious symbolism in political rhetoric. While I have translated it here as "impostor," the word also refers to the notion of the Antichrist *(dijāl al-masīh)*.

41. Lilienthal wrote that he visited Riyadh and Jidda in 1955, but made no mention of his trip to Dhahran.

42. *Al-Fajr al-Jadīd* 2 (March 19, 1955), quoted in al-Qasha'mī, *Al-Bidayāt al-sahifa*, 60–62.

43. Hawshan's recollection of the conversation is consistent with Lilienthal's later political writings about Israel, in which he renounced Zionism and sought to build understanding between Arabs and Israelis.

44. Hawshan quoted in al-Qasha'mī, *Al-Bidayāt al-sahifa*, 60–62.

45. Yusuf al-Sheikh Yaqub remarked subsequently that he believed his decision to run the article was likely the main factor behind the government's decision to close the paper just two issues later, although he had no definitive proof. Letter from Yaqub to Qasha'mi, in al-Qasha'mī, *Al-Bidayāt al-sahifa*, 80–88.

46. Vitalis, *America's Kingdom*, 145–151.

47. *Akhbar al-Dhahran* 26 (January 27, 1956). Parts two and three appeared in issues 27 (February 3) and 28 (February 10).

48. *Akhbar al-Dhahran* 27 (February 3, 1956).

49. "Rid the Municipality of Qatif of This Administration," *Akhbar al-Dhahran* 14 (August 19, 1955).

50. Ibid.

51. From 1954 to 1964 residents elected these local councils in the kingdom; there are no public records available of the names or identities of council members. Each major region or city maintained its own municipal council, which administered the area around it. I was unable to locate any existing Saudi Arabian records related to the councils, their membership, and the elections. Aramco did maintain election-observer records, some of which are available in the William E. Mulligan Papers, Special Collections, Georgetown University Libraries.

52. "Rid the Municipality of This Administration," *Akhbar al-Dhahran*.

53. Ibid.

54. It is often assumed that the state clearly expected Aramco to handle the affairs of infrastructure building and other development in the Eastern Province. Saudi rulers did exert pressure on the oil company to aid in certain areas, although it is unclear that even the regime had articulated a clear program for what was expected. However, as Robert Vitalis outlines in *America's Kingdom*, the company had little intention of undertaking expensive operations that it considered a distraction and a drain on its resources. What is clear from the letters published in *Akhbar al-Dhahran* is that residents in the east were under the impression that the state and its local institutions were responsible for fulfilling the needs of the region's communities.

55. *Akhbar al-Dhahran* 17 (October 3, 1955).

56. Ibid.

57. Ibid.

58. Ibid.

59. Dammam, al-Khobar, and Dhahran were not Shia cities.

60. The terms "rural," "urban," and "civilized" would have been familiar to commentators such as Ibn Rashid, as they were made popular by the fourteenth-century scholar Ibn Khaldun. Arab scholars, including Sunni and Shia thinkers from across the Arab world, several of whom

are cited in this volume, continue to rely on Ibn Khaldun's framework for understanding Arab civilization in their analyses of events and social relationships. See al-Hassan, *Al-Shiʿa fil-mamlaka al-ʿarabiyya al-saʿudiyya,* and Fandy, *Saudi Arabia and the Politics of Dissent.*

61. *Akhbar al-Dhahran* 18 (October 18, 1955).

62. Ibid.

63. *Akhbar al-Dhahran* 19 (November 1, 1955). Interestingly, this anonymous writer also thanked the paper for allowing the discussion to take place, underscoring the important role played by "the free press" in society.

64. He further remarks that "as for the rest of the article, it [offers only] attacks on and accusations toward all those known to have accused them with corruption from the moment that they entered the administration." He also mentioned that he was "satisfied with the second [Ibn al-Asima's] article" and that he intended to address additional issues here.

65. *Akhbar al-Dhahran* 19 (November 1, 1955).

66. Al-Juhayman mysteriously noted that while some had written in support of continuing the discussion, others had requested that the subject be closed, although he did not suggest who the advocates for silence were. *Akhbar al-Dhahran* 20 (November 16, 1955).

67. "The Municipality of Jubail Is in a Deep Slumber," *Akhbar al-Dhahran* 21 (December 1, 1955).

68. *Akhbar al-Dhahran* 23 (December 31, 1955).

69. Abdullah bin Khamis, who contributed to the first issue of *Akhbar al-Dhahran,* wrote an article on the shortage of modern machine tools in al-Hasa, and the shortcomings of development, for *Al-Yamama* magazine (no. 33). His article in *Al-Yamama* sparked interest in a reader from Hail, in Najd, who surveyed farmers in his hometown about the use of modern tools. The farmers also complained about the shortage, leading the reader (Ibn Tay) to write an article on the subject for *Al-Ishaʿāʿ,* criticizing the Ministry of Agriculture for its inability to properly manage the agricultural affairs of the state. See *Al-Ishaʿāʿ,* year 1, issue 13 (August 1957): 18.

70. *Akhbar al-Dhahran* 25 (January 16, 1956) and *Akhbar al-Dhahran* 28 (February 10, 1956). The anonymous author of the February 10 letter wrote "[We] waited for long to no avail [for the Municipality to act].

You [author of January 16 letter] disregarded this and said that they represent the people. But . . . Abu Farawis probably [best] expressed the sentiments of the citizens of this country . . . And all agree with what Abu Farawis said. Therefore, your call is futile . . . Your foolishness increased when you said that you welcome impartial criticism. Why, if Abu Farawis did not depart from the path of criticism, don't you face and admit the situation? I say clearly without hesitation or embarrassment that you will lose the battle and that you will return a refugee and a failure."

71. *Al-Isha'ā'*, year 1, issue 13 (August 1957): 44.

72. Phebe Marr, "Public Health Conferences," December 15, 1960, William E. Mulligan Papers, Special Collections, Georgetown University Libraries.

73. Phebe Marr, "Municipality Election," December 19, 1960, William E. Mulligan Papers, Georgetown University Libraries.

74. Ibid.

75. One of the most notable figures to be arrested and eventually driven from Saudi Arabia was Nasser al-Said, a Sunni Arab nationalist who grew disillusioned with the Al Saud while working for Aramco. In addition to organizing labor unrest, al-Said wrote several works critical of the royal family, including political poetry.

76. Al-Hassan, *Al-Shi'a fil-mamlaka al-'arabiyya al-sa'udiyya.*

6. The Wages of Oil

1. The decision to stage the Ashura celebration in public was a specifically political act. Because it had long been banned in the kingdom, marking the ceremony served notice to the government that Saudi Arabia's Shia community sought to exert its communal will and challenge state efforts that not only prevented them from observing religious rituals but also, as the Shiites believed, suppressed them politically.

2. Communist Party of Saudi Arabia (CPA), *Ahdāth nufimbir (al-muharram) 1979 fī sa'udiyya,* December 1979, 42.

3. The uprising compounded what already constituted a political crisis in the Arabian Peninsula, one that directly threatened the security of the House of Saud. The unrest overlapped with the occupation of the

Grand Mosque at Mecca by a group of religious radicals headed by Juhayman al-Utaybi and his band of neo-Ikhwan. The occupation of the mosque in Mecca, which lasted several weeks and required the use of Saudi and French special sources to bring it to an end, shook the kingdom to its core. Meanwhile in the east, because the vast majority of the residents, and therefore those who took part in the rebellion, were Shia, the uprising suggested the popular appeal of the revolutionary message of Ayatollah Khomeini—who was a direct threat to the Saudi regime.

4. Jacob Goldberg, "The Shi'i Minority in Saudi Arabia," in Juan Cole and Nikki Keddie, eds., *Shi'ism and Social Protest* (New Haven, Conn.: Yale University Press, 1986), 239.

5. Madawi al-Rasheed, *A History of Saudi Arabia* (New York: Cambridge University Press, 2002), 147.

6. James Buchan, "Opposition in Saudi Arabia," in Timothy Niblock, ed., *State, Society and Economy in Saudi Arabia* (London: Croom Helm, 1982), 119.

7. Noting the symbolic significance of the Islamic Revolution for Saudi Shiites, David Lesch states that the Saudi uprising "indicated to all interested observers that the reverberations from the Iranian revolution would be more than just fitful" and that "the emotional atmosphere produced by the ashura [*sic*] celebration naturally led to riots amid loud support for the Ayatollah Khomeini." David Lesch, *1979: the Year that Shaped the Modern Middle East* (Boulder, Colo.: Westview Press, 2001), 61.

8. Joseph Kostiner, "Shi'i Unrest in the Gulf," in Martin Kramer, ed., *Shi'ism, Resistance, and Revolution* (Boulder, Colo.: Westview Press, 1987), 177–179.

9. See Nikki Kiddie, *Modern Iran: Roots and Results of Revolution* (New Haven, Conn.: Yale University Press, 2003), an update of her 1981 book *Roots of Revolution: An Interpretive History of Modern Iran;* Misagh Parsa, *The Social Origins of the Iranian Revolution* (New Brunswick, N.J.: Rutgers University Press, 1989); and Ervand Abrahamian, *Iran between Two Revolutions* (Princeton, N.J.: Princeton University Press, 1982).

10. Information based on interviews I conducted with Saudi Arabians in

Qatif, September 2003. See also the excellent work by Laurence Louër, *Transnational Shia Politics: Religious and Political Networks in the Gulf* (New York: Columbia University Press, 2008).

11. Based on interviews conducted in Qatif, 2003.

12. Information based on interviews conducted in Manama, Bahrain, February 2005.

13. Their close contact in Bahrain was driven in part by coordination between offices, but they also had familial connection, as Hadi al-Mudarrisi, along with his older brother, Muhammad Taqi al-Mudarassi—currently grand ayatollah of Iraq and one of two successors to al-Shirazi—were al-Shirazi's nephews.

14. Abdullah Nasir al-Subaiʻi, *Iktishāf al-naft wa ātharuhu ʻala al-haya al-iqtisadiyya fī al-mantiqa al-sharqiyya, 1933–1960* (Riyadh: Shariif Publishers, 1989), 30.

15. Hamza al-Hassan, *Al-Shiʻa fil-mamlaka al-ʻarabiyya al-saʻudiyya*, vol. 2 (Muʻassasat al-Baqī li-Ihyaʼa al-Turāth, 1993), 236–237. See also Muhammad Ali Salah al-Shurafa, *Al-Mantiqa al-sharqiyya min al-mamlaka al-ʻarabiyya al-saʻudiyya*, vol. 1 (Dammam: Al-Madukhil Publishers, 1994), 43–45.

16. Al-Subaiʻi, *Iktishāf al-naft*, 132; al-Hassan, *Al-Shiʻa fil-mamlaka al-ʻarabiyya al-saʻudiyya*, 232–279; al-Shurafa, *Al-Mantiqa al-sharqiyya*, 42–51.

17. Twelver Shiites, who make up the largest branch of Shiism in the world, believe that the twelfth imam, their highest religious guide and a direct descendant of the prophet, went into occultation in the ninth century. They believe that he will eventually return from hiding and usher in an age of greater justice.

18. It is impossible to accurately determine the population totals at virtually any time, as the Saudis published only one census, in 1974, and did not distinguish citizens based on faith. Goldberg cites various estimates from 200,000 to 440,000. He settled on the figure of 350,000 for reasons that are not entirely clear, although he seems to rely on the work of James A. Bill for that determination. With a total Saudi Arabian population of 6 million at the time, that would place the Shia at approximately 6 percent of the total—a contested number. Other estimates suggest that the minority probably constituted anywhere from 10 to 15 percent of the total, although no figures can be considered abso-

lutely reliable. See James A. Bill, "Islam, Politics, and Shi'ism in the Gulf," *Middle East Insight* 3 (1980): 6; Goldberg, "The Shi'i Minority in Saudi Arabia," 230.

19. Within the Shia branch of Islam, two theological schools dominated in the twentieth century: the Usuli and Akhbari schools. In Saudi Arabia both are represented, the former in Qatif and the latter in al-Hasa. According to Juan Cole, the differences arise in the relationship between Shia religious leaders and the community around them—with adherents of the Usuli school having a more complex relationship with the community—as well as in matters of interpretation of the Quran. Akhbari *mujtahids* tended toward a greater degree of literalism when interpreting various texts and proved, according to Cole, to be more independent and conservative. Although their theological differences were most important in matters of law, and certainly helped define the different religious practices of the two communities, the significance of the split proved even more important in the turbulent era of the Iranian Revolution. The embrace by Qatifis, but not by al-Hasawis, of Ayatollah al-Shirazi, an Usuli, is explained in part by these connections.

20. F. S. Vidal, *The Oasis of Al-Hasa,* Arabian American Oil Company, Local Government Relations, Arabian Research Division (1955). See also Ibrahim S. al-Abdullah al-Elawi, "The Influence of Oil upon Settlement in al-Hasa Oasis," Ph.D. diss., University of Durham, 1976.

21. Organization of the Islamic Revolution in the Saudi Arabian Peninsula (OIR), *Intifadat al-muharram fil-mantiqa al-sharqiyya (witha'iq al-intifada), 1979* [The Intifada of Muharram in the Eastern Province, vol. 1: Documents of the Intifada, 1979]. In other materials, the group dropped "Saudi" from its name.

22. OIR, *Intifadat al-muharram,* 2.

23. Ibid., 3.

24. Ibid., 4.

25. Ibid.

26. Ibid., 5.

27. Ibid., 7.

28. Kingdom of Saudi Arabia, Ministry of Planning, *Second Development Plan, 1975–1980* (Riyadh: Ministry of Planning), 4.

29. *Al-Yawm,* May 27, 1979.

30. Ibid.

31. *Al-Yawm*, May 28, 1979.

32. OIR, *Intifadat al-muharram*, 1–7.

33. Letter from Ahmad bin Abd al-Aziz, Deputy Minister of the Interior, to Prince of the Eastern Province [1977], document 50 in al-Hassan, *Al-Shiʿa fil-mamlaka al-ʿarabiyya al-saʿudiyya*.

34. The pages of *Al-Yawm* contain numerous articles critical of local government officials and institutions. These remarkable pieces of journalism are rare in the history of Saudi Arabia, as the kingdom has long monitored and discouraged open political discussion. While the efforts of *Al-Yawm* journalists to document social problems and government responsibility were not unprecedented in the kingdom, they were and are very rare. After the events of 1979, the state reined in the paper and stopped the critical writing.

35. Hussein al-Tantawi, "The Drinking Water Project in al-Hasa Demands Another Look," *Al-Yawm*, April 22, 1979.

36. *Al-Yawm*, May 6, 1979.

37. Muhammad Abd al-Rahman, "In 3 Years . . . ," *Al-Yawm*, April 21, 1979.

38. Muhammad Abd al-Rahman, "Tarut Island," *Al-Yawm*, June 20, 1979.

39. Abd al-Rahman, *Al-Yawm*, June 20.

40. Ibrahim al-Ghudair, "From the Municipality to the Civil Defense and No Solution," *Al-Yawm*, June 24, 1979.

41. Ibid.

42. Ibid.

43. Ali Yusuf al-Jarudi, "The Municipality and the Indefinitely Postponed Projects of Qatif," *Al-Yawm*, September 22, 1979.

44. Ibid.

45. Abdullah al-Dubaisi, "Qatif, Oh Respected Officials of Ours," *Al-Yawm*, September 9, 1979.

46. Ibid.

47. Faisal al-Qu, "New Projects for the Center of Social Services in al-Jafar to Raise the Standard of Health of the Community," *Al-Yawm*, March 8, 1979.

48. Abdullah al-Falah, "Social Assistance for Citizens of Qatif," *Al-Yawm*, May 1, 1979, and Abdullah al-Falah, "The End of the Qatif Health Project," *Al-Yawm*, May 9, 1979.

49. Falah al-Sughair, *Al-Yawm*, April 28, 1979.

50. Abdullah al-Ghashri, *Al-Yawm*, May 7, 1979.

51. Abdullah al-Ghashri, *Al-Yawm*, September 8, 1979.

52. "Seminar on the Level of Services in al-Hasa," *Al-Yawm*, April 12, 1979.

53. Ibrahim al-Muqaiteeb, *Al-Yawm*, May 2, 1979.

54. Goldberg, "The Shi'i Minority in Saudi Arabia," and Guido Steinberg, "The Shiites in the Eastern Province of Saudi Arabia (al-Ahsa'), 1913–1953," in R. Brunner and W. Ende, eds., *The Twelver Shia in Modern Times: Religious Culture and Political History* (Leiden: Brill, 2001).

55. CPA, *Ahdāth nufimbir*, 26.

56. Ibid.

57. Buchan, "Opposition in Saudi Arabia," 119. Buchan wrote, "The demand came at a time when the General Directorate of Intelligence . . . was acutely concerned at possible subversion by Iranian pilgrims both in the *haramain* (Mecca and Medina) and in the villages."

58. Kostiner, "Shi'i Unrest in the Gulf," 179.

59. "Bahrain Welcomes Support by Holding a Gulf Foreign Minister's Meeting," *Al-Yawm*, September 13, 1979.

60. *Al-Yawm*, October 2 and October 3, 1979.

61. The Arabic original was "*Ya Khalid shīl īdak, kul ash-sha'b ma yurīdak*."

62. While there is virtually no documentation available from the Saudi security forces, the OIR managed to obtain copies of various administrative letters and materials that give a sense of the state's direct approach to protest. In one, published regarding the summer of 1979, the Saudi chief of police in the Eastern Province warned security forces about possible Shia unrest during the month of Ramadan, purportedly at the urging of broadcasts from Radio Tehran. Encouraging them to deal swiftly and powerfully with possible unrest, the letter directed the security forces to "be vigilant, attentive, and resolute in oppressing any aggressive act they [the Shia] undertake with no leniency or carelessness." Kingdom of Saudi Arabia, No. 3049, 1400/9/26, in the monthly newsletter of the OIR, *Al-Thawra al-Islamiyya* 54 (October 1984): 38.

63. Ibid., 28–29.

64. Ibid., 28. The Communist Party of Saudi Arabia corroborates the OIR's account of events, although the CPA claims that al-Qalaf was killed November 27; see CPA, *Ahdāth nufimbir*, 23.

65. Information based on CPA, *Ahdāth nufimbir*; interviews conducted during fieldwork from 2003 to 2005.

66. Committee for the Defense of Human Rights in Saudi Arabia, cited in CPA, *Ahdāth nufimbir,* 31–42.

67. CPA, *Ahdāth nufimbir,* 36.

68. Ibid., 22–23. The CPA also claims that public events were staged in more than seventy communities, a number that likely takes into account each village in the Eastern Province.

69. Mamoun Fandy, *Saudi Arabia and the Politics of Dissent* (New York: Palgrave, 1999), ch. 7.

70. Ibid., 198.

71. Al-Rasheed, *A History of Saudi Arabia,* 147. See also Madawi al-Rasheed, "The Shiʿa of Saudi Arabia: A Minority in Search of Cultural Authenticity," *British Journal of Middle East Studies* 25, 1 (1998): 121–138.

72. Hussein Musa, *Al-Ahzab wa-l-harakat al-islamiyya fī al-khalīj wa al-jazira al-ʿarabiyya* (Manama, Bahrain: n.p., 2004), 52–53. Hussein Musa is the pen name of a Bahraini political dissident who lived in exile for more than thirty years.

73. Ibid., 7.

74. Ibid.

75. Ibid., 53.

76. The OIR shaped Saudi-Shia relations for a decade and a half after the 1979 uprising, agitating for mass action, such as demonstrations in February 1980 on the anniversary of Khomeini's return to Iran, and publishing a militant monthly newsletter, *Al-Thawra al-Islamiyya* (The Islamic Revolution), which became *Al-jazira al-ʿarabiyya* in the early 1990s.

77. OIR, *Intifadat al-muharram,* 18.

78. Ibid., 19–21.

79. Ibid., 22–23.

80. Ibid., 21–23.

81. OIR, *Al-Thawra al-Islamiyya* 54 (October 1954): 37.

82. See Goldberg, "The Shiʿi Minority in Saudi Arabia," 243.

83. OIR, *Intifadat al-muharram,* 25.

84. Ibid., 27.

85. Ibid., 27–38.

86. Helen Lackner, *A House Built on Sand: A Political Economy of Saudi Arabia* (London: Ithaca Press, 1978), 99. Lackner argues that this was

the first organization "in which Saudi Arabians met and developed a political perspective."

87. CPA, *Ahdāth nufimbir,* 22.

88. CDHR materials, reprinted in ibid., 36.

89. Ibid., 32.

90. Ibid.

91. Joseph Kechichian, "The Role of the Ulama in the Politics of an Islamic State: The Case of Saudi Arabia," *International Journal of Middle Eastern Studies* 18, 1 (February 1986): 53–71.

92. Gwenn Okruhlik, "Empowering Civility through Nationalism: Reformist Islam and Belonging in Saudi Arabia," in Robert W. Hefner, ed., *Remaking Muslim Politics: Pluralism, Contestation, Democratization* (Princeton, N.J.: Princeton University Press, 2005), 189–212; Joshua Teitelbaum, *Holier Than Thou: Saudi Arabia's Islamic Opposition,* Policy Papers 52 (Washington, D.C.: Washington Institute for Near East Policy, 2000).

7. Nature's Retreat

1. See Thomas Hegghammer and Stephane Lacroix, "Rejectionist Islamism in Saudi Arabia: The Story of Juhayman al-'Utaybi Revisited," *International Journal of Middle East Studies* 39, 1 (2007): 103–122.

2. Joseph Kechichian, "The Role of the Ulama in the Politics of an Islamic State: The Case of Saudi Arabia," *International Journal of Middle Eastern Studies* 18, 1 (February 1986): 53–71.

3. The government reportedly invited French commandos to assist Saudi paramilitary forces in rooting out the hundreds of militants in the Grand Mosque. See Yaroslav Trofimov, *The Siege of Mecca: The Forgotten Uprising in Islam's Holiest Shrine and the Birth of al Qaeda* (New York: Doubleday, 2007), for a gripping account of the takeover and the struggle to end the rebellion.

4. This continues to be true. In interviews I conducted during fieldwork in Saudi Arabia in 2003 and 2005, Saudi Arabian Sunnis in Riyadh and Dammam—both in and outside government—said they still believe that the 1979 Shia uprising was coordinated by forces in Iran.

5. Saudi leaders also viewed Khomeini as a regional threat. The fear that Iran would achieve hegemony in the Persian Gulf and Central Asia led the Saudis to finance Iraq in its decade-long war with Iran in the 1980s, and led to the kingdom's decision to send people, weapons, and money to fight in Afghanistan, which Saudi leaders viewed as under siege not only by the Soviets but also by Iran, which borders Afghanistan on the west.

6. See Toby Jones, "The Iraq Effect in Saudi Arabia," *Middle East Report* 237 (Fall 2005). The most infamous book, *Tabdid al-zalam wa tanbih al-niyam ila khatar al-tashayyu' 'ala al-muslimin wa al-islam* [Removing the Darkness and Awakening to the Danger of Shiism to Muslims and Islam], was written by Ibrahim Sulaiman al-Jabhan (Riyadh, 1980). The Pakistani author Ihsan Ilahi Zahir composed a number of anti-Shia screeds that circulated widely in the kingdom, including *Al-Shi'a wa al-Sunna* [The Shi'a and the Sunna] (Lahore, 1988) and *Al-Shi'a wa ahl al-bayt* [The Shi'a and the Prophet's Family] (Lahore, 1983).

7. Juhayman gathered around him a band of several hundred followers who shared similar convictions. He justified the seizure of the Grand Mosque in Mecca by arguing that his colleague Muhammad al-Qahtani was the Islamic Mahdi, an apocalyptic figure whose appearance heralded the end of days. In spite of Juhayman's criticism of the ulama, the kingdom's main religious scholars refused to condemn him for his political critiques of the Saudi political system, although they did refuse his proclamation of the Mahdi. Their decision was significant, for it demonstrated that while they disagreed with his theological worldview, they shared his frustration with their subordination in the Saudi political system.

8. Joshua Teitelbaum, *Holier Than Thou: Saudi Arabia's Islamic Opposition*, Policy Papers no. 52 (Washington, D.C.: Washington Institute for Near East Policy, 2000), 10–12.

9. Toby Craig Jones, "The Clerics, the Sahwa, and the Saudi State," *Strategic Insights* 4, 3 (March 2005): 2.

10. See Gwenn Okruhlik, "Empowering Civility through Nationalism: Reformist Islam and Belonging in Saudi Arabia," in Robert W. Hefner, ed., *Remaking Muslim Politics: Pluralism, Contestation, Democratization* (Princeton, N.J.: Princeton University Press, 2005), 189–212; Gilles

Kepel, *The War for Muslim Minds: Islam and the West* (Cambridge, Mass.: Harvard University Press, 2004).

11. Okruhlik, "Empowering Civility through Nationalism," 194.

12. Ibid.

13. Ibid., 195.

14. "The Kingdom of Saudi Arabia," address by King Fahd ibn Abd al-Aziz (Riyadh: Ministry of Information, 1983).

15. *Al-Yawm,* December 2, 1979.

16. Ibid., December 11, 1979.

17. Ibid., December 12, 1979.

18. Ibid., December 15, 1979.

19. Jacob Goldberg, "The Shiʿi Minority in Saudi Arabia," in Juan Cole and Nikki Keddie, eds., *Shiʿism and Social Protest* (New Haven, Conn.: Yale University Press, 1986), 244.

20. Ibid.

21. Ibid., 245.

22. See Hamza al-Hassan, *Al-Shiʿa fil-mamlaka al-ʿarabiyya al-saʿudiyya,* vol. 2 (Muʾassasat al-Bāqī li-Ihyaʾa al-Turāth, 1993), documents 5–8, 423–429, for local letters appealing to state authorities for an end to violence and the release of political prisoners. It seems that the kingdom's leaders took such action in answer to pleas for kindness, rather than initiating it.

23. Saudi Shiites took up temporary residence in various cities around the world, including in Iran and the United States.

24. Committee for the Defense of Human Rights, in Communist Party of Saudi Arabia, *Ahdāth nufimbir (al-muharram) 1979 fi saʿudiyya,* December 1979, 40.

25. Interviews conducted during my fieldwork in 2003.

26. Copies of several of the petitions are available in al-Hassan, *Al-Shiʿa fil-mamlaka al-ʿarabiyya al-saʿudiyya,* 465–468.

27. Ibid., document 30, 468.

28. By the 1980s fewer than 25 percent of Saudis were engaged in agriculture. Richard F Nyrop, ed., *Saudi Arabia: A Country Study* (Washington, D.C.: Department of the Army, 1985), 185.

29. Eliyahu Kanovsky, *The Economy of Saudi Arabia: Troubled Present, Grim Future,* Washington Institute Policy Papers 38 (Washington, D.C.: Washington Institute for Near East Policy, 1994), ch. 6.

30. Reuters, "Saudi Arabia to End Wheat Program," January 9, 2008.
31. Elie Elhadj, "Saudi Arabia's Agricultural Project: From Dust to Dust," *Middle East Review of International Affairs* 12, 2 (June 2008).
32. Ibid.
33. Nyrop, *Saudi Arabia: A Country Study,* 190.
34. Elhadj, "Saudi Arabia's Agricultural Project."
35. Reuters, "Saudi Arabia to End Wheat Program."
36. Kanovsky, *The Economy of Saudi Arabia,* ch. 6.
37. Elhadj, "Saudi Arabia's Agricultural Project."
38. Kanovsky, *The Economy of Saudi Arabia,* ch. 6.
39. Reuters, "Saudi Arabia to End Wheat Program."
40. Based on interviews I conducted in Saudi Arabia in 2003.
41. Based on interviews conducted during my fieldwork, 2003 to 2005.
42. "Saudi Arabia Looks for Farms Abroad," *Economist,* August 21, 2008; Andrew England, "Saudis Plan to Grow Crops Overseas," *Financial Times,* June 13, 2008.
43. Andrew Rice, "Is There Such a Thing as Agro-Imperialism?" *New York Times,* November 22, 2009.
44. Ibid.

Epilogue

1. Abdullah's policies have been both inconsistent and ineffective on the reform front. See Toby Jones, "Violence and the Illusion of Reform in Saudi Arabia," *Middle East Report Online,* November 13, 2003; Toby Jones, "The Iraq Effect in Saudi Arabia," *Middle East Report* 237 (Winter 2006); Toby Jones, "Embattled in Arabia: Shiʿis and the Politics of Confrontation in Saudi Arabia," Occasional Paper Series, Shiʿa Militancy Program, Combating Terrorism Center at West Point, West Point, N.Y., June 3, 2009.
2. Toby Jones, "Saudi Arabia's Silent Spring," *Foreign Policy,* February 2009, www.foreignpolicy.com.
3. See www.kaust.edu.sa/about/kingsmessage.html.

Acknowledgments

This book is the result of a number of long journeys. Along the way I have made many friends and enjoyed the camaraderie of fellow travelers. And I have also accumulated numerous debts to many people. To them I owe more than mere appreciation. Lindy Biggs patiently and enthusiastically encouraged me forward and helped me find my way as a historian. Joel Beinin shaped my identity as a scholar. He was just as influential in shaping my identity as an activist and my belief that historians can and should use their craft to speak truth to power. I continue to be in awe of his passion and commitment to political justice. I owe a similar debt to Gabrielle Hecht. Gabrielle has always, unfailingly, even in hard times for her and her family, been a source of support, encouragement, and intellectual inspiration. Gabrielle's influence is evident on every page of this book. For this and more I am thankful.

I was fortunate to learn from a remarkably diverse group of people at Stanford University, including Robert Crews, Ahmad Dallal, Tim Lenoir, and Richard White. I arrived at Stanford surrounded by brilliant young talent and a group of people whose influence I continue to feel. Stephen Andrews, Catherine Yoonah Bae, Holly Case, Charly Coleman, Ben Kafka, Chad Martin, Shira Robinson, Max Weiss, and Brandon Wolfe-Hunnicutt were sources of intellectual and personal strength. I am equally grateful to a second group of friends and colleagues made while studying in the Middle East. From June 2001 to June 2002, I spent a bittersweet year as a fellow at the Center for Arabic Study Abroad (CASA) at the American University in Cairo. My wife, Sandy, Jennifer Derr, Sherine Hamdy, Nathalie Peutz, Ian Straughn, and especially Justin Stearns and I spent a tremendously challenging year together. Each shaped me and this book in innumerable ways. Most of the research for this book was carried out in Saudi Arabia in 2003. I was generously supported by a Fulbright-Hays fellowship. Getting to Saudi Arabia to do research was very difficult. Researchers, particularly those with an interest in politics, are not always welcome in the kingdom, and the only way to gain entry for any length of time is to have a Saudi host. The U.S. embassy staff in Riyadh and especially John Burgess somehow convinced the scientists at the King Abd al-aziz City for Science and Technology (KACST) in Riyadh to host me for more than ten months. I still consider this something of a miracle and myself to be the beneficiary of great fortune. The department of petrochemical engineering at KACST was wonderful. Suleiman al-Khowaiter, the chair of the department, was particularly gracious and accommodating, providing me with a computer and office space in which to carry out my work. Abdulhamid al-Sayigh befriended me and helped me survive several difficult months alone, as the Saudi Ministry of the Interior did not grant Sandy a visa. The library staffs at KACST, the King Fahd National Library, and the King Faisal Foundation were equally generous, allowing me to take materials home or to bring in my computer in order to scan many of the documents and other materials that serve as the empirical foundation for this book. Friends in the Eastern Province and in Bahrain took me in and opened many doors. Having lived in difficult circumstances all of their lives, and in spite of the risks of helping an American historian with a politically sensitive research project, they enthusiastically showed me the way. While the political situation in Saudi Arabia has improved considerably, particularly for minorities, many of my conclusions and arguments are provocative enough that I have chosen not to name my Saudi friends. I only hope my private thanks will suffice.

I have had the very good fortune of asking for and receiving the support of a number of wonderful historians and political scientists whose work focuses on Saudi Arabia. Gwenn Okruhlik and Pat Conge were also in Riyadh in 2003. We endured together the tribulations and challenges created by the U.S. invasion of Iraq and a violent al Qaeda campaign against Westerners in Saudi Arabia. Personally and professionally I owe them both a tremendous debt. Greg Gause, Bernie Haykel, and Robert Vitalis have been sources of steadfast support. Greg and Bob have been selfless beyond any reasonable expectation. Bernie graciously brought me to Princeton in 2008–2009 as a fellow with the Oil, Energy and Middle East Project, where I completed this book. The experience transformed my understanding of oil and it transformed the book. Bernie is as generous, kind, and supportive as anyone I have had the pleasure to know. He has also been one of the most thoughtful critics of my work, pushing for clarity and analytical caution. Bernie will not agree with everything I have written here, but I hope he knows that I have struggled to account for his careful consideration of my work. Sam Blatteis helped me track down important materials.

As has been the case for many students of modern Saudi Arabia and oil, I owe more than a mere intellectual debt to the Arabic novelist Abdelrahman Munif and his brilliant multivolume epic, *Cities of Salt (Mudun al-Milh)*. An inspiring account of the considerable political, social, and environmental costs of oil, Munif's work remains unparalleled. Readers of this and any other history of oil and politics in Saudi Arabia would be well served to read and reread Munif's novels.

Alan Mikhail read the introduction to the book and offered his typically sharp insight. Karl Appuhn also read several parts of the manuscript and offered generous and compelling suggestions for improvements. Thanks also to Miriam Lowi, David Patel, Cyrus Schayegh, and Arang Keshavarzian for their helpful comments and suggestions.

My colleagues in the History Department at Rutgers University in New Brunswick have been especially wonderful. Several of them read various parts of the book. Others provided an audience while I discussed the myriad details and hopes I had for the project. Michael Adas, Indrani Chatterjee, James Delbourgo, Ann Fabian, Paul Hanebrink, Jochen Hellbeck, Al Howard, Temma Kaplan, Seth Koven, Jackson Lears, Julie Livingston, and Keith Wailoo all helped me improve the book. Rutgers is a remarkably collegial and vibrant place. As the beneficiary of the goodwill and genuine support of those around me, I consider myself very lucky to be here.

I have presented parts of the book at many institutions over the years and received much valuable feedback. Thanks to audiences and panelists at Princeton, Yale, Michigan, NYU, Cornell, and the annual meetings of the American Historical Association and Middle East Studies Association.

A shorter and earlier version of Chapter 6 was published in 2006 as "Rebellion on the Saudi Periphery: Modernity, Marginalization and the Shi'a Uprising of 1979" in the *International Journal of Middle East Studies*. I am grateful to the journal and to Cambridge University Press for allowing me to include it here.

It has been a pleasure to work with Joyce Seltzer at Harvard University Press. She has been an enthusiastic supporter of this project since I first met her in 2008. A careful reader, a sympathetic listener, Joyce is a joy to know and work with. I am thrilled that this is but our first project together. Julie Hagen was a great help in improving the writing and the book.

Since moving to New Jersey I have also had the good fortune to be surrounded by a number of friends who have helped keep me sane. Thanks to Michael Jenks, Todd Kruger, Richard Thompson, and Mark Vareschi for their friendship and for logging thousands of cycling miles together.

The greatest source of inspiration, indeed a source of awe, has been my family. My parents and my wife's family have always been genuinely curious about my work. They did not always understand the decisions we made, but they always made certain that nothing stood in our way as Sandy and I pushed ahead. More often, they made pushing ahead possible. In good times and bad, I have been able to count on their love and guidance. Sandy has given me more than I can ever repay or even begin to acknowledge. For years, she sacrificed her own work so I could finish mine. We traveled almost every step together, and when she could not join me she was supportive from afar. I cannot imagine this book or anything else without her. Our two daughters, Mackenzie and Danielle, were born while I wrote this book. It will be many years before they know it exists. I hope they understand then that it is their love and the joy they have brought me that matter the most. I have dedicated this book to them and to Sandy, but that is trivial compared with what they have done for me.

Index

Abd al-Aziz, King, 58, 146, 277n1; al-Hasa conquered by, 90–91; and al-Kharj project, 261n8; cult of, 84–85; death of, 56, 59; as founding monarch, 8–9, 257n16; and material incentives, 62; relationship with Crane, 36–37; relationship with Twitchell, 36–37, 39, 41, 47, 53; relations with Ikhwan warriors, 8–9, 74–75, 80, 93, 251n18, 258n18, 267n3; and taxation, 256n13; and water resources, 36–37, 39, 40, 41, 91

Abdullah, King, 239–244, 294n1

Abir, Mordechai: *Saudi Arabia in the Oil Era*, 250n15, 262nn10,11, 278n15

Abohassan, Atalla Ahmed, 273nn65,66,70

Abrahamian, Ervand: *Iran between Two Revolutions*, 285n9

Adas, Michael: *Dominance by Design*, 252n25, 260n48, 276n115; *Machines as the Measure of Men*, 276n115

Afghanistan, 216, 292n5

Africa: Saudi land purchases in, 234–235

Agrawal, Arun: *Environmentality*, 251n20

Agriculture: alfalfa, 274n80; al-Kharj project, 44, 59, 261n8; Bedouin/Ikhwan farming communities (*hujjar*), 9, 29–31, 33, 74–75, 80, 257n17; dates, 26, 27–28, 48, 91, 102, 105, 107, 108–116, 121, 122, 123, 127, 132, 141, 189, 228, 256n13, 271n44, 272nn50,54, 274n80, 278n8; Faisal on, 67, 70, 88; Faisal Settlement Project, 75–76, 80–83, 266n67; and family structure, 129–130, 132–133; food security/self-sufficiency regarding, 62, 94, 125, 227–229, 234–235; irrigation, 25–26, 31, 40–41, 46, 56, 71–72, 73–74, 81, 95, 102, 111–115, 116, 120–128, 131–137, 141, 176, 183, 184, 195, 229–232, 233–234, 255n6, 256n13, 257n17, 272n54, 274n79,80, 275n95; Ministry of Agriculture/Agriculture and Water, 32, 50, 58, 64–65, 67–68, 69, 70–74, 76, 81–83, 89, 111, 116–117, 121, 123, 125, 128, 196, 197, 224, 255n6, 263n21, 266n67, 283n69; number of Saudis working in, 32, 40, 121, 132–133, 228, 293n28; per capita income from, 68; as percentage of GDP, 68, 89, 228, 264n36; purchase of African farmland, 234–235; relationship to political authority, 5, 6, 9, 10, 16, 24, 25–29, 27, 29–32, 33, 40, 46, 47–48, 54–55, 56, 64–69, 70–72, 73, 74–75, 85–86, 89, 94, 135, 217, 224, 227–234, 236, 237, 241; rice, 132, 189, 274n80; Saudi Arabian Agricultural Bank, 64–67, 68–69, 85, 89, 264n30; soil surveys, 12, 43, 44, 71, 72, 81, 83, 120; and taxa-